Writing for Academic Success

Writing for Academic Success

A Postgraduate Guide

GAIL CRASWELL

SAGE Publications
London • Thousand Oaks • New Delhi

First published 2005
Reprinted 2006

SAGE Publications Ltd
Oliver's Yard
55 City Road
London EC1Y 1SP

SAGE Publications Inc.
2455 Teller Road
Thousand Oaks, California 91320

SAGE Publications India Pvt Ltd
B-42, Panchsheel Enclave
Post Box 4109
New Delhi 100 017

British Library Cataloguing in Publication data

A catalogue record for this book is available from the British Library

ISBN 1 4129 0300 9
ISBN 1 4129 0301 7 (p/b)

Library of Congress control number 2004096556

Typeset by C&M Digitals (P) Ltd., Chennai, India
Printed in Great Britain by Athenaeum Press, Gateshead

Summary of contents

Contents

Acknowledgements

The procedural advice and strategies presented in this book have evolved over many years of working individually with graduates at all levels of study in different disciplines, from presenting workshops, seminars and courses tailored for different groups of graduate students, sometimes independently and sometimes in collaboration with professional and academic staff, and from developing institutional level programmes on academic and professional skills training for research students. So a special thank you to all the graduates, past and present, for providing me with such a rich learning environment.

Thank you also to the many colleagues with whom I have worked over the years. I would particularly like to thank Jan Robbins, Stephen Milnes, Maurice Neville, John Clanchy and Brigid Ballard for their valuable insights in commenting on draft chapters, and the sharing of their expertise. And thank you to Annie Bartlett and Stephanie Fadini for time out – the best.

Introduction

The communication needs of graduate coursework and research students are complex and remarkably varied in practice. Hence, the major focus of this book on writing, presenting and publishing. While the text is essentially about the many aspects of writing, issues unique to presenting and publishing are given independent treatment in the final two chapters.

Every new level of study is a learning experience, and a learning experience that takes place in a particular context, with all communication being influenced by that context. This context can be thought of as the social context in which you are writing, presenting or publishing – what may be thought of as your 'discipline'. As you may be engaged in cross- or inter-disciplinary study or research, I use the term 'disciplinary' broadly to refer to any social context.

Because disciplinary or course requirements exert considerable influence on the perceived appropriateness of end products (for example, submitted papers or theses), it is difficult to write or present well without understanding these requirements, including the variations of practice within disciplines or courses. I have consequently emphasized repeatedly the need to ground my advice in disciplinary/course contexts, to follow advice, written or otherwise, given by lecturers and supervisors on producing texts, and to consult with them frequently.

Nevertheless, not all academic writing practices seen to constitute good practice are disciplinary or course-dependent. Conciseness in writing is valued in general by the academic community, as is treating information critically, attending to audience needs, consistency in the mechanics of academic writing, careful referencing of sources, coherent development of texts, sound logic and evidential support in argument, and so forth. Material of this type is covered in Chapters 2, 3, 4 and 5.

Other aspects of context may also feature prominently in graduate communication. For example, disciplinary influences on style and language are much reduced where there is a broad audience for, say, a conference paper, or with publications in journals targeting a more general audience. While audience needs are a crucial consideration in all communication, at times they exert primary influence on both the treatment of information and the language, style and formatting of a paper or talk.

The aims of the book

The general aim of this book is to ease the path towards successful communication of your study and research. It is in that sense a developmental guide based on my understanding that graduates are not interested in a *quick fix* but rather in building on skills and strategies already in place so as to take control of the different communicative situations in which they find themselves.

The usefulness of the book lies in your following through on suggestions and testing their appropriateness in the context of monitoring your own practices, attempting the exercises or following step-by-step procedures where relevant, applying strategies in practice, and opening up conversations with lecturers, supervisors, conference convenors and editors or publishers where uncertainties remain.

The book does not attempt comprehensive coverage of every type of academic writing, which would be impossible. Nor is it possible to cover in detail the varied and complex communication challenges graduates encounter. Nevertheless, much of the material covered in Chapters 1, 2, 3 and 4 will apply in most situations of writing, and the different types of self-help strategies presented throughout the book should prove useful if you encounter types of writing not covered in the book.

Organization of the book

The book's underlying organization mirrors a developmental movement from consideration of general issues in academic writing and communication in Part One, to coverage of issues specific to different types of writing, presentations and publication processes in Part Two.

The book begins by considering in Chapter 1 some key psychological and physical stressors and effective management strategies with a view to enabling a more positive writing environment.

Chapter 2 initially outlines the complexity of the graduate writing culture, where it is not a matter of being literate but of being multi-literate in various types of writing, which can have different communicative purposes and so require new practices or different combinations of new and known practices.

The exercise that follows under 'Mastering (inter)disciplinary writing practices' in Chapter 2 is a primary learning tool that should help you to recognize the interplay of contextual influences affecting writing in specific contexts, and assist with orientation to new types of writing you may be attempting. I then take up information issues preparatory to writing. Effective communication is not just about the act of writing, it is about careful preparation in the information-gathering stages, about having the best and the right information for the writing task in hand, and being able to retrieve that information efficiently.

Chapter 3 reviews standard expectations of academic writing. It provides an opportunity to reflect on your current practices in terms of approaching the writing, the mechanics of academic writing, plagiarism and referencing, and key aspects of style. Chapter 4 addresses whole text development, including the structural scaffolding framing academic writing in general, whereas issues specific to structuring different types of writing are discussed at appropriate points in Part Two.

The impetus behind Chapters 2, 3 and 4 is three-fold. It is hoped these chapters will raise awareness of your current practices to counter the negative effects of the learning by *osmosis* that many graduates mention. Because they have had no training in academic writing and presenting, having just picked up their practices along the way, graduates can find it difficult to know what is good practice and what is not, why some of their efforts attract more positive feedback from supervisors/lecturers than others, and how they might readily appropriate, adapt and apply known practices in different situations of writing and presenting, and when they need to develop new practices. It is also hoped that these three chapters will reinforce confidence in your current practices, and/or allow you to identify areas that might be improved, using the strategies offered.

Chapter 5 focuses in detail on prominent types of written assessment in many graduate courses: research essays, book or article reviews and coursework exams papers of various types. Chapter 6 continues with a detailed focus on other significant academic genres: the literature review (really a sub-genre), different types of reports and research proposals.

Chapter 7 is devoted exclusively to thesis writing, though information in Chapters 2, 3 and 4 is also critically important for thesis writing.

Chapter 8 moves to full consideration of the topic of presenting. The chapter divides into two parts: the first considers issues relevant to different types of presentations – tutorials, seminars, conferences and posters; the second part examines a range of issues integral to the planning, formatting, rehearsal and delivery of a presentation. Chapter 9 takes up issues specific to journal article and book publication.

Terminology and other practices

I have tried to keep the terminology in the book as simple as possible. This means you may find it does not necessarily fit the understanding current in your institution (for example, under some systems Course = Unit or Subject and Programme = Course). When I talk about a 'programme', I mean the whole programme in which you are enrolled or thinking to enrol, your degree programme. The term 'course' refers to one particular subject or unit you are taking within that programme.

I make only three distinctions as regards degree structures: degrees by coursework (no research component), degrees by coursework and research, and degrees by research only. These distinctions do not allow for the wonderful array of titles given to different graduate degrees or the variable structures of degrees, but they are recognizable distinctions easy to apply to your own situation.

I sometimes use the term 'thesis' to apply to any type or level of thesis writing. At other times I find it necessary to distinguish between shorter and longer theses. I also use some terms interchangeably, for example, thesis and dissertation, and where noted, 'thesis' is also used in reference to a position being developed; and degree and programme, which seems to be common in research-only degrees. Where I am using terms in a rather precise way, I provide definitions

All identifying signifiers have been removed from illustrative materials taken from graduate student writing. Instead of including actual details of source references, I substitute '[reference]', and where countries, authors, etc. have been named in the writing, I substitute X, Y, Z and so forth. This is to protect the interests of the graduates on whose work I draw for illustration.

Part One

General Issues in Academic Writing and Communication

1 Managing the Writing Environment

Developmental Objectives

By applying the strategies, doing the exercises and following the procedural steps in this chapter, you should be able to:

- Take a pro-active approach to reducing the psychological and physical stress that typically accompanies academic writing and communication.
- Identify a range of strategies for managing more efficiently yourself and your writing in the context of your life commitments and goals.
- Ensure results-oriented communication with your lecturers and supervisors, including email communication.
- Understand some cross-cultural challenges in terms of writing and communication, why these exist and how you might address them.

It is common for graduates to experience ups and downs with academic writing and communication. Your feelings of confidence, excitement, self-doubt, disinterest, frustration, lack of motivation, isolation and so forth may alternate, and it is important to recognize such mood swings as typical rather than unusual. This chapter covers a broad range of management strategies designed to reduce stress and improve the quality of your writing environment.

Effective self-management

While networking requires effort, it can be worth the investment of your valuable time, particularly if you are enrolled in a longer research degree.

NETWORKING FOR SUPPORT

These networking strategies should help alleviate stress while contributing to a greater sense of integration in the academic community at large.

Generate peer support: local, national and international Students in your course or research group will prove an excellent support resource, so be proactive in making yourself known to them. Make contact too with the graduate student organization within your institution, if there is one. Such organizations usually provide a range of social and academic support, are often advocates for resolution of issues of concern to graduates, and may represent graduates' interests on important institutional committees.

Understanding more about what is going on for graduate students in general can afford a welcome sense of solidarity. Ask whether there is a national student organization representing graduate interests that you should know about. Websites of these organizations can contain informative material regarding the current status of graduate and research education in your country (see for example: *National Postgraduate Committee* <http://www.npc.org.uk/>; *Council of Australian Postgraduate Associations* <http://www.capa.edu.au/> or the US site, *National Association of Graduate-Professional Students* <http://www.nagps2.org/frame-top.cfm>). Government departments responsible for higher education also produce publications that you might like to browse in, again with a view to becoming more informed.

There are numbers of international graduate student and dissertation support sites on the Internet. Many enquiries about writing are posted on such sites, as is copious information about 'surviving' graduate studies. Even joining a chat group with other graduates sharing your interests can lend support – discuss this possibility with peers and academics in your area.

One well-established international site is the *Association for Support of Graduate Students* <http://www.asgs.org/>, a US site that provides a news and reference bulletin for graduates writing theses and includes *Doc-Talk*, a free, moderated email discussion list about doing a thesis (lots of useful tips). Another is the *Postgraduates' International Network* <http://www.postgrad.org/>. This is a European-founded organization (with rather a strong science focus) aimed at promoting international cooperation among graduate student associations and facilitating communication within the international graduate community. The site is still under development and may contain more information specific to writing and communication issues in the future.

Identify institutional resources available for developmental assistance There is now considerable academic learning assistance offered within institutions at different levels of the institution and in various contexts – graduate schools, faculties, centres and departments, academic skills or writing centres, or by lecturers and supervisors.

You should thoroughly network your institution's website home page to find out what supplementary assistance is on offer. Network across institutions too as you may locate the precise materials you need on another institution's site, where these are accessible. Academic skills, learning or writing centres of different institutions in different countries often provide electronic resources specific to graduate writing and communication that may prove useful. Whatever you turn up that seems relevant, do check with your lecturer/supervisor that the advice is sound in their view.

Make use of visiting scholars and other disciplinary experts Introduce yourself to visiting scholars and attend any conferences/seminars they give while at your institution. Where the research interests coincide, a visiting scholar may be willing to give advice on communication tasks, and even provide feedback on your drafts. You could also benefit from contact with other disciplinary experts.

CASE STUDY Example

Box 1.1 Other disciplinary experts can be a valuable resource

A doctoral student realized when writing up that there was a gap in her reading (not an unusual occurrence!). She needed an overview of one aspect of a famous philosopher's work about which she knew little, as she was not a philosophy student. A quick database search turned up literally hundreds of potential sources that left her, as she said, *'totally depressed'*. So she rang around to identify an expert in nineteenth-century philosophy, and asked him if he could refer her to an appropriate source for what she needed. This he did. And, in her own words: '*This saved me heaps of time – there were just so many sources – really put me on the right track with my reading.*'

Actively elicit understanding of close ones You may be relying on partners, family and friends for primary support when writing. But sometimes it can be difficult for those closest to accept what appears to them to be inflexibility, or even selfishness on your part, when you are unavailable for a social invitation or a request for help. A doctoral student struggling with this very dilemma had this to say:

My biggest problem in the whole business is time-management … it's hard for me to claim the 'right' to sufficient space for the job in hand, telling myself too often that I can mind a grandchild, have coffee with someone, or take time out to go shopping when it's really not a good idea at the time. This is probably a very common problem, especially for women in my position who have a partner, children, grandchildren, friends and elderly parents or relatives – all claiming a piece of one's life which one feels is their due anyhow. There is no definitive answer, I feel, apart from progress in the art of self-assertion, and self-discipline, along with the realization that the university is paying (in the case of a scholarship student) for a task to be done and therefore has a right to expect full value for money.

By identifying peak writing periods in advance (see the next section), you will be able to give partners, family and friends ample warning.

Of course you may be the one who is paying for your degree, and paying dearly. That aside, as this type of dilemma is not unusual, you may need to work at gaining more understanding of those close to you (see also the balanced self-management exercise below that encourages building relationship goals into your time management). Tell them well in advance that there will be times when you will not be available, and remind them of this when such occasions arise. Perhaps, too, keep reminding them, and yourself, that whatever the duration of your studies, the period will come to an end.

Network your own resources It is not easy to find the right words to express complex ideas, to structure or organize material on the scale of, say, a dissertation, a long report or essay, or to develop subtle arguments and discussions. Writing is an intellectually demanding task and one that rarely goes smoothly. As one student said: '*Writing is a matter of thinking writing, thinking writing, thinking writing – it is never just writing.*'

There will be difficult spots. At such times there can be a tendency to be harshly self-critical, even to resurrect inner saboteurs ('I've never been any good at writing'), to use negative reinforcers that cement a sense of failure. It is then necessary to network your own resources with a view to positively reinforcing your efforts, to recall past and present academic successes, to be patient with yourself, to remember that the act of writing is always about learning to write (it is little different with presenting), to genuinely value your own efforts, and to visualize that degree certificate in your hand – it will happen.

PRE-PLANNING: MAXIMIZING EFFORT

On a global level, maximizing effort involves effective self-management in all sectors of your life. It is near impossible to maximize effort in terms of communication activities in a course of study or research if other significant areas of your life are under strain. Stephen Covey's *The Seven Habits of Highly Effective People* (1994) invites the understanding that how we respond to time, how we understand time, how we behave in time and organize our time is nothing but habit, and all habits can be changed to meet changing circumstances, which is sometimes necessary.

Exercise: balanced self-management

Step 1

Review closely the 'The self-management matrix' in Figure 1.1. Thinking about the implications of these four quadrants for your own situation may prove illuminating, particularly if you are writing a thesis in a research-only degree, where there are no course deadlines to meet.

Effective self-management means avoiding the trap of Quadrant 1 (all too easy for busy graduates), of being driven to the time-wasting distractions of Quadrant 4 because of Quadrant 1 pressures and stress, or of attributing undue importance to the activities of Quadrant 3, which need to be monitored closely. It means training yourself to reside comfortably in Quadrant 2 as much as possible, for as Covey says:

> The way you spend your time is a result of the way you see your time and the way you really see your priorities. If your priorities grow out of a principle center and a personal mission, if they are deeply planted in your heart and in your mind, you will see Quadrant II as a natural exciting place to invest your time. (1994: 158)

If study/research is a deeply embedded, principle-centred priority in your life, then work towards embedding this priority as a set of balanced life activities. Generate expectations focused on preserving and enhancing relationships and on achieving results. Develop a clear idea of the results you desire in your life, and organize and execute around priorities aimed at these results.

	Urgent	Not Urgent
Important	**Quadrant 1** *Shrink 1: Move Across* **Immediate commitments** • Deadline-driven projects • Crises • Pressing problems • Always putting out fires • Problem-minded • Fragmentation • Controlled by events • HIGH STRESS – burnout	**Quadrant 2** ☺ **Empowering activities** • Proactive, *principle-centred* • Balance: *relationships and results* oriented (holistic) • Prioritization, clarifying values, assessing worth of activities • Specific goal setting – long, intermediate and short term • Scheduling time to meet goals • Opportunity-minded • Synergy • Fun and relaxation • In control • LOW STRESS – flexibility
Unimportant	**Quadrant 3** **Proximate activities (need to watch these)** • Interruptions, some phone calls • Some social and popular activities • Some mail/email • Some meetings • Many proximate and pressing matters	**Quadrant 4** ☹ **Time wasters (in context of work)** • Escape activities • Irrelevant email • Much social chit chat • TV, computer games, Internet, some phone calls • Endless housecleaning • Trivia, busywork • More busywork

FIGURE 1.1 **The self-management matrix (adapted from Covey, 1994: 151)**

Step 2

Detail all regular commitments, and include prioritized weekly goals in terms of desired results. Do this for each of the four sectors tabulated below, with the aim of achieving balanced self-management:

Research/Study/ Writing	Work/Teaching	Relationships	Individual/personal development
		Partner? Children? Other family members? Friends?	Physical Mental Emotional Spiritual
(Detail priorities and specific goals for the week in terms of desired results) ←			→ *(It is important not to exclude your private/ personal needs)*

Step 3

Set up a **weekly timetable**. Build in flexibility – allow for (at least in your mind) the unanticipated 'urgent' of Quadrant 1. A scheduled activity might need to be passed over because of a higher value (for example, a sick child). Better still, is a **yearly diary** in which you can detail goals, and activities to meet those goals, week-by-week.

Step 4

Set up a timeline that gives you an overview of your whole course (whether a research or coursework degree):

Starting date **End date**

Mark along the timeline **priority dates** (for example, due dates for items of coursework assessment, or dates for seminar/conference papers, progress review papers, thesis outlines or chapters, etc.). As these become known, include in your yearly diary advance deadlines and dates for preparatory activities to meet those deadlines.

Focusing your energies On a more immediate level, individual circumstances, course requirements, personal preferences and peak energy flows can influence when you write and how you organize your writing time and other communication activities. Some students concentrate better in shorter periods, taking frequent short breaks. Others prefer longer writing periods with fewer but longer breaks. Some work a 9 to 5 day, or stay up half the night and sleep late. Some see no choice but to write at night after full-time employment and/or when the children have gone to bed. But is this the only choice?

CASE STUDY Example

Box 1.2 Maximize effort by harnessing your natural biorhythms

One graduate in full-time employment and with a young family presented with anxiety because he was '*getting behind*' in the writing of a long research report. He felt confident about writing the report, but said he was *'just too tired to write at night'* and doubted he could '*get it done*'. As he thought of himself as *'a morning person'*, it seemed reasonable to suggest he reorganize his writing time: rise two hours earlier in the morning to write (5 days a week), and reserve every Sunday from 10am to 2pm for writing until the task had been completed. He enlisted support from his partner in this and found it worked well for him.

Regularizing your writing pattern Whatever your circumstances, try to establish a regular writing pattern that is viable for you, allows you to write when you are likely to be most productive, given your various commitments, and that can be adjusted when necessary. Graduates have reported that regularizing the writing pattern helped them in these ways:

- Reduced the anxiety often associated with the 'I'll write when I can' approach, an approach that easily leads to writing being put of.
- Encouraged thinking through the setting up of a detailed writing schedule.
- Provided a stronger sense of working steadily towards completion of the writing task.

- Increased confidence in completing the task given their many and varied commitments.
- Allowed them to forewarn family and friends of their unavailability at certain times, which in turn reduced household stress.

Boosting your motivation Motivation is another issue frequently raised by graduates. It is of course impossible to remain highly motivated month in, month out over the years of a long research degree, or even during a shorter degree. Motivation levels do fluctuate. But your inner 'motivator' may at times need a full recharge. Perhaps your interest in your project is depleted – you feel bored, or your confidence has plunged and you seriously doubt your potential, or you are frustrated because you cannot get the help you need, or a troubled relationship is claiming all your attention, or you are oppressed by financial struggle, or it all seems a terrible grind. Any one, or a combination of these factors, can make you feel flat, not motivated at all.

At this point **STOP!** Try to pin down what is causing you to feel so unmotivated. Address the particular problems sapping your motivation, perhaps by talking these over with a professional counsellor, so as to take control of the situation.

CASE STUDY Example

Box 1.3 Significant life changes may be necessary to recharge your inner motivator

This is how one doctoral student (two years into a research degree), who presented as *'totally unmotivated'*, being '*bored with the whole thing*' and just wanting *'out'*, turned his situation around:

- Lifestyle changes to achieve a better balance, which included improved diet and joining a gym with his partner.
- Development of a comprehensive time plan so that he could alert his partner to periods of peak demand in advance and so alleviate pressures on the relationship.
- Visualization strategies from a counsellor to build confidence.
- Regular advice and assistance from an academic skills adviser to overcome a fear of failure centred on writing.

Engaging in pro-active strategies to manage physical stress is no less important than for psychological stressors.

AVOIDING OCCUPATIONAL HAZARD

More attention is now being given to the health hazards accompanying long hours of sitting at a computer or desk. It is best to vary your activities as much as you can. Intersperse computer work with other tasks such as reading, organizing or reviewing notes, working out graphs, tables or figures, monitoring experiments, drafting ideas for the next chapter, outlining an essay or report and so forth, anything that you might be able to do *off* the computer. Make your tasks multi-various, particularly when producing lengthy texts like theses and long reports.

Also, get advice or material from the occupational health service in your institution on how best to avoid Occupational Overuse Syndrome (OOS), which can lead to such disabilities as Repetitive Strain Injury (RSI). Overuse injuries appear to be increasing among graduates. The tips provided in Figure 1.2 will help you to manage the physical strain of working with a computer.

Managing the writing

While effective self-management itself aids management of the writing, other issues may arise.

MANAGING MULTIPLE COMMUNICATION TASKS

Managing communication tasks can be complicated, particularly if you are a coursework student with several items of assessment for different courses due around the same time. This type of situation tends to cause coursework graduates much anxiety. As a research student, you may also have converging deadlines, and feel the resulting pressure. To improve your management of multiple communication tasks, consider these procedural steps well in advance.

WORKSTATION ENVIRONMENT EXERCISES

WHAT TO DO

- Sit upright – chair supporting lower back.
- Keep thighs and forearms parallel (or angled slightly down) with floor, feet flat on floor, neck straight, and elbows at waist.
- Place mouse on same level as keyboard to avoid raised shoulder; mouse close to side of keyboard and body to avoid an outstretched arm; alternate sides each week.
- Position screen, use document holder and learn to touch type in order to attain a straight neck posture.
- NOW: RELAX ALL BODY PARTS

WHAT TO AVOID

- Resting wrists on desk when keying or pausing.
- Chair too low; chair pressure on back of knees.
- Sustained neck flexion and/or twisting.

TAKE CARE

- Eyes – if you experience vision problems at the computer, consult your optometrist. If you perform more than 25% VDU work, have your eyes checked regularly.

Head and Neck

Head and Neck
Gently turn head to left, then to right. Lower chin gently to chest, and then raise head until looking straight ahead. Repeat several times.

Upper Back

Upper Back
Grasp raised arm below elbow. Gently pull elbow towards opposite shoulder. Repeat with other arm.

Shoulders

Shoulders
Roll shoulders forward in a circular motion five times, then reverse direction.

Wrists

Wrists
Extend arms in front of body. Raise and lower hands. Repeat several times. Rotate hands in one direction several times, and then reverse direction.

Hands and Fingers

Hands and Fingers
Form fingers into a fist, then release by spreading fingers wide apart with palm down. Repeat several times.

FIGURE 1.2 **Occupational health and safety tips for working with computers**
(Source: Brochure *Don't let your posture cost you!* Produced by The Occupational Health and Safety Unit at The Australian National University)
(NOTE: VDU desk should be a minimum of 900 mm deep × 1200 mm wide)

Exercise: multiple communication task planning

Step 1

Count the number of days that remain to the due date of your last item of assessment.

Step 2

Work out how many days from your total number of days you wish to allot to each item of assessment. Consider the value of each item of assessment in doing this – an item worth 20 per cent does not warrant time equal to an item worth 80 per cent.

Step 3

Nominate an end-date for completion of all tasks for each item of assessment. Your end-dates will not be the same as *actual* submission dates or exam dates, as indicated below for three hypothetical items of assessment to take place in one week in June:

(lst essay due 16 June): end-date for completion 9 May
(2nd essay due 18 June): end-date for completion 3 June
(Exam on 20 June): end-date for all revision 19 June

The end-dates here signal completion of one item before moving on to the next. You may prefer to work simultaneously on specific tasks associated with two or more items (for example, database searching for the second essay while drafting the first).

Step 4

Discriminate tasks needing to be done to meet your end-date for each item of assessment. For example, for an essay (see 'The research essay' in Chapter 5), these tasks might be:

- Search for appropriate source material after brainstorming the topic (see 'Topics or (questions)' in Chapter 5).
- Read identified source material and take notes.

- Produce an essay outline (see 'Visual mapping of material' and 'Sequential outlining' in Chapter 4).
- Draft the essay (one, two or three drafts?).
- Proofread, check accuracy of references, tables and other illustrations, and polish presentation.

Step 5

Now set up timelines for the different items of assessment. Include rough estimates of time to complete the specific tasks for each item of assessment, as indicated below by way of my essay example:

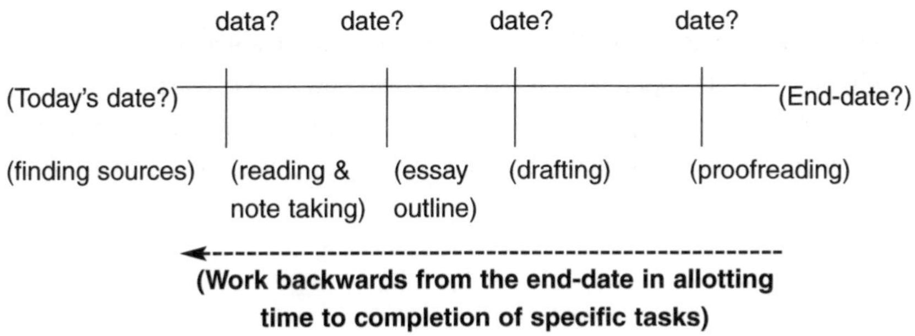

Pin your different timelines above your regular workstation so that you can monitor your progress in meeting deadlines. As writing is hard intellectual work, in setting up timelines of this type do allow sufficient time for drafting and completing papers.

BEING REALISTIC ABOUT THE DEMANDS OF WRITING

> **Writing is intellectually hard work. So do be generous in allotting time to complete your writing tasks.**

You may have concerns about the time and effort it takes to write (many graduates do), and such concerns may linger even if you seem to be progressing well. Whether there are actual problems requiring attention, or whether the amount of time and effort expended is to be expected given the difficulty of the writing task, can be a moot point. If you do have serious concerns along these lines, consider the following exercise. Interesting patterns and insights can emerge from this type of close scrutiny of your own writing.

Exercise: self-monitoring when writing

Step 1

On the next occasion of writing, monitor under what conditions you feel stuck (for example, generating ideas about your topic; uncertainty about how to proceed with the type of writing you are doing; organizing your paragraphs or linking parts of your discussion; marshalling evidence in an argument and ensuring logical development of your ideas; or writing up a theory section or chapter).

Step 2

Take concise notes about these instances. Note what is actually happening, why you think it is happening (if you can), and how long it takes you to overcome the difficulty – a matter of hours? days? or what? Also monitor how many days/weeks it takes you from the first phase of writing to completion of the draft.

Step 3

Make an appointment with a lecturer, supervisor, or a language, learning or writing adviser to discuss your notes.

Confronting the 'writing block' As many students phrase their difficulties in terms of 'writing blocks', the subject does need airing. This is a somewhat fuzzy concept that generally translates as: 'I just can't write.' But do take heart. Writing blocks can usually be traced to quite identifiable factors, often interrelated. Typical factors are:

- Confusion about specific task requirements, such as uncertainty about how to proceed with a particular type of writing or part of it, or not having to hand the type of information needed to complete the task (see 'Preparing the ground' in Chapter 2).
- Uncertainty about expectations of academic writing practices and how to take control of specific situations, like avoiding plagiarism (see 'Reflecting on current practice' in Chapter 3).
- Insufficient control of strategies for whole text development (see 'Whole text development' in Chapter 4).

- An incomplete understanding of subject matter, perhaps because time pressures have thwarted attempts to build up a thorough understanding of your material, in which case review your time management.

Computers too can feature in writing problems. Computers allow you many advantages when writing, including shifting chunks of material within and across documents. But shifting material around can contribute to incoherence in writing. Print out texts that you have altered by shifting material around. It seems to be easier to identify disruptions to the flow of a discussion, and other substantive problems, by reading a printout than by moving down a screen.

Nevertheless, deeply rooted psychological problems (for example, a fear of writing or over-perfectionism) can cause severe blockages in which case they may need to be worked through with a professional counsellor at your institution. These few tips should otherwise help you to cut through writing blocks:

- Ensure you do allow sufficient time to complete your writing tasks. Sometimes the stress occasioned by having to rush the writing to meet deadlines itself becomes a block.

- Do not delay writing. As I repeatedly stress, it is important to start writing early and to keep writing. To begin writing a first draft of a thesis or long report without having produced writing along the way that will feed into it is not a good idea.

- If you are finding it difficult to start writing, access the writing at a point at which it seems least difficult. Usually some parts are easier to write than others. Do not concern yourself too much with issues of focus and structure – just get ideas down.

- Try not to leave off writing at a point at which you feel blocked. This makes it harder to return to the writing. Knowing where you are going in your writing provides incentive to return to it.

HANDLING CRITICAL FEEDBACK

Another important issue in managing the writing concerns critical feedback. Criticism is a valuable feedback mechanism. Understandably though, students can be sensitive to criticism of their drafts and presentations. Where the criticism is perceived as unduly harsh, some become so upset their confidence plunges and they are left feeling vulnerable. If this should happen, it is important to remember that it is your writing that is being criticized (or it should be), not you:

- Seek immediate support from your institution's counselling centre if you are very upset.
- Put aside your draft for a few days until you can assess the criticisms with more detachment.
- Think carefully about the usefulness of the criticisms in terms of your research focus and objectives, your arguments, structure and so forth.
- Discuss the criticisms further with your lecturer/supervisor if you feel the need.
- Where you do decide to reject certain criticisms, think about *why* so that you can communicate your reasons clearly to your lecturer/supervisor.
- If you think it will help, seek assistance from an academic skills, learning or writing adviser when redrafting.

Sometimes though, it is not the criticism itself but the tone of the criticism that upsets. You may perceive comments as overly aggressive or condescending. Take this up with your supervisor/lecturer if you feel able to. Let them know that, while you value their critical feedback, you were upset by the way this was given; have an example or two to show if they ask: 'What do you mean'?

Many students also mention the unbalanced nature of critical feedback on their writing. They say that lecturers and supervisors seem to perceive useful feedback as consisting solely in negative comments and give no positive feedback at all. Yet as one student astutely observed of her supervisor:

> *I'm sure my supervisor has no idea how destructive it is to constantly rip apart my writing – it makes me feel so stupid. But I know he means to be helpful – he makes lots of effort when he reads my drafts – thinks about everything – makes lots of suggestions. He's a good supervisor in many ways – he's great to discuss ideas with, and tries to help. He probably thinks he's doing the right thing.*

Supervisors may well perceive detailed criticism as the most effective method to help you revise your drafts. If the criticism is overly negative, next time you submit a draft ask your supervisor to comment on the positive aspects as well as areas for improvement. Most importantly, try to extract value from the criticism and use it to improve drafts and presentations – do not take it too personally.

Communicating with lecturers and supervisors

Good communication is the key to establishing positive working relationships with your lecturers and supervisors. Never think that you may be thought inadequate because of some question (however trivial) you want to ask – you are always learning and your lecturer/supervisor is there to help you progress. Also, never assume that your supervisor will recognize that you do need help – supervisors are busy, preoccupied people too, and may think that all is going well for you if you do not tell them otherwise.

> **Ask questions – any questions you want to ask – and keep asking them until you understand, until the matter is clarified or resolved.**

RESOLVING UNCERTAINTIES

Simple communication queries may be quickly answered in class or even in casual conversation with your lecturer/supervisor at a chance meeting. If, however, you have more substantive enquiries, or indeed are having serious problems, you will need to take action to resolve these by arranging a meeting with your lecturer or supervisor.

Exercise: resolution action planning

Step 1: clarifying the nature of your uncertainties

Clarify the nature of your uncertainties before the meeting takes place by considering questions of this type:

- What precisely do I need to clarify or sort out (detail these)?
- Under what conditions do my uncertainties about writing/communication arise (try to be specific)?
- What outcomes do I hope for in a meeting with my lecturer/supervisor (jot these down)?

Step 2: setting up a discussion agenda

Setting up a discussion agenda is a useful strategy when initiating meetings with your lecturer or supervisor. When you have clarified precisely what you wish to discuss and reasons for doing so:

- Make a concise dot-point list for discussion (your agenda).
- Give your lecturer/supervisor a copy of your agenda before the meeting so that she/he has time to review your points.

Step 3: at the meeting

It is very easy for any meeting to become sidetracked, and when you meet with your lecturer/supervisor, you want the discussion to remain focused on your concerns:

- If the lecturer/supervisor begins to digress (students often report this), try to re-focus his/her attention on your agenda, those points worked out during the clarification process.
- Keep an eye on time so that you will be able to get through all the points on your agenda.
- You want the meeting to be helpful to you, so do not hesitate to say so if you are still not clear about what your lecturer/supervisor is advising.

EMAIL COMMUNICATION ISSUES

Email communication between students and lecturers/supervisors is increasingly popular, convenient, easy to use and may afford a welcome degree of anonymity not possible in face-to-face conversation. It can be an appropriate and effective medium of communication. Still, where there is a choice of communication media (for example, face-to-face-talk, telephone or email), it is worth considering whether email is the best option given the nature of your subject matter, the purpose of your communication and a possible need for privacy. Certainly, issues do arise in terms of the appropriateness and effectiveness of email as a medium of communication between graduates and their lecturers/supervisors.

Appropriateness

- Will your lecturer/supervisor welcome your emails? If yes, clarify the purposes for which email communication is to be used before dashing one off. Determine whether there are any restrictions on what types of emails lecturers/supervisors might welcome and when (for example, making an appointment might be welcomed whereas expecting written comments – let alone copious comments – on an attached draft might not).

- Email communication may seem a less confrontational forum for discussing sensitive or difficult matters, but it may not be the most appropriate for resolution of these matters. It can be difficult to encode in written communication nuances of feeling, to achieve a fuller understanding without those non-verbal cues that can be so vital in resolution dialogue. Perhaps a telephone conversation or face-to-face-talk might be a better option.

- Avoid dashing off an email if you are feeling angry or upset about something, one that may antagonize or alienate the recipient. It is most important to practise self-censoring – sit on the email for a day or night until you have calmed down. Think further about the wording of your email before hitting the send button, or maybe you should not send it at all.

- Privacy or confidentiality can never be assured with email, and deletion does not mean final erasure. Emails can go to the wrong address, others may have access to the recipient's computer, the recipient can pass emails on without a sender's permission, and they can be retrieved from servers after deletion. So think twice about using this medium if confidentiality is a high priority.

Effectiveness

- The quality of the relations between you and your lecturer/supervisor will influence the effectiveness of your email communications. Where there is trust and openness, these should work well. But where tensions exist, particularly in a context of unequal power relations, email might not be the best choice. At least think about it.

- The desired timescale of the communication can also affect effectiveness. Many students report frustration at delayed responses, or no response at all. This might mean that the lecturer/supervisor is away, that the email is not welcomed, that it has been accidentally overlooked in a hundred other unread emails (a big problem) or that the pressure of overall responsibilities has prevented the lecturer/supervisor from providing a timely response. A follow-up email may help, but not necessarily – you may still need to telephone or make a face-to-face appointment if possible.

- Clarity of communication is also important. As with any written text, it is important to think carefully about audience needs and overall text quality to ensure a message will be clearly understood by the recipient. It is easy for misunderstandings to arise with hastily put together emails, and so invite an unhelpful or negative response.

- Providing critical feedback on (sometimes lengthy) texts via email is, in my experience of doing this, a somewhat unsatisfactory option for both lecturer and student, but perhaps the only option. The on-line medium itself constrains development of the more task-sensitive dialogue developed in face-to-face communication, which is so valuable in negotiating understanding about textual production and settling on strategies for improvement. So bear this in mind if the email feedback seems somewhat brusque or even insensitive.

As a final point, where sensitive issues are being dealt with via email over time, keep hard-copy records in case there is a future need to review this 'conversation' as, for example, in resolving differences of opinion about what transpired in the course of events.

Issues in cross-cultural writing and communication

Many of the writing and communication challenges experienced by international students are similar to those experienced by other graduates, so do review the previous discussions. None the less, it is unwise to assume that what has previously worked for you will do so now, and equally unwise to attribute all communication difficulties to a problem with English if English is a second language, perhaps even a third. Cross-cultural issues of the following type may arise because of your embedded expectations about teaching and learning and the conduct of relations between students and academic staff.

- **Taking a fully critical approach:** It will be expected that you do take a fully critical approach to all materials being worked in your writing and communication. If the need for analysis, critical appraisal and argument in writing is proving difficult and challenging, the section on 'Treating information critically' in Chapter 2 will help; also review 'Evidence and reasoning' in Chapter 5.

- **Using the disciplinary language:** Using the disciplinary language (as distinct from English) may also cause you concern when writing and presenting, in which case spend more time on 'Linguistic features' in the exercise under 'Mastering (inter)disciplinary writing practices' in Chapter 2.

- **Acquiring independence as a researcher:** If you come from a culture where the teacher/supervisor is viewed as the authority from whom the student is to learn, you may expect that your supervisor will direct every stage of your studies or research. A major expectation in Western universities is that students be self-directed, with guidance from a lecturer/supervisor. This is a crucial reason to talk through a supervisory relationship early, so that you are clear about what will be expected of you and what you can expect from your supervisor. What you find out could be very different from what happens in your home country. Also, different supervisors will have different expectations.

- **Accepting guidance as a researcher:** If you are returning to study from a position of authority and respect in your home country (perhaps even as a senior academic), you may find it hard becoming a student again. Your adjustment in this case may invite strategies quite the opposite of those mentioned above. You might need to work at not being too independent, at accepting an appropriate level of guidance from your supervisor. Some supervisors mention that occasionally international students are inclined to totally ignore their advice and guidance. Doing this is not recommended. Supervisory input is important for many reasons, including ensuring the thesis meets the standards appropriate for the level of the degree, of which supervisors will certainly have the best understanding.

- **Entering the 'conversation' in a tutorial:** You may find the tutorial meeting a somewhat strange affair, with everyone talking at once. You may perhaps even think students disrespectful to the lecturer, and the tutorial unhelpful in providing instruction. But this is a matter of different cultural behaviour. Because of the emphasis on critical engagement, lecturers often choose not to provide answers, but will prefer instead to stimulate students to think for themselves by asking questions of them, allowing them to discuss issues as a group, to challenge each other's viewpoints and the lecturer's own, and to argue and debate at will. Some international students can find it difficult to join in, being too polite to interrupt others. If you have this problem, ask for your lecturer's help; try at every tutorial meeting to have just one point from your reading you want to introduce into the discussion – ask your lecturer if he or she could invite you to speak at an agreed-on signal. You will gradually become confident enough to enter this 'noisy' conversation.

- **Speaking confidently in English:** Most graduates worry about giving tutorials, seminars or conference presentations (see 'Oral and Visual Presentations' in Chapter 8), though not all have the added burden of speaking in a language not native to them. If pronunciation is a particular concern, ask an English-speaking friend, your lecturer/supervisor, or some other appropriate person to run through your paper with you to practise pronouncing words about which you are uncertain.

- **Conducting interpersonal relations:** In conducting interpersonal relations with lecturers and supervisors, you may find marked differences. You may need to be more pro-active in asking questions, in negotiating the terms of, say, a relationship with your supervisor, in adjusting to different forms of address (for example, using first names), or in setting discussion agendas for meetings with your supervisor. If you are asked to do the latter, between meetings with your supervisor keep notes on:

  (a) Interesting ideas about or interpretations of your readings and data.

  (b) Ideas you have about your overall research plan.

  (c) Suggestions for changes in focus or direction of your research.

  (d) Any uncertainties about or difficulties with content or research procedures that need discussing.

  (e) Anything else you consider important to discuss.

If English language/expression is preventing you from communicating clearly in writing, consider various avenues of assistance:

- Find out what assistance your lecturer/supervisor is prepared to provide.

- Investigate assistance provided by academic skills, learning or writing services within your institution.

- Search for helpful Web materials or on-line services that focus on English grammar/expression/pronunciation.

- Identify whether there are courses for credit in English for Academic Purposes that you may be able to take.

Most useful is to practise your English in context. By this I mean in situations where you are actually in the process of producing the various texts required in your degree, or preparing your presentations. While this type of developmental assistance will help you to improve your control of English, it will not necessarily extend to a full editing service – that is to say, fixing the grammar. Where I consider there is a further need to profile second language issues, I do so in the appropriate context throughout this book.

Summary Comments

- Colleagues, friends and family can be wonderful sources of support if you cultivate their understanding.
- By taking steps to manage yourself and your writing you will reduce stress and increase your enjoyment of writing and other communication activities.
- Never be afraid to ask questions (however trivial they may seem) of your lecturers and supervisors who are there to help you develop skills and take control of writing and communication tasks.
- Be aware of, but not unduly anxious about, cross-cultural challenges you may need to address in writing and communication – you will overcome these.

2 Preparing the Ground

Developmental Objectives

By applying the strategies, doing the exercises and following the procedural steps in this chapter, you should be able to:

- Understand the powerful shaping influence of genre (type of writing) and (inter)disciplinary practices on all academic writing and communication.
- Build on your current bank of skills by studying genre and (inter)disciplinary writing practices suited to the different types of writing you now have to produce.
- Develop competence in treating information critically so that you do have the right *type* of information for your writing tasks.
- Appreciate that having the best information means accessing *quality* academic sources, both print and electronic.
- Understand the importance of clearly defining research goals/aims before proceeding to data collection so as to ensure task-focused information.
- Identify strategies to read effectively for different purposes, define reading goals to meet specific task requirements, cut down on unproductive reading, and improve information retrieval to reduce frustration when writing.

This chapter covers information management practices, which are vitally important in ensuring you will have the best and right information to successfully complete a specific writing task, whether that task involves writing a report, a research essay, a thesis, or any other type of writing.

The graduate writing culture

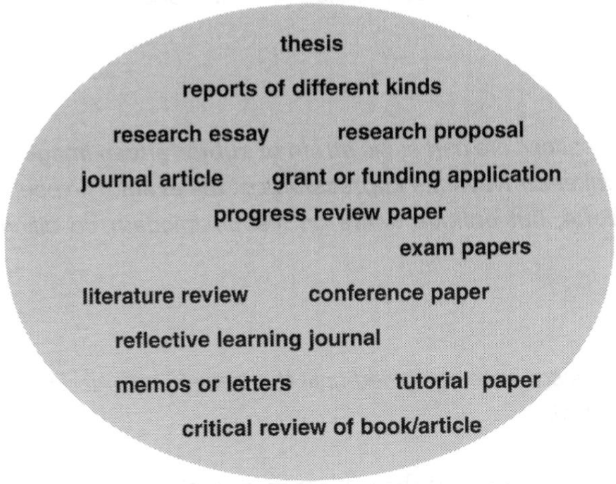

FIGURE 2.1 **A representative sample of graduate genres**

The graduate writing culture is indeed complex. You may find yourself producing different types of genres, a representative sample of which I show in Figure 2.1. Because different academic genres have distinctive purposes, they can have different underlying conventions that affect the language, style, structure and treatment of information, all of which are further influenced by preferred disciplinary practices.

Because of this complexity, you could find yourself confronting unanticipated challenges: doing types of writing with which you are unfamiliar; or finding your understanding of a particular type of writing is now insufficient (for example, you have experience of writing reports in the workplace or in an undergraduate degree, but find you need to change/ adapt your practices to meet specific requirements of report writing in your present course); or discovering that the *types* of questions raised in treating familiar concepts/information are now different in your present course.

> **Take time to orient yourself to specific requirements of course genres if you are transferring disciplines at a graduate level, returning to study or research after many years in the workforce, or have not previously studied in Western universities.**

Or perhaps you are grappling with a new disciplinary language because you are transferring disciplines. By disciplinary language, I mean language of the type I have emphasized in these extracts from different disciplinary writers:

Law

In ACTV and Nationwide, a majority of the Justices ***drew the implication*** *of a freedom of speech from the overall structure or fabric of … X argued that* *freedom of speech regarding political matters is required for the proper working of government and as such* ***ruled the relevant sections*** *of the Political Disclosures Act 1991 (ACTV) and the Industrial Relations Act 1988 (Nationwide) as invalid [reference].*

English
These snippets of conversations are part of the ***strain of subterranean imagery through which the speaker conveys his impressions of the event.*** *The poem can be seen as a* ***forceful, but oblique satire*** *on the 'postmodern' condition [reference].*

Systems Engineering
Reports from the sonar sensor were combined until ***the belief*** *converged to be equal to or greater than 0.99.*

You will see that it is not just the nature of the subject matter (the content) that is different in each case, as expected. In the Law example, the phrases emphasized are distinctly legal; we would not normally talk about drawing the implication of 'a freedom', or ruling 'relevant sections'. Equally distinctive are the 'literary' language of the English example, and the unusual use of the word 'belief' – meaning 'probability distribution' – in the Engineering example.

MASTERING (INTER)DISCIPLINARY WRITING PRACTICES

The first step then in preparing the ground is to clarify expectations of the type of writing you now have to do. Of course your lecturers/supervisors may advise you on what is expected, but you can teach yourself if needs be. The exercise below is designed to help you gain control of genre and disciplinary practices.

Exercise: mastering (inter)disciplinary writing practices

You are already highly trained to read for content, what an author is saying. It is also possible to train yourself to focus on how a text is put together, what it does rather than what it says.

Step 1

Select a sample of the specific type of writing you now have to do (for example, an essay, report or thesis) – ask your lecturer/supervisor to provide you with a good model or to refer you to well-written theses that have passed examination. If working from a published article, select one that you find enjoyable and easy to read regardless of the difficulty of the content, as not all publications are equally well written.

Step 2

Set aside regular time to focus on aspects of language, style, expression and structure – perhaps an hour or two twice a week. Identify those aspects of the disciplinary language and writing on which you wish to focus.

Step 3

Set yourself specific tasks. Remember, you are not primarily concerned with what the author is saying about the subject, but how the author goes about discussing the subject – the composition processes. Decide to focus on *one* thing at a time, as selected from the categories below:

Treatment of information:

- The *types* of information writers include in different sections of their text, as in the parts of a thesis or report.
- How writers treat their information, the questions they raise, the issues they think are important, the theories, models, methodologies they apply, and so forth (important in contexts of disciplinary transfer).
- How writers handle theory in their discussions, develop arguments, provide supporting evidence, present and discuss results or data.
- The type of material that seems to go into Appendices rather than the body of the writing, and how such material is used and referred to in the body of the text.

Linguistic features:

- Typical terminology or phraseology being used by discipline writers.
- The language/phraseology used to describe specific procedures or methods or other processes.

- Whether first person 'I' is used in some parts of the text, or not at all.
- Verb tenses chosen to report on other scholars' work, or verb tenses preferred in different parts of a text, or the range and type of reporting verbs used (see 'Selecting a reporting tense/verbs' Chapter 3).
- Language choices. Think about how obvious, predictable, unusual, striking, effective the language is, and also the range of the vocabulary, which may become a way of extending your own vocabulary.

Organizational features (see also 'Whole text development', Chapter 4):

- How writers divide up the overall text by way of parts and/or chapters. Scrutinize the actual headings. Think about whether these provide a sense of how the whole text fits together.
- Whether it is usual to use sub-headings, and if yes, how effective these headings are in focusing the main theme of the text beneath, how much text appears under sub-headings, whether these sub-headings are numbered and/or titled, and whether there are explicit or implicit attempts to link the different divisions.
- How an introduction, a conclusion, a literature review, a results, a discussion, a theory or methodology section, or any other part of the writing is composed. Look at what the writer is actually doing, the step-by-step moves, and think about why this organization suits that writer's purposes.
- The structure of a paragraph, and how writers link paragraphs, the implicit or explicit strategies they use, the actual words or phrases used (see 'Developing texts' in Chapter 4).
- How writers lay out tables, figures or graphs, or present maps, and how they refer to these in their texts.
- How writers of large theses organize their bibliographies, whether they divide their sources into categories by way of sub-headings or not.
- Under what conditions writers signpost what they will do and where they are going, how obvious or subtle such signposting is, and how effective writers are in taking care of audience needs, your needs as the reader.

You could reserve a special book in which to build up sets of notes relating to disciplinary practices for easy future reference.

CASE STUDY
Example

Box 2.1 Students report significant benefits from studying (inter)disciplinary writing practices

A second-language student experiencing difficulty in using English verb tenses gathered an impressive set of examples on their complex usage in thesis writing in her discipline of Archaeology, which helped her to overcome the problem. Another graduate reported that he felt he had '*learnt*' the art of argument by studying: as he said, *'how they put their arguments together and what evidence means'*. Yet another student having difficulty writing strong discussion sections studied organizational strategies of *'discussions'* in published articles and said he felt *'much more confident about how to do it'*.

Treating information critically

How you read or treat material can affect whether or not you will have the necessary information to produce your texts.

In extracting factual information from source materials, your focus will be on the details of what is being said. To illustrate, you might need to distinguish clearly the different anatomical functions of the human body, or to model accurately the plan of a complex irrigation system. You will need to know the facts. Similarly, your purpose could be to identify details such as when certain events took place, where these occurred and on what dates, and who was involved. Again you will need to know the facts, a fact being information that is accepted as true, and is not contested in the literature as some so-called facts are.

Questions such as What? When? Where? and Who? tend to stimulate the recall of information for the purpose of reproducing knowledge. This is a legitimate and important purpose in writing, which may dominate the process at times, and at other times complement critical evaluation, which is fundamental to all academic writing and communication.

CRITIQUING: CRITICALLY EVALUATING SOURCE MATERIALS

The term 'critique', meaning the critical art, or critical evaluation or analysis, seems more appropriate for the academic context than the term 'criticism', with its embedded negative connotations. Critiquing involves evaluating strengths and weaknesses of discussions/arguments across a range of authors, bearing in mind that the generation of knowledge tends to turn on the clash of ideas emanating from the community of world.

Still you will need to be clear about what is being said, not always easy in itself. You will also need to extend your range of questions when dealing with source material to engage questions to do with the why and how of the research: to hold your sources in relation, to compare and contrast the positions of different authors, to draw out the issues being debated and so forth.

Critical evaluation requires holding your sources in relation.

Exercise: practising critiquing

The scenario

Imagine you are required to read reports, articles and other studies about the topic 'Greenhouse effects on the global environment' in order to produce a report advocating measures to reduce greenhouse emissions. On reading, you discover that there is considerable disagreement amongst scholars about which measures should be introduced, and why.

The challenge

How then do you begin to evaluate the experts? If your previous tertiary experience was one in which critiquing was not common, this could prove challenging. But the challenge will seem less if you recognize that where there is difference of opinion in scholarship the different viewpoints themselves will provide material for your critique. It is often explicit or implicit in one author's discussion what is problematic in another's.

The critique (question-raising)

In conducting the critique, you would be drawing on your knowledge of the subject, which may include valuable general, specialist, experiential and/or cultural knowledge that you have. At the same time, you would be raising questions of this type in order to map central issues in the arguments and debates surrounding the subject:

What is the full range of measures identified by the different authors? List these as you read, and perhaps categorize them too in a way that seems useful. To what extent do the authors agree or disagree about which measures should be implemented: is there considerable agreement? a reasonable amount? hardly any? Draw up a list of measures commonly agreed on, another where there seems to be a reasonable amount of agreement, and another where there seems to be strong disagreement, presuming this sort of division applies.

In the process of clarifying what is being said, think about *why* authors take the positions they do. The first question to ask yourself is: what are the issues here? What *are* the points on which authors disagree and why? Identify and consider these carefully: list points and reasons. One issue on which authors might disagree could be the division of costs across state boundaries; another, whether or not there should be *compulsory* reduction targets for *all* nations.

Continue your questioning. What reasons do authors give for the measures they prefer? Is there any overlap here? How do these measures line up in terms of advantages and disadvantages, and for whom? From where do these authors draw their evidence? Are their sources reliable? What types of evidence do they present in advocating different measures? Do they use statistics, examples from scientific reports or what as evidence? Are the statistics sound? Do the examples make sense to you: why? why not? Could a discussion be too narrow (or too broad) because important information is left out? Perhaps you can recognize this from reading other authors. Can you see any biased assumptions behind the evidence, perhaps because of the methodology or theory framing their discussions, or cultural biases (for example, the East/West divide)? In short, how convincing are the reasons they give for the measures they advocate?

During reading, you will generate further questions as you refine your understanding of the subject.

The outcome

By the end of the critique a transformation will have taken place in your knowledge base, as you will have used a range of authors to deepen and clarify your thinking about the subject. The intelligence and creativity with which you handle source materials, and the subtlety of your insights, are matters of individual judgement that will influence the position or point of view you take on any topic. *You* have to decide which authors or aspects of their studies convince you and *why they do*, and which do not and *why they do not*. In rearranging all that you have taken apart in the analysis of a topic – any topic – when you write your paper you will be making a new synthesis, with your position at the centre of that synthesis.

CRITICALLY EVALUATING THEORY

If theory does feature in your writing, you will need to critically engage with it. Reading and critically evaluating theory, or philosophical works applied in analysis, can be particularly challenging, as can the critique of models or methodologies. It could be that your course includes much new theory so that you do not feel you have a sound knowledge base from which to exercise your critical judgement. Or you may be unpractised in critiquing theory, having never before done this in an academic context.

The term 'theory' is often used loosely in the academic community. The meaning I follow is: 'The formulation of abstract knowledge or speculative thought; systematic conception of something' (*New Shorter Oxford English Dictionary*). I think of a theory as a clearly identifiable, abstract body of knowledge, one that has been conceived systematically.

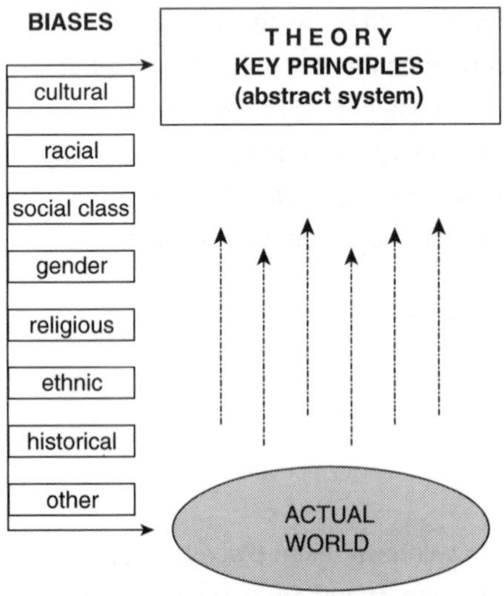

FIGURE 2.2 **How theories work**

Theories are abstract systems in which certain aspects (the key ideas or principles of a theory) are privileged by an author over other possibilities. Theorists abstract from the chaotic, actual world of everyday events and activities that which they consider most significant to explain that world, or some aspect of it. Theories are useful for their explanatory value, and perhaps their predictive value. They can open up different possibilities in ways of perceiving and understanding complex events and happenings important in your context of academic enquiry, and so prove to be valuable tools of analysis. But they do have their limitations.

You will need to critically evaluate how well the particular theory does in fact explain what it sets out to explain – its strengths and weaknesses. Critiques by other scholars or schools of scholars, and those of your lecturers/supervisors, can provide a sound starting point for your own critical evaluation of a particular body of theory. Before conducting your critical assessment, however, you will first need to know what the theory is really all about – not always easy in itself.

All established disciplines have specialist dictionaries (or reference works). Making use of these is a useful orientation strategy before you read more deeply and comprehensively in the theoretical literature.

As you read, probe the assumptions about the nature of the world that underpin the key ideas or principles of the body of theory you are studying. Think about whether these assumptions are biased or not (see Figure 2.2). Cultural bias, for example, would be evident if the assumptions underlying a theory of human behaviour proved to be strongly Western-centric and not inclusive of all cultures.

Refer to a specialist dictionary or reference work in your discipline to gain an initial overview of a theory or unfamiliar terms/ concepts.

Just one final point. If you are asked to develop a theoretical framework, an analytical framework or a conceptual framework for your thesis or other writing, you may be uncertain about what distinguishes these. (Students often mention this type of confusion.) In Figure 2.3, I attempt to distinguish these frameworks by way of how they might function in writing. Do confirm with your lecturer/ supervisor though that these understandings will apply.

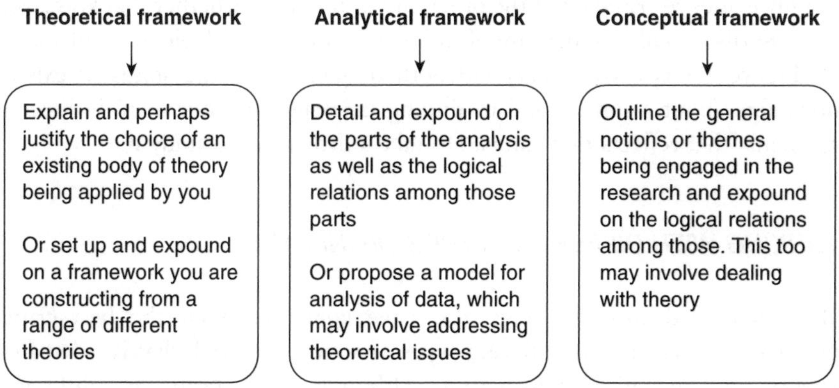

FIGURE 2.3 **Different types of frameworks**

Percentage guide	Quantity	Frequency	Probability Adverbs/adjectives	Verbs
100%	all/every/each most	always	certain(ly) definite(ly) undoubtedly probably/probable	will is/are must/have to should
	a majority (of) many/much a lot (of) enough some	usual(ly) normal(ly) general(ly) regular(ly) often	likely	ought to
	a number (of) several a minority (of) a few/a little few/little	frequent(ly) sometimes occasional(ly) rare(ly) seldom hardly ever scarcely ever	perhaps possibly/possible maybe unlikely	may might can could
0%	no/none/not any	never		will is/are can could } + not

FIGURE 2.4 **Scale of qualification (Jordan, 1980: 60)**

CRITICAL ENQUIRY AND THE STATUS OF EXISTING KNOWLEDGE

Recognizing the status of existing knowledge on a subject can also be important when exercizing your critical judgement: the extent to which that knowledge is strongly evidence-based or, at the other end of the scale, whether that knowledge is necessarily speculative because of the scant evidence available to scholars.

Figure 2.4 is a vocabulary aid both to identifying the status of existing knowledge about a subject and to finding language for your own discussions/arguments that reflects that status. Do take a little time to study it.

WORKING WITH DIFFERENT TYPES OF INFORMATION

Like other graduates, you may also have concerns about the best critical approach to working with different types of source material, that is, what I call primary and secondary information, although these terms are differently understood across academic areas.

By primary information, I mean

- Raw data generated by you through, for example, tests, experiments or field research; data sets from pre-existing databases generated by others; archival materials (for example, journals, diaries or letters written by, say, historical figures, or original historical documents); policy documents generated by, say, governments and other organizations; state and international legal legislation – also court judgments; literary, art or religious works; and so forth.

By secondary information, I mean:

- Any texts that provide critical commentary of whatever sort on texts categorized under primary information above, such as journal publications, books or chapters in scholarly books, book reviews, etc.

One issue that does arise is whether it is better to read primary information (for example, a complex piece of legislation or a literary work) before secondary information or vice versa. It will be difficult for you to critically evaluate secondary source materials providing commentary on a primary source, without first having a reasonably sound understanding of that primary source. So I suggest a circular approach:

- Start with the primary source, move to secondary sources, return to the primary source and continue to move between the two types as you refine your critical judgement.

FOLLOWING YOUR HUNCHES

Your greatest asset is your own critical intelligence. You will have hunches as you read: something does not seem right, or the argument does not convince you, or

you sense that some approach or procedure is problematic, or you think perhaps there is a better way, or the data appear dubious, or the underlying assumptions just do not seem to add up, or you suspect the theory being used has skewed the interpretation, or the questions being asked do not seem to be the right ones, or something mentioned in passing strikes you as important but has not been recognized as such. These hunches may be vague and imprecise: half-formed ideas, questions marked by uncertainty, sceptical or doubtful responses or passing intuitions about other possibilities.

It is easy to let these hunches, these instinctive responses, slip away as you push on with the reading. But try not to do this. Stop and ask yourself why you might be responding as you are. It may be that your hunch arose spontaneously from the fact that your general life or work experience suggested something different from what was being reported, or that other disciplinary knowledge you have was pushing you to respond sceptically. While it may take time and further reading to clarify the reason for your response, having such hunches come to fruition in a reasoned argument is the peak of treating information critically.

> **Hunches can be the seeds of the best critical insights, the subtlest ideas, the very ideas you want to bring to the writing of your texts.**

Ensuring task-focused information

It is possible to have masses of data and source material but still to lack the information you need to successfully complete your writing task. There are different reasons why this occurs, four major ones being:

1. Uncertainty about how to proceed with a particular type of writing, or parts of the writing, as perhaps with what to cover in a specialized report and how to structure it, or what to include in an introduction as opposed to a discussion section of a paper, and how each part might be focused and developed. Uncertainty about how to proceed with a specific writing task inhibits prediction of information needs. This is a matter given considerable attention in Part Two of this book, which looks closely at different types of writing and presentations.

2. Uncertainty about how to pin down the best information when searching large databases or conducting general Internet searches. This type of uncertainty often leads to information overload as well as inadequate information, and is most stressful.

> **To refine search techniques, find out what information literacy training programmes are available in your institution.**

3. Insufficient attention to assessing the academic merit of potential source material.

4 Proceeding with information-gathering without first defining information-gathering goals as these relate to the writing task in hand.

Points 3 and 4 occupy my attention in the subsequent discussions of this section. Initially, I take up point 3. I then discuss point 4 from two angles: generating data and reading the literature.

ASSESSING THE ACADEMIC MERIT OF SOURCE MATERIALS

To produce a quality paper you will need the best information possible, so do think carefully about the academic merit of all potential source materials, both print and electronic. A definite danger in this regard is the tendency to rely on general Internet searching for source materials. This is what I now concentrate on.

Evaluating sources on the Internet Although there is copious information on the Internet, which can be accessed quickly, much of it has not been through the traditional reviewing processes in place for print sources. There are informative and valuable websites with solid, reliable publications (for example, government, industry or organization sites such as the United Nations, or academic sites including electronic journals). There is also a lot of junk, which, however interesting to read, is worthless for your academic research.

> **Ensure that your online sources have equal academic merit with your print sources.**

Do take care, just as you do with traditional print sources. Maintain a healthy scepticism. The following are a few questions and points for you to keep in mind.

- What is the purpose of the website and who is its intended audience? Are these made clear? Can you identify any particular agenda (political, ideological, religious, etc.) behind the site's formation? If yes, the information presented might be biased rather than balanced, and therefore unsuitable for academic research.

- Who is the author of the site? Is it an individual, organization or institution that has some credibility and authority? If so, how is this demonstrated? Does the site allow for multiple contributions and what appears to be the status of the contributors; is there any evidence of scholarly credentials?

- What does the site contain? How comprehensive is it? Is there enough information? Is there too much information? How will the site complement other sources you are using?
- How up-to-date is the site? When was the site created? When was the last time it was updated and how often is it updated?
- How available is the site? How likely is it that the site will be traceable, at least in some form, in the future – in a week? a month? a year? longer? For example, is the site published as an electronic book or journal, or affiliated with a reputable organization or institution?
- What particular benefit does the site offer? How does the content compare with that of other sites you have accessed, or to related print-based materials? How confident are you that the content is accurate and reliable? Is there equivalent or better information readily obtainable from more stable and verifiable sources?
- Is the site presented so that the content is easily accessible, and the access path clear? This is important because your reader may wish to follow up sources you have used.

Just as you need quality academic source materials to ensure the best information, you also need the right type of information to successfully complete writing tasks.

AVOIDING THE URGE TO RUSH INTO DATA-GATHERING

The intricacies of data-gathering, collation, analysis and writing up are complex across disciplines and quite beyond the scope of this book. Nevertheless, be aware that problems of relevance may arise if you rush into data-gathering.

For example, using surveys and/or interviews attracts many researchers across a range of disciplines as a primary method of data-collection. But, as suggested: 'Many students make the mistake of rushing out to do premature and ill-prepared surveys before the research question … and the concepts involved have been properly defined' (Preece, 1994: 97). Preece further notes that *'surveys do require careful thought, advice, discussion with more experienced researchers and time for preparation, and … the role of surveys within the organization of the research needs to be clearly defined'* (1994: 97; emphasis in original).

Interviews also need careful thought. Martyn Denscombe provides an excellent short discussion of interview methods, concluding with a nine-point 'Checklist: preparation for interviews', which begins with these questions:

1 Is the interview method appropriate in terms of:

- The *topic* of the research?
- The need for detailed information?
- Access to informants?
- Necessary time and funding for the interviews?

2 Do I have a clear vision of the *issues* to be *discussed* during the interview?

3 Can the interviews be *scheduled in good time* to allow for the subsequent transcription and analysis of the data? (1998: 121; emphasis in orginal)

The above discussion highlights the importance of discriminating information needs in the process of designing data-gathering instruments.

Clarifying the precise details you should be recording What I say here may be less relevant if you are doing team research, though perhaps not. What details you record when collecting data and how you go about recording them will of course depend on the nature of your research. For example:

- It might be necessary to accurately record instrument-dependent factors (for example, time, temperature, order), to calibrate an instrument, tube or gauge to determine the correct value or weight of something, and to note this.
- Or perhaps there is a need to monitor closely, and record, aspects of the physical environment (for example, the weather, season, time of day, geographical position, etc.) where data-gathering is taking place.
- Or you may need to record contextual factors such as behaviour, action or interaction among group members, which is important in qualitative research.

Do clarify precisely which details you should be recording (and why), and be rigorously consistent in your recording methods.

In deciding which details to record it may be necessary to return to your research goals, to the issues you are engaging with in your research, and to talk further with your supervisor and others in your test or research group before final decision-making. Insufficient or incorrectly recorded details are time-consuming to redress later, and cause considerable stress when writing.

It could also be instructive to compare your chosen method of recording data with those of other practitioners. There may be better ways of organizing the information, and it is useful to realize this at the outset. If you are keeping a lab book, for example, is it possible to improve the quality and accuracy of your notes by recording information in a different style and format?

DEFINING READING GOALS

Much time can be lost to unproductive reading, however fascinating it all may be. So identify your precise goals before embarking on the reading of any material by considering questions of this type:

- Why am I reading this?
- What *type* of information do I hope to gain from this?
- Will this information suffice for my present information needs?
- How much effort should I expend on reading this?
- Do I need to read all of it or only parts of it?
- Is it worth reading at all?

Do avoid reading in a vacuum. Define your information-gathering goals, particularly as these relate to whether:

- You are attempting a broad understanding of the literature, as when trying to get on top of the literature for a big research project.
- You are searching for more focused information to meet already defined research goals of a specific writing or presentation task in your course, as with an essay or report.

READING INTENSIVELY AND SKIMMING

At times you will need to read intensively, by which I mean read every word of a text from the first to the last word. This is likely when:

- There is a set text for a course, perhaps to be read gradually throughout a semester.
- You are trying to build up basic but in-depth knowledge about some area of research or a new discipline.
- You are conducting archival research or need to read primary texts in detail (for example, literary texts, legal or historical documents).
- You have to read difficult, dense texts (for example, legal, scientific or philosophical texts or those that are highly theoretical). Such texts or parts of them may even need re-reading to improve understanding.

Deciding whether a source is worth reading intensively is not always easy. Quick review will not necessarily confirm its appropriateness for your task information needs. This is when you should activate **skimming**. Skimming is particularly useful:

- When you are conducting a broad survey of the literature to determine what has been done generally, perhaps with a view to identifying a suitable topic for research.
- When you are trying to extract only key points or general information from a text. In this case, you would be trying to by-pass the multitude of detail typically embedded in academic analyses and arguments – **key word skimming** might prove useful.
- When you have set up your own topic, having thought through the precise type of information you will need to meet the research goals/objectives of that topic.
- When you have been given a set assignment or project in which the research goals/objectives and scope have been explicitly laid out.

The last two points are particularly relevant if you are a coursework student.

Unproductive reading leads to the information gathered being insufficient to the task, only marginally relevant or even irrelevant. Skimming can cut through unproductive reading, thus giving you time to search out more useful source materials.

> **The time constraints on completing writing and presentation tasks in coursework degrees mean it is imperative not to lose time to unproductive reading.**

First, consider these questions preparatory to skimming:

- In setting up my own topic or project, have I defined my goals/aims/objectives and scope clearly enough to begin, or to refine, information-gathering?
- In addressing a topic set by the lecturer, have I brainstormed the topic to ensure I can deal fully with the central concerns of the topic – all of them? (See 'Topics (or questions)' in Chapter 5).
- Am I clear about the type and extent of information I will need to write the different parts of my text? For example, in the discussion section of a report you will need to situate your findings in relation to those of others, so you will need a full critical understanding of other relevant studies in order to do this.
- Will the information I am gathering allow me to answer the research questions or meet the research goals of my paper, and meet expectations of the type of writing I am doing? Check during the process of information-gathering that you are on target with relevant information.

A major objective of skimming is to determine what precisely the author is discussing or talking about at different points in the text. This will help you to decide whether to read the whole text intensively, or only parts of it because only those parts will meet your present information needs.

Skimming can work because of the way academic texts are organized, as discussed in Chapter 4. To recap briefly, in academic writing paragraphs tend to be built around main ideas that are often placed in the first or last sentence of the paragraph, so making it easy to identify precisely what an author is talking about.

Exercise: skimming texts

Step 1

When reading a **large document** (for example, a book):

- First review the table of contents, then read the introduction intensively to find out the author's goals. Then skim the chapters and sub-divisions to identify which sections/pages might serve your information needs. Note these, but continue with skimming until you have covered the entire document. If there is an index, this too is useful to browse in at this point.

- Read the conclusion intensively to clarify the author's findings.

Step 2

With a **shorter document** (for example a journal article):

- Read the abstract (if there is one) and the introduction intensively to determine the author's objectives, issues to be addressed or arguments to be presented.

- Now begin to skim the text. Read sub-division headings, main ideas in paragraphs so as to identify the subjects under discussion – what the author is talking about. Do try to identify the *precise* subject being covered. To recognize, for example, that an author is talking about economic recession in the USA in a specific period is not enough; you need to know precisely what the focus is – the *effects* (immediate/long-term?) of the recession, the *causes* of the recession, the *impact* on other countries, or what.

Step 3

- Continue reading through the entire text, marking as you go any parts, sections, pages, etc. that seem directly relevant to your information needs.

Step 4

- Now return to those areas you have marked and read them intensively in order to take notes.

Ensuring task-focused information is no less important in the following situation.

> **It is vital to clarify the precise objectives and procedures for assessment. If the instructor delivers these verbally at the beginning of a practical, take careful notes.**

Student laboratories, clinicals and practicals The common component of student laboratories, clinicals and practicals (as distinct from tutorials) is that you learn by doing in a context of practical training suited to future employment. Such learning usually takes place in a structured environment under the guidance of a demonstrator, instructor or lecturer, which puts considerable pressure on your listening, note taking and questioning skills – asking the right questions of the lecturer.

Know exactly which details you should be recording:

- Will you have oral and/or demonstration and/or written tests (for example, a laboratory report, an essay or an exam)?
- Will you, for example, be tested on your ability to describe accurately particular apparatus or equipment, or procedures for using these, including how to adjust, say, the tension on a piece of equipment?
- Will you be tested on your knowledge of requisite safety procedures in using particular materials or equipment?
- Will you be expected to detail the nature of responses taking place under certain stimuli or to codify the underlying principles of such responses (not the same thing)?
- Will you be tested on the effectiveness of your communication skills, say, with patients, including your understanding of cross-cultural communication needs?

Clarify the precise practitioner knowledge, skills and competencies you are required to develop before the start of a practical, and what communication tasks will be expected of you in assessment.

Strategies for information storage

You will also want to retrieve information efficiently so as to reduce the frustration of time wasted when writing. To expand possibilities, talk to other staff and students (over coffee) about how they store information – whether they use computers, cards or electronic managers, such as 'Inspiration' or 'EndNote' – what types of filing systems they set up, and what they see as the advantages of their approach.

By obtaining a variety of views, you should be able to decide on strategies that will allow you to retrieve information more efficiently when you write:

- Do use an electronic reference manager if possible. These take practice to master but can also improve retrieval efficiency, with **key word searching** being a favoured and effective strategy, particularly where the imported database is not very extensive. Your institution may have a site licence for a particular reference manager that you can access free, and may run training courses on how to use it.

These further strategies can be used in tandem with an electronic reference manager or independently of such usage:

- When you have a rough idea of how you might divide up your thesis chapters, however general (for example, theory, methodology chapters), set up separate folders for each chapter. Many students find it useful to set these up quite early in the research. With these folders in place, you can add source materials to the appropriate folder, plus ideas, thoughts and hunches – anything that might be at all relevant – as they occur to you along the way (keep paper and pen beside your bed for those brilliant 3 a.m. insights!). If your chapter organization subsequently changes, then you can re-sort the material into new folders, discarding what you no longer want.

- Categorize information for storage by using different card indexes for different purposes. One card index might be an annotated bibliography of all you have read. Other sets of cards might be categorizations of, say, key concepts, themes, issues, theories or methodologies, or perhaps subject categories.

Figure 2.5 provides a hypothetical illustration of one card from a bibliographical index (*left*), and the formatting of one from a different index covering central themes (*right*).

Where the research is heavily reading-based and there is an extensive literature, category card indexes can assist the streamlining of information retrieval. The 'Euthanasia' theme card in Figure 2.5 would be a useful memory organizer in beginning to write on that topic in that it groups relevant sources and provides comparative commentary, and allows quick access to full bibliographic details of each author as well as more extensive evaluative commentary on each. Cards are not the only option, however. One student reported storing information by way of subject categories on a Microsoft access database; another used her electronic reference manager to set up theme categories.

BIBLIOGRAPHICAL INDEX

Brown, P.Z. (1996) 'Living to die: debating moral right'. *Philosophy Today*, 12:4, pp. 234–65.

Include your own evaluative comments (perhaps in relation to ideas of other authors), plus any direct quotations or paraphrases of interest

Also note whether or not you have photocopied the whole or parts of this article

THEME CARD INDEX

EUTHANASIA

Brown, P.Z.—philosophical approach to the morality of Euth. practices—very good
Chin, K.—see bibl. for direct quotes (interesting case studies)
Parker, T.Q.—dilemmas facing medical practitioners—'medical' issues well covered
Paque, J.—unusual angle on supporters of Euth.—(yes—see paraphrase on bibl. card)
Smith, S.T.—weak challenge to Parker

FIGURE 2.5 **Indexing different types of information**

Summary Comments

- By studying models of the type of writing you now have to do, you can gain insight into composition processes: how a text is put together in terms of focus and structure, how information is treated in the whole or parts, typical phraseology and other composition practices – what the text *does* rather than what it *says*.
- Exercise your critical intelligence when reading: question the underlying assumptions, consider the possibility of theoretical or methodological biases, assess the soundness of the data or evidence, the logic of the arguments and so forth.
- Before embarking on the exciting journey of data-gathering, determine what data you need, why you need these data and what purposes they will serve in terms of your overall research goals and design.
- Never read in a vacuum. Identify what information you need to gather for what precise purposes in terms of your research goals/aims or specific topic objectives, and vary your reading strategies to improve efficiency.

3 Reflecting on Current Practice

Developmental Objectives

By applying the strategies, doing the exercises and following the procedural steps in this chapter, you should be able to:

- Understand whether your current practices will suffice, or whether you need to modify, adapt or develop new practices to meet the communication demands of your course.
- Assess the efficiency of your approach to writing, determine whether there is room for improvement and identify strategies for improving.
- Renew your acquaintance with standard academic writing practices, including the need for consistency, that contribute to the overall quality of the writing.
- Avoid practices that can be construed as plagiarism: understand when to reference sources and why you should do so; and identify strategies for integrating source material, selecting an appropriate academic referencing style and manipulating reporting tenses/verbs effectively.
- Develop understanding of the complex role of the reader and identify strategies for accommodating the reader when you write.
- Identify strategies to ensure clarity in the writing, conciseness (as opposed to wordiness), appropriate use of voice and tone, and to invigorate your writing with precision and energy.

You will already possess a bank of general ideas about writing along with specific textual knowledge, skills and strategies built up from previous tertiary study and/or work experience. While these are indeed valuable, this chapter provides an opportunity for reflection on your current practices. As you may be uncertain about the value of these practices, I also hope that the chapter will provide positive reinforcement.

Reviewing your approach to writing

How you approach writing is not necessarily a problem. Graduates do approach writing quite differently, often relying on established practices.

A QUESTION OF EFFICIENCY

It has been suggested that there are two distinct types of academic writers: **serialists** and **holists**.

> 'Serialists', ... see writing as a sequential process in which the words are corrected as they are written and who plan their writing in detail before beginning to write.
>
> 'Holists' ... can only think as they write and compose a succession of complete drafts. (Lowenthal and Wason, cited in Phillips and Pugh, 1994: 65)

You may shift between these approaches depending on the difficulty of your text, or parts of the text you are producing: for example, you may exhibit serialist behaviour when writing a straightforward data chapter, but revert to holist behaviour when tackling a difficult theoretical chapter.

Another notable approach is to start with a reasonably structured, but basic first draft that is repeatedly expanded on – filled in so to speak – as research continues and you refine your subject knowledge and understanding. This might be called a **layered approach** to writing.

The important question in all of the above is how efficient is your approach? Does your approach work for you or should you change? Serialists generally find their approach efficient, though a few suffer from over-perfectionism, correcting every little detail over and over again, so that progress is exceptionally slow. If this should happen to you, do seek professional help from a counsellor at your institution.

Holists (sometimes called 'get-em-all-outers') often hold the preconception that their approach is indeed inefficient, but this may not be so.

CASE STUDY
Example

Box 3.1 The 'holist' approach is not necessarily cause for concern

One (holist) student did not write outlines or plans, preferring instead to write several drafts of each chapter, expanding, reworking and refining each successive draft. He claimed, and his supervisor confirmed, that he estimated he had written well over 200,000 words to produce a doctoral thesis of around 90,000 words. This might seem an amazing case of inefficiency. Yet, while on a three-year research scholarship, this student completed his PhD in two years and nine months (and passed with only minor amendments). Very few research students – serialists or holists – manage so well.

As a holist, you will prefer to go straight to the computer and start writing. Little thought will be given to structure, the idea being to work out what you want to focus on, to explore your material and what you think about it through writing, to generate ideas about your topic.

Incoherent or rough writing of this type serves a useful function. And, of course, the polished end products of communication (submitted papers) never reflect the messy, uneven process of production. Style and structure can be improved through successive revisions of your drafts (See 'Developing texts' in Chapter 4). If, however, you think your holist approach is holding you back, review 'Visual mapping of material' and 'Sequential outlining' in Chapter 4.

The mechanics of academic writing

Information about the mechanics of academic writing can usually be found in style manuals. The discussions that follow in this chapter draw attention to some standard practices with which you may wish to reacquaint yourself.

ENSURING CONSISTENCY OF PRACTICE

Consistency is expected of all academic writing. Consistency refers to just about everything: the way you write dates, numbers, percentages, foreign words (non-English), refer to other scholars and set up bibliographies, hyphenation and capitalization practices, typography and so forth. Decide how you will write something and stay with that practice throughout your text.

Work out which fonts (italics, bold, underline, plain) and font sizes (9, 10, 12, 14, etc.) and combinations of these you want to use for specific purposes, and follow these rigorously. It can be time-consuming to alter formatting and typography later, if you are not using a reference or style manager. Even then, inconsistencies might need to be manually addressed, for example, if italics, bold type and underlining have been used inconsistently throughout for emphasis. If you are uncertain about what practices to follow:

Finalize formatting and typography decisions before writing a first *full* draft.

- Review author practices in relevant refereed journals and follow those. While certain practices may vary from article to article or journal to journal, you should find internal consistency in the texts of individual authors.

More is said about this matter of consistency in ensuing sections.

SPELLING, GRAMMAR AND PROOFREADING

A computer spell-checker can help standardize your spelling, and it will pick up many errors. But it will not pick up everything, including incorrect substitutions (for example, 'an' when you mean 'and', or 'form' when you mean 'from'). Grammar-checkers also serve their purpose but they are more intuitive than logical, so that suggestions given are sometimes dubious, and even wrong.

Applying grammar-checkers can aggravate rather than alleviate second-language error if you do not have the confidence to assess the validity of suggestions.

Yet many graduates now report sole reliance on spelling- and grammar-checkers. Apart from their already-mentioned limitations, these will not help you to identify more substantive textual problems, such as flow problems due to shifting bits of text around on the computer, missing or incorrect references, flawed illustrations or illogical arguments, and so forth.

Do proofread, preferably in hard copy, as it is easier to detect errors/textual problems in this way.

Proofread your texts carefully before submitting them.

Even better, organize exchange proofreading with a fellow student if possible, as it is less taxing to proofread another's work than your own.

PUNCTUATION

Punctuation is part of the meaning of a text. So you will need to know how to punctuate correctly, whether you incline to minimal or heavy punctuation. Preferred disciplinary practices, the complexity of sentence structure and personal preference can all influence the extent of punctuation. If you are troubled by punctuation practices, refer to the detailed document on punctuation (under *Electronic resources*) on the website of the *Academic Skills and Learning Centre* at the Australian National University, or try other Internet sites by keying in 'punctuation'.

Plagiarism and referencing

In producing your texts, you will also need to apply rigorous academic standards when acknowledging and referencing source material.

AVOIDING PLAGIARISM

While deliberate plagiarism is viewed as cheating (for example, downloading unsourced material – sometimes whole essays – from the Internet), much plagiarism is unintentional. This latter type of plagiarism occurs for different reasons, including the following:

> Honesty is crucial in study and research.

1 Insufficient understanding of conventional practices governing the use of source material in academic writing.

2 Insufficient understanding of the *task-specific* uses to which source material will be put.

3 Failing to distinguish when you are drawing on source material and when you are interpolating your own comments.

I will look at each of these areas in turn.

Practices governing the use of source material When you write, you need to acknowledge the hard work (including mental work) of those scholars on whose work you draw. You will need to cite your sources, including sources from the Internet, in situations such as the following.

> **If English is a second language, do take care. It is all too easy to introduce second-language errors into direct quotations and time-consuming to check the correct wording of the flawed quotations.**

- When you **quote directly** from another author. This means when you reproduce the *exact* words of the author in your own text – and do make sure they are exact. Signal direct quoting by using double ("….") or single ('….') quote marks around the extract. Or indent longer quotes (usually over four lines) about five spaces from the margin. Sometimes writers use a different font for indented quotations, or they change the line spacing.

  If you insert anything into a direct quotation or change anything in that quotation, it is usual to indicate this by placing square brackets […] around the word/s you have inserted or changed. If something unusual appears in the original quotation (for example, a misspelling), place [*sic*] meaning 'thus' after the misspelt or otherwise seemingly incorrect word or expression. '*Sic*' communicates: 'This is how I found it in the source – it is not my mistake.'

  While the colon (:) is commonly used to introduce a direct quotation, it is not always an appropriate punctuation mark. Follow correct punctuation practices in introducing quotations, just as you normally would in writing.

- When you **paraphrase** what another author has said. This means when you put what another has said into your own words. Make sure you do use your own words. Paraphrase is a favoured technique in many situations of writing, but one in which source materials will need to be thoroughly worked and understood if paraphrase is to be effective.

- When you **summarize, refer to or use** another author's ideas, theories, methodologies, models, procedures, arguments, results, insights, interpretations, information or data. All these require intellectual, and sometimes manual, effort on the part of another and you need to acknowledge this.

- When you **use distinctive language or phrases** from another author, including those phrases that have been coined by an author to denote a concept or specific meaning. For example, 'goals mapping blueprint' is a distinctive phrase coined by a doctoral student to conceptualize a specific process. In using this phrase in writing, it would be necessary to acknowledge the author, and perhaps explain in a footnote what the phrase meant in its original context if this were not clear in the body of your writing.

When taking notes from reading, work out a system that clearly distinguishes the following:

- Direct quotations from other sources, that is, where you are reproducing the *exact* wording of an author (note page number/s).

- Material from other sources that you are *paraphrasing*, putting into your own words. Note page number/s if you are referring to a specific piece of information somewhere in the text, but these will not be necessary in referring to the overall discussion/argument.

- *Your* observations, views or comments that you wish to document.

Task-specific uses of source material I now consider my second point above by way of a case study example.

CASE STUDY Example

Box 3.2 Plagiarism can arise from the misunderstanding of task-specific objectives

Three graduates for whom English is a second language were referred to me by a course lecturer because they were not using their 'own' words when paraphrasing source material; in effect they were plagiarizing. In discussing the problem with each of them in separate consultations, it soon became clear that their real difficulty lay elsewhere. Their writing task involved critically evaluating a published article. But the students had not understood that their lecturer did not want them to *report* on, or simply repeat, what the author was saying, but rather to *assess* the strengths and weaknesses of the paper. With this new understanding in place, the students were encouraged to concentrate on formulating the key points *they* wanted to make in developing their critical review, to think about why they were taking that position, how they would develop their key points, and to use material from the paper to back up these points (by way of summary comment, by incorporating key words or phrases as direct quotations, and by using only page references). As all three students were able to verbalize their critical insights, it was clear that they had already thought deeply about the article. The true cause of their apparent plagiarism was a misunderstanding of writing task objectives.

Clearly distinguishing source material and comment Plagiarism may also be suspected if you do not make clear whether the ideas being discussed belong to another or are your own comment. Take the text below, where in the original version it is impossible to determine which ideas belong to X (the source) and which to the writer:

Original text:
X's critique of truth [reference] is based on his analysis of discursive procedures. The relation between truth and power is one between truth and discursive practice. Truth is not a stable and independent entity.

Amended text:
X's critique of truth [reference] is based on his analysis of discursive procedures. The relation between truth and power is ***[seen by him as]*** *one between truth and discursive practice.* ***[This suggests]*** *that truth is not a stable and independent entity.*

It is clear from the inserted material shown in bold type in the amended text that the ideas in the first two sentences belong to the source (X), on whom the writer is drawing, and that she herself is interpolating her own comment in the third sentence.

Nor is placing a reference at the end of a succession of paragraphs a sound practice. If all the ideas in a paragraph are being taken from a single source and you are not interpolating any comments of your own, then simply phrase your lead sentences to indicate that this will be so, as in my examples:

- The following discussion draws on an empirical study undertaken by X (2001).
- Further support for this type of intervention is found in X's argument (2003), as now discussed.
- The extent of military interference in the political process is attested to in an extensive study undertaken by X, Y and Z (2002).

As lead sentences in paragraphs, sentences of this type would set up reader-expectation that all that follows in that paragraph is taken from the nominated source. Of course, to avoid plagiarism, you will need to have in place an acceptable academic referencing system.

CHOOSING AN ACADEMIC REFERENCING STYLE

There are two, dominant academic referencing styles, and many variations within each of these:

- Consecutively **numbered notes** (1, 2, 3, etc.) at the foot of the page (footnotes), or at the end of a document/chapter (endnotes) to provide source details.
- The **Harvard style** of in-text referencing (e.g. Smith, 1983: 64). Footnotes or endnotes can also be used with the Harvard style, but only to include additional information (such as referring readers to additional sources or expanding discussion of a point mentioned in the body of the text). Notes of this type should not clot the text, however. It is distracting for a reader to have to plough through masses of these notes because discussions in the body of the text are inadequate or incomplete without reference to them. Such overuse signals a structuring problem.

  With the Harvard style, omit the author's name with the referencing details if you have already mentioned the name in the body of your sentence. For example: 'Wilkinson argues that "people power will force a change in political will" (2001: 7)'.

If you are using an electronic reference manager (EndNote, for example), selecting a referencing style is as simple as pressing a button, with standardization being automatic; styles can also be switched at any point to accommodate course/disciplinary or publication preferences. If you are not using such software, consider these strategies:

- Ask your lecturer/supervisor to refer you to an acceptable style manual (these are usually located in the reference sections of libraries). Style manuals provide information on how to reference, or cite, in the body of a text, and how to write the 'Bibliography', which usually includes all sources consulted in producing a text. A 'References List' or a 'List of Works Cited' usually includes only those sources to which you actually refer in the body of your text. Such manuals also illustrate the differences in style for citing sources in your text and putting these in a bibliography. They further illustrate how to cite a range of different items, for example, an article, a book by several authors, a television documentary, a play, an unauthored document, a CD, a multi-volume reference work, different types of Internet sites, etc.

- Follow the referencing style used by authors in a quality journal in your area.

- Search the Internet, which has numerous sites on academic referencing. Key in 'harvard referencing' or 'footnotes referencing', depending on the generally preferred style in the journals you are reading.

Be rigorously consistent in using the referencing style you do adopt. Such consistency extends to types and placement of punctuation marks, the use of capitalization, whether titles or works published independently are underlined or italicized, whether an item published within another publication (for example, journal articles or chapters in a multi-authored edited volume) is in inverted commas or not, and so forth.

In preparing a bibliography:

- Arrange items in alphabetical order of authors' names.

- Insert an unauthored source alphabetically by way of the document's title.

- Make sure your bibliographic style is rigorously consistent in every respect.

CITING SOURCES FROM THE INTERNET

Up-to-date style manuals also include information on citing sources from the Internet. As when citing print sources, give enough detail on online sources to enable your reader to identify the source and easily access it:

- The author's surname and first name or initial (if known), and/or the title of the document used, and/or the name of the organization or institution.

- The title of the site, and the 'host' website, if there is one and it is different.
- The full address (location) of the site – the URL.
- If possible, the page number(s) or other marker(s) identifying the page or section of the site you have used.
- (Perhaps) when the site was last updated, or modified, or revised, if this is shown.
- The date on which you accessed (read or visited) the site. *This is mandatory.*
- Where the site is complex, provide sufficient information on the access path itself to assist reader access.

SELECTING A REPORTING TENSE/VERBS

While the verb tense you select to report on other scholars' findings may be governed by disciplinary/course practice, consistency in usage is nevertheless important. Use:

Either: the *present* tense or *present perfect* (these two tenses are interchangeable) – Smith *argues* or Smith *has argued.*
Or: the *past* tense – Smith *argued.*

Both present and past tenses should not be used randomly in a single text. Consistency does not, however, mean rigidity. Look at the verb tenses I have highlighted in the following example, where the present/present perfect is favoured, but with a variation in the first sentence:

> *In an early study conducted in 1990, X* ***suggested*** *that the decline in living standards was due solely to changes in government policy at that time [reference]. This suggestion* ***has subsequently been challenged.*** *Y [reference]* ***has identified*** *three interlocking factors as contributing to the decline ... Z [reference] too* ***acknowledges*** *these same factors as important and* ***further points out*** *that ...*

The choice of past tense in the first sentence is due to the writer's desire to emphasize that X's suggestion was made in the past, in 1990. This is also an interesting example of the subtle effects of reporting tense choice, as the selection of past tense gives the impression that the study in question should also be confined to the past!

Reporting verbs – verbs selected to refer to other scholars' work – tend also to have subtle effects in conveying your attitude towards your sources. Skilful use of reporting verbs serves in part to position the reader to respond to your text in certain ways (see also 'Engaging the reader' in Chapter 9). While the groupings in Box 3.3 are rough, they should help you with an initial appreciation of this point and provide a range of choices, something graduates often request.

Box 3.3 Reporting verbs can have subtle attitudinal effects in writing

Words that tend to convey a neutral attitude (though how neutral depends on the commentary in the surrounding text):

X points out/argues/suggests/indicates/describes/observes/comments/remarks/reports/recommends/maintains

Words that tend to convey some degree of uncertainty about findings (perhaps because you wish to mount a challenge):

X alleges/declares/speculates/postulates/contends/claims/asserts

Words that tend to imply agreement:

X establishes/affirms/confirms/proves/convinces/demonstrates/shows

Words that convey the attitude of the original too: source (you might agree or disagree with the view):

X refutes/discards/stresses/advocates/proposes/urges/declares/contradicts/challenges, etc.

Attending to audience needs

Always take into account audience needs to ensure effective communication with readers.

When immersed in complex trains of thought while writing, it is easy to forget that you are always writing *for* someone. Just who your audience will be depends largely on the specific objectives of the communication task in which you are engaged. This is why the subject of audience is taken up in different contexts throughout this book. Still, in many cases your audience will be your lecturers/supervisors, who may also be your examiners; and, in the case of some dissertations, your external examiners. This is the group I now consider, with initial emphasis on the all-important matter of disciplinary practices from the angle of the reader.

THE READER AS DISCIPLINARY PRACTITIONER

Academics will bring to the reading of your text the expectation that it will evidence appropriateness, that is to say, what they 'judge' to be appropriate (see Fairclough, 1992). Reader expectations of the style and structure of say, an Engineering report, an Engineering essay involving sustained argument, or an Engineering research proposal, will be different. Academic readers will also expect appropriate treatment of subject matter, which is important to recognize when transferring disciplines. For example, an Anthropologist, a Sociologist, a Political Scientist or an Art Historian will engage different questions and issues when treating the same subject of 'identity'.

As another example, if your writing task were a 'briefing paper' intended to address, say, a particular group of farmers, then your lecturer would expect you to take full account of the nature, make-up and interests of that audience – the group of farmers. In reading your paper, your lecturer would assess how effectively you had managed to address that particular audience.

In making these observations about appropriateness, I do not mean to imply that academic readers will not allow for and welcome creativity in your writing. There is much room for you to manoeuvre creatively within the framework of (inter)disciplinary writing practices, just as the experts do. Still, as Mikhail Bakhtin, the Russian philosopher and theorist observes: 'genres must be fully mastered to be used creatively' (1986: 80).

THE READER AS SUBJECT SPECIALIST

Your lecturers and supervisors are subject specialists. But is it a good idea to fix on the fact that you are writing for experts in the content when you write? Doing this can lead to insufficient textual explanation, underdeveloped ideas, definitional and other problems because you assume that your lecturers/supervisors (as experts) will know what you mean. They may well do – but is this the point?

Some lecturers and supervisors say it is useful to focus on reader expertise when writing, but not all do.

CASE STUDY
Example

Box 3.4 Not all supervisors advise writing with an 'expert' in mind

This advice was offered by one supervisor to a large group of doctoral students (my paraphrase):

Imagine you are writing for your Aunt Sally, who, although unfamiliar with your discipline, is a bright, intelligent and interested reader. You need to include enough detail in your discussions to ensure Aunt Sally can follow quite well what you have to say even if she doesn't understand some of the terms you use. Aunt Sally is intelligent enough not to be convinced by an argument that does not provide detailed evidence to back up the assertions.

As the advice in Box 3.4 was offered in the context of more accessible texts in the humanities and social sciences, it may not be seen as relevant for difficult theoretical, philosophical, scientific or legal texts. Still, it does have broadly applicable value in that it places the burden of clear communication on you the writer, and appropriately so. More important then, is not to focus on what your reader knows, but to direct your efforts to demonstrating that *you* have a thorough critical understanding of all materials being worked in your text, that you do know what you are talking about. In this way, you are more likely to forestall criticism from your readers, those subject specialists your lecturers and supervisors.

SIGNPOSTING: SIGNALLING YOUR INTENTIONS

Regardless of their being subject specialists, your lecturers and supervisors will not have travelled your particular research path and so cannot be expected to follow your line of discussion unless you help them.

Your readers do expect you to recognize that they are certainly not experts in the decisions *you* make (for example, the meanings *you* give to terms, phrases, etc., what *you* choose to focus on, why *you* take the approach you do, how *you* organize and develop discussions, etc.). You will need to signal your intentions, which is sometimes called 'signposting'.

Do accommodate your readers. Tell them at appropriate points what you are doing, why you are doing it, how you are going to go about doing it, and so forth (for example, in the introductory chapter, between sections, between chapters, and in the introduction for each chapter). At least ensure sufficient signalling of intentions to help your reader follow, as these writers do:

> **International Relations:**
> *This essay proposes that the issues involved in this debate are issues of power relations. Accordingly, the paper will treat racial violence and sexual violence as two manifestations of a type of violence, which happens across the power divides that exist in society.*
>
> **Biochemistry and Molecular Biology:**
> *To provide an adequate background to these studies, the introductory section contains information about the structure and function of mitochondria and a consideration of the properties of the ATPases located in the inner mitochondrial membrane, the plasma membrane and the membrane of the sarcoplasmic reticulum.*
>
> **Law:**
> *As pointed out above, the introduction of these revitalised Programs has occasioned a shift in attitude among participant organisations. My purpose in the following section is to detail the nature of the Programs; full critical assessment of these is reserved for Chapter IV, which considers the broader international context.*

How subtle or obvious such signalling is does vary, usually because of preferred disciplinary practices. Regardless, respect the intelligence of your readers – avoid clotting the text with too many such signals.

Signalling a digression in mid-discussion In departing from the main line of your discussion, signal your intention to do so:

> *The broader implications of this ruling for international law are well documented, as shown above. In terms of this research, however, an important issue is the extent of controversy occasioned by the case. Just why the case has generated so much debate is itself a matter of debate, one that requires careful scrutiny before proceeding with this [literature] review.*

Note that there is a sound intellectual reason for the digression in terms of argument development. Many of the style issues now discussed are also audience issues at some level.

Clarity: the first rule of style

Good writers are addicted to clarity.

Clarity of course encompasses much more than style (for example, the whole of the next chapter might be invoked), but it is also the first rule of style. It is a rule that will serve you well in all your communication activities.

In 1985, US economist Donald McCloskey wrote a substantial article entitled 'Economical Writing'. His is a lively, rich probing of the bad 'habits of style' of economists. It is an impassioned plea for stylistic reform and the ways to reform. Essentially, McCloskey's article is a eulogy to clarity that has generic value. He belongs with a host of writers similarly concerned, including George Orwell, more famous for his novel *1984* than his spirited essay of 1946 'Politics and the English Language', which continues to be resurrected and can be accessed on the Internet.

One topic McCloskey alludes to is the 'affliction' of abstraction, a disease that obscures rather than clarifies meaning, an affliction found everywhere, and typified in this extract:

> *What I would put forward, however, is that presenting the tortured body as only a symbolic static referential point of meaning often subsumes the victim under the wider 'objective' theoretical framework and assumes an emphasis upon a pre-objectified reality which shifts attention away from the location of direct and subjective embodied experience, itself the inescapable locus of meaning creation and active negotiation.*

Graduates and I have struggled together over publications loaded with abstract language of this type in trying to make sense of them, as you may have done yourself. Unfortunately, some students think that this is the writing to which they should aspire. But it *is* possible for you to deal with complex theory, ideas, abstract concepts and the like in a way that makes meaning easily accessible for your reader.

Good writers are as concerned not to be misunderstood as they are to be understood.

Think about this. Good writers do not rely on highly inflated abstract language to impress. Good writers impress with the quality of their research, the complexity of their thinking, the soundness of their reasoning, the subtlety of their insights, the rigour and crispness of their prose, the sophistication with which they use the disciplinary language and engage the theory. Good writers prefer language that is 'definite, specific, concrete' (Strunk Jr. and White, 2000: 21). They care about readers and readability. They can be found everywhere, in all disciplines, across the academic community of writers. And you can be one of them.

You will quickly recognize these writers when you come across t students always do. Take a close look at the stylistic features of their texts and you will see why you have so enjoyed the reading, regardless of the difficulty of their content.

CONCISENESS (LOW FAT WRITING)

Conciseness aids clarity. But do not confuse conciseness with density. Whereas conciseness is a positive attribute of writing, density is not. If your text is dense, a reader will find it difficult to follow your line of discussion because of cognitive leaps, insufficient detail, marginal signalling, underdeveloped ideas, missing links and so forth.

Conciseness is the opposite of wordiness, by which I mean taking too many words to say what you have to say, a practice that pads the writing, sometimes so much so as to obscure main points. Excess wording takes up valuable space that can be put to better use, such as bringing in more points to support a position you are developing.

The writer in this example not only had a problem of wordiness but also difficulty integrating source material in the writing:

Original text:

There is certainly a parallel relationship between the dramatic growth of social violence and current media practices: between the rising incidents of murder, malicious wounding, child abuse, rape and paedophilia and the media's greater emphasis on Rambo-style violence, more explicit sex in cinema and on TV, and an increased number of pornographic publications [references]. But the existence of such a correlation does not necessarily point to the media being the sole cause of increased violence in the community. It may be that the changes in cultural patterns relating to violence and sex have produced greater permissiveness in the media, rather than the other way about [references]. Even if the media have played a role in these social changes, they are probably not solely responsible [references], though X's large study [reference] suggests the media are the 'primary causal agents' of increasing social violence. Regardless, there is disquiet about media values in the minds of those forced to contend with unwanted changes. This disquiet cannot be brushed aside as somehow 'imaginary', or seen as an over-anxious response by hypersensitive people. Many share the concern and it needs to be addressed. (189 words)

Tightened text:

Several studies [references] confirm a correlation between the growth of social violence and current media practices: between rising incidents of murder, malicious wounding, rape, child abuse or paedophilia, and repeated graphic depictions of such events in different media. But attributing causality here is problematic. Some scholars [references] argue that changing social patterns have induced greater permissiveness in the media; others [references] that there is a cross-influence effect, while X's extensive study [reference] identifies the media as 'primary causal agents.' Regardless, media values remain a community concern that needs addressing. (90 words)

The tightened text is more concise (although perhaps some vividness is lost by cutting metaphors like 'Rambo-style violence'). As well, the logic of comparison of scholarly views to support ideas being developed is now reflected in the parallel sentence structure itself: 'several studies confirm', 'some scholars argue', 'others that ... while X's extensive study identifies'. The improvement in the text in this example bears out what one lecturer wrote beside a student's wordy paragraph: 'practise brevity'. I can give no better advice.

Exercise: developing conciseness

Step 1

Select a wordy paragraph from your own writing, preferably a long one. Your objective is to reduce the number of words by about one-third while conveying the same information.

Step 2

Scrutinize each sentence carefully. Be ruthless. Identify unnecessary words and repetitious material. Substitute one word for several, for example, 'now' for 'at this point in time', or 'yearly' for 'on a yearly basis'; cross out adjectives/adverbs (often superfluous); re-work sentences to convey information more concisely. Exclude details that add nothing to your discussion; but do not exclude important details needed to support ideas you are developing, which is unfortunately often a first choice for students wanting to cut back on length. Take this sentence, which is quite sound in itself:

Original text:
RRV is the etiological agent of epidemic polyarthritis, a disease which was first described in 1928 [reference]. Epidemic polyarthritis has a wide geographic distribution in X [country named], occurring regularly as epidemics in eastern X and as sporadic outbreaks in other parts of X [references]. (43 words)

Tightened text:
RRV is the etiological agent of epidemic polyarthritis, first described in 1928 [reference]. This disease occurs regularly as epidemics in eastern X, and as sporadic outbreaks elsewhere in X [references]. (30 words)

What I cannot know is whether or not this writer thought it important to particularly emphasize the point about 'wide geographic distribution', in which case my revision might not be acceptable as it merely implies this point. That is another consideration to keep in mind when you are doing this exercise: what ideas do you want to profile?

ASPECTS OF VOICE AND TONE

Voice is remarkably complex, in being shaped by individual style, academic and disciplinary practices, and specific task requirements – including audience needs, the tonal qualities of a text or presentation, elements of style and so forth. I now consider briefly two simple aspects of voice frequently brought to my attention by students, because their lecturers/supervisors have suggested that they use one or the other and they are uncertain about the difference between the two, as you may be. I then discuss tone.

Impersonal versus personal voice The impersonal mode of the third person, the 'it' form, is often preferred over the first person 'I' in academic writing. The third person is thought by some to sound more objective, to confirm the idea of researcher as detached observer, and to ensure that a reader remains focused on the discussion itself, undistracted by the intrusive 'I' of the writer. Yet students from different areas, even the sciences, do use the personal 'I', usually with restraint (for example, in introductions only) and only very occasionally without, as in the next example.

CASE STUDY
Example

Box 3.5 Less restrained use of the personal 'I' is occasionally seen in science theses

One science student felt so strongly about positioning herself as participant researcher in the writing of her dissertation that she chose to flout convention of the time by including this type of commentary in several places, obviously without penalty, as she was awarded her doctorate:

> *Since I brought to this study a set of previously developed values, beliefs, attitudes and skills, it seemed important to augment these in order to produce some tangible and practical outcomes that 'would make a difference'. Instead of standing outside a community offering advice, as a rural person originally, I wanted to stand alongside other rural people in their quest for sustainable management of the local environment.*

While you may choose not to use 'I' in the body of a text, you may use 'I' in, say, the parts of an introduction detailing topic focus, research questions or objectives and procedure indicating overall structure.

Some disciplines favour use of the first person throughout a text. In some quarters, such usage is even considered a matter of principle, one argument being that writers should take personal responsibility for their research and ideas, and embody this responsibility in their writing by using 'I'. But voice is not just about the choice between personal and impersonal modes.

Active versus passive voice Lecturers/supervisors in their comments on student texts often express a preference in terms of voice (for example, 'use active voice' or 'use passive construction'), and/or advise students on preferred practice. The assumption is that students will know the difference between active and passive, although they often do not.

When the active voice is used, the agent/producer/instrument of the action expressed in the verb is foregrounded. The reverse is true of the passive construction. Take the following examples:

Active construction:

Management **introduced** new measures to address output problems. (Foregrounding the agent of change, 'management'.)

Passive constructions:

(a) New measures **were introduced** by management to address output problems. (Foregrounding the 'new measures', while acknowledging the agent of change, 'management'.)
(b) New measures **were introduced** to address output problems. (Foregrounding 'new measures', while obscuring the agent of change, 'management'.)

The active construction, which is more direct and energetic, does not necessarily involve using the personal mode, as seen in these examples:

Active constructions:

(a) Results **confirm** an increase in the incidence of this type of crime. (Passive would be: An increase in the incidence of this type of crime **is confirmed** by the results.)
(b) Interventionist policies of the British colonial government **aggravated** tensions among ethnic minorities. (Passive would be: Tensions among ethnic minorities **were aggravated** by the interventionist policies of the British colonial government.)

Pause to consider the different effects of voice in the examples below:

(a) Chapter 3 **analyses** concepts of management and how these have influenced medical practice.
(b) Concepts of management and how these have influenced medical practice **are analysed** in Chapter 3.
(c) In Chapter 3, **I analyse** concepts of management and how these have influenced medical practice.

In (a), active voice is used and the agent of the action is foregrounded as the Chapter; it is the Chapter that is doing the analysing. This is strange when you think about it, but a common practice nevertheless. Example (b) uses a passive construction in which the agent of the action is obscured; there is no mention of who is doing the analysing. Example (c) uses an active construction while acknowledging that it is the writer who is doing the analysing. All three of these constructions are commonly found in academic writing, but different academic areas often display distinct preferences, as do individual lecturers/supervisors, so be guided by them.

Strategic use of tone Tone is a device that can be manipulated in writing to achieve desired effects. One way to think of tone is as your attitude towards:

- yourself as the writer;
- the subject matter you are discussing; and
- your readers and/or listeners.

Whether you recognize it or not, the tonal qualities of your text convey emotional and/or mental attitudes that can be influential in shaping audience response to your text.

Tentative language (for example, perhaps, it appears, it seems, it could be) is appropriate to use when commenting on possibilities, as when speculating. But too much of such language throughout a text may trigger the reader-response that you lack confidence:

> **More confident writer:**
>
> This study **shows** that ... *or* This study **suggests** that ...
> In section 2, I **assess** the reasons for ...
>
> **Less confident writer:**
>
> This study **might mean that** ... *or* It **seems that the author is saying** ...
> In section 2, I **will try to assess** the reasons for ...

Neutral, impartial or judicious tones, with varying degrees of engagement, tend to characterize formal academic writing. Where ideology is a shaping influence on the writing, the attitude towards readers may be somewhat exclusive, alienating those unlikely to share similar views.

Or take this example from a student text:

> *What is needed is reform, and quickly. For this to occur, there needs to be a thorough investigation of the nature and extent of 'damage' caused under the existing law; analysis of this damage in terms of individual, economic and social costs to the community; clear identification of areas to be targeted for reform; and canvassing of members of the legal fraternity to gain support for reform.* ***This last recommendation is likely to prove the most difficult.*** *(my emphasis)*

The tone of this last sentence could be seen as disputatious, aggressive, condescending, engaged and perhaps alienating of the very people from whom support is sought. But then, perhaps the writer intended this in seeking to stir a response, to shame legal professionals into action.

Exercise: voice and tone

It can be informative to interrogate the use of voice and tone by scholars you are reading:

- Are the best writers using personal or impersonal voice, and in what situations of writing if there is a mix?
- Do they favour the active or passive voice, or is there a mix and in what situations of writing?
- What is the writer's attitude towards her/himself, towards the subject matter, towards readers? How do these encoded attitudes influence *your* response to the text?

Apart from voice and tone, other significant aspects of style may need review.

OTHER STYLE ISSUES

The strategies now suggested may require vocabulary extension if you wish to apply them; but then, extending vocabulary is important for effective communication. Do try for language that invigorates the prose, adds some zest. An excellent starting point is scrutiny of verb choices, as the English verb is a singular carrier of energy. Not only do active verbs enliven prose, so too do more striking verbs and other diction. Pause to consider the effects of the following verb choices in terms of energy levels:

(a) These reforms led to more interest in conservation programmes.
These reforms accelerated interest in conservation programmes.

(b) These reforms increased the desire for conservation programmes.
These reforms energized the drive for conservation programmes.

Try also to avoid clichés, worn out words and phrases that will depress your writing, drain it of energy. One prominent example is the repeated use in a text of the tired phrase 'has played a role in' (and its variations). The writing could be energized by selecting a variety of simple replacements, for example: has *influenced*, *affected*, *shaped*, *contributed to*, or whatever seems appropriate in context, as illustrated below by way of three examples taken from a page and a half of one student's writing:

(a) *The organization played a leading role* [***was instrumental***] *in stopping ...*
(b) *The organization has played a disproportionately large role* [***has been pivotal***] *in moving ...*
(c) *The organization played an important role in* [***exercised a shaping influence on***] *...*

On this issue of variation, do take care though. It is helpful to vary language for reader interest, but not just for the sake of variation itself so that the reader becomes confused:

> Elegant Variation uses many words to mean one thing, with the result that in the end no one, not even the writer, really knows what the thing is. A paper on economic development used in two pages all these: 'industrialization,' 'growing structural differentiation,' 'economic and social development,' 'social and economic development,' 'development,' 'economic growth,' 'growth' and 'revolutionized means of production.' With some effort one can see in context that they all meant about the same thing. (McCloskey, 1985: 210)

This is another illustration of the same problem from a student text:

> *As I do not speak Mandarin, I had to use* ***interpreters*** *with newly immigrated Chinese.* ***Translators,*** *however, create a screen between researcher and informants. The researcher has to rely on the accuracy of* ***interviewers*** *in translating both questions and responses.*

While all three emphasized words actually meant the 'interpreters', a reader will struggle to recognize this because of unhelpful variation.

It is also important to respect the meanings of words. Words like *aspects, features, issues, elements, factors, parts, concepts and ideas* are sometimes used interchangeably to have the same meaning when they have distinctive meanings. *Issue*, meaning 'the point or matter in contention', is repeatedly misused in writing. Issue is selected when not really discussing an issue at all, but rather a subject or topic, a particular fact, a theoretical concept, an idea or notion. Do clarify the meanings of even commonly used words of this type if you are uncertain – use a good dictionary or a thesaurus, or a dictionary of synonyms and antonyms can also be a useful resource.

Avoid, too, practices certain to cause vagueness in writing. A typical example is use of the old media favourite 'dramatic': 'a dramatic increase,' 'a dramatic turn around,' 'a dramatic slump or fall or drop,' 'dramatic changes'. A word such as dramatic does not convey the type of rigour expected of graduate writing. Instead of the vague 'dramatic increase' be more precise: 'exports rose by 89%,' or 'exports doubled in 1993', or 'exports increased from around $US1.5m to $US2.3m', or even 'exports increased significantly'.

The English language offers such variety it can be fun to work on style, and very rewarding too.

Summary Comments

- Good practice involves close attention to academic standards of consistency and accuracy in terms of writing practices, formatting, spelling and punctuation. Computer spell and grammar-checkers will not suffice: careful proofreading is essential.
- Integrating source material, referencing sources and understanding the conventions that apply in doing so can be like crossing a minefield of uncertainties. If needs be, do not hesitate to ask your lecturers/supervisors (or anyone else who can assist you) for clarification. Having a recommended style manual to hand will help you manage the many queries that tend to arise in the context of academic referencing conventions.
- It is vitally important to understand and take into account the needs of your audience on every occasion of writing. No matter how impressive your ideas and insights, these will be lost if your readers cannot follow what you are doing or understand what you are saying.
- Style is not merely decorative but part of the meaning of a text. Improving aspects of style can increase the overall effectiveness of communication.

4 Whole Text Development

Developmental Objectives

By applying the strategies, doing the exercises and following the procedural steps in this chapter, you should be able to:

- Develop understanding of whole text development so as to avoid practices that lead to common writing problems.
- Identify strategies to gain control of coverage through brainstorming or mind mapping, and sequentially outlining a text.
- Understand how to use sub-headings as an effective structuring device contributing to argument development and overall coherence.
- Develop paragraphs logically around *main ideas* that, in turn, contribute to the development of a unifying point of view or thesis (as in argument).
- Identify strategies for linking paragraphs to ensure the logical or coherent development of ideas throughout a text.
- Learn how to manipulate sentence structures so as to give focus to important ideas and avoid monotony in the writing.
- Appreciate the necessity of discarding even well-written material that does not fit the context.
- Improve the overall structure of texts.

My concern in this chapter is with whole text development or overall textual design, the logic of the arrangement of parts at different levels of the text – their relatedness or interconnectedness. Insufficient attention to matters discussed in the chapter accounts for many (but not all) problems evident in graduate writing – fragmented text, disruptions to flow, repetition, labouring the point, under-developed ideas, cognitive leaps, irrelevant material and so forth. The focus on the structural scaffolding framing academic writing in general is supplemented by discussions in subsequent chapters that address structural issues specific to different types of writing.

Visual mapping of material

Visual mapping of material is a useful way to begin to gain textual control. The idea here is to mine the extensive knowledge you have on emerging from reading or other information-gathering, knowledge that often goes unrecognized by students themselves.

BRAINSTORMING

A brainstorming plan can take any shape you wish. One student favoured the image of an upside-down tree; another liked to work with free-floating and intersecting boxes. You might need more than one of these plans: for a whole thesis, for each chapter, or for each sub-division.

First write your topic – or use a working title of, say, a chapter or section – in the centre of a large piece of paper, then branch out from there with lines going in all directions. The idea is to brainstorm *coverage* so as to work out what you need to cover, to identify issues and to generate ideas that you want to develop.

Jot down quickly anything at all that springs to mind. It does not matter how disorganized or messy your brainstorming plan is, just let your imagination float free. Get as much information into your plan as possible, and ignore structural issues at this point. You can use different coloured highlighter pens for different purposes.

To give you an idea if you have not used this method before, Figure 4.1 shows a partially complete plan, but yours could be quite different depending on your research interests, visual inclination and imagination.

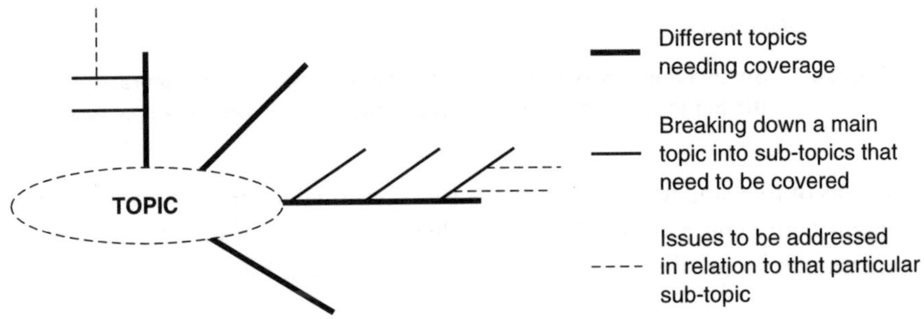

FIGURE 4.1 **Simple brainstorming plan**

To illustrate further, if this were a brainstorming plan for a chapter, then the different topics could be used to generate sub-division headings in terms of what is being covered; the sub-topics could be a means of focusing more precisely what needs to be covered in each sub-division; and the issues could be

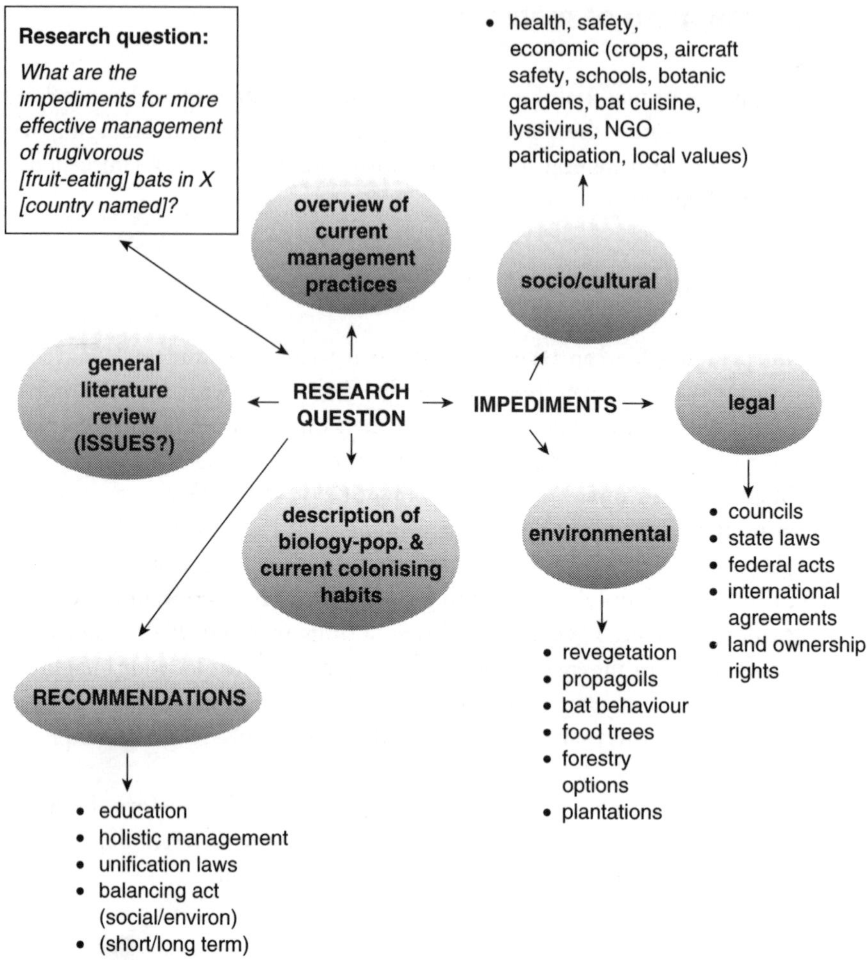

FIGURE 4.2 **Sample mind mapping outline. The circles represent chapters: note how the big topic of impediments was broken down into three chapters**

a means of focusing more precisely the sub-division headings in terms of *why* the topic is being covered (see 'Using sub-division headings' below). But do not be constrained by my illustration; your needs might be different.

MIND MAPPING

Rather than brainstorming, you may prefer to mind map on the computer, using the central research question as a starting point. Your overall objectives will still be the same as when brainstorming: mining information to pin down coverage. A mind map of a 30,000 word thesis is illustrated in Figure 4.2.

Sequential outlining

> **It is not just a matter of sequencing what to cover, but sequencing *stages* in a discussion or argument.**

Brainstorming plans and mind maps can be as simple or as complex as you choose. They are particularly useful in gaining control of coverage, and they can be further developed to show a host of textual relations. Sequential outlining is equally useful for determining the logic of relations among parts of a discussion, that is, the order in which topics and sub-topics are to be covered – your overall textual design.

Basically, divisions in academic texts turn on one or a combination of the choices depicted in Table 4.1.

TABLE 4.1 **Basic choices in dividing up a text**

Division into parts	Division into chapters	The addition of sub-divisions	The addition of further sections within a sub-division	No divisions at all
Sequentially numbered: Part 1, Part 2, Part 3, etc.	Sequentially numbered: Chapter 1, Chapter 2, Chapter 3, etc.	Usually indicated by specific headings	There could be just one or several layers of these	This might be the case in a very short essay, or be a preference in some disciplines for certain types of writing
Sometimes given titles	Usually given titles	Sometimes sequentially numbered as well	Sometimes indicated by specific headings	
			Sometimes sequentially numbered so as to indicate the level of layer after a numbered sub-division	

All this looks simple but is far more complex under the influence of structuring practices suited to different types of writing in the different disciplines, which is why the issue of structuring is taken up in other contexts in this book.

For the time being, I want to emphasize just a few principles important in sequential outlining of texts:

- Take account of word length where there is a designated word length.
- Consider the *appropriateness* of information for the different parts, chapters, etc.
- Determine the *logical relations* between parts, chapters, etc. in order to ensure coherent sequencing. The idea is to experiment with different sequential arrangements until you come up with one that seems to have a strong flow-on effect in terms of the point of view you are developing.
- Ensure that, in the ordering of material, the reader will have sufficient information, at each point, to follow the sequential arrangement you settle on. Ensure that definitions of key concepts, terms, theories, etc. are given before these are applied in discussions.

This last point may need further clarification.

It is not sound practice to introduce phrases, concepts or terms, even those representing an entire body of theory, into a discussion and then:

- Not define the meaning of such terms, or even signal where they will be defined.
- Define their meaning only long after their first usage, say, in a later section or even chapter.
- Freely use such terms in chapters or sections prior to the one that discusses in detail the theories or key terms and their relevance for the overall research.

Do think about whether the sequencing you adopt will allow a reader to follow clearly your overall line of discussion.

Table 4.2 provides an example of a sequential outline of a thesis of around 15,000 words. The writer has taken into account logical sequencing of chapters, the approximate word length for each chapter and subject matter to be covered in each chapter.

A next step towards further refinement of this level outline would be to:

- Include working titles for chapters and sub-division headings.
- Designate material to be covered in the different chapters under the newly set up sub-division headings. Be as precise as possible (you may already have done this on a mind map).
- Jot down any main ideas/points you have in relation to material to be discussed in the different sub-divisions of the different chapters – ideas around which your discussions will be built.

TABLE 4.2 **Sequential outlining of a shorter thesis**

Research question	**How do contemporary Indonesian intellectuals justify the practice of Jihad?**
Introduction	Relevant background, aims, objectives, Indonesian context – **approx. 1500 words**
Chapter 1 (title?)	Methodological considerations; justification for approach – **approx. 2500 words**
Chapter 2 (title?)	The Islamic notion of the state (define). The reductive notion of Jihad as 'holy war'. Jihad as an instrument of state power, as universalizing agent of Islamic law, as agent of socialization (power effects: internal, external) – **approx. 3000 words**
Chapter 3 (title?)	Islamic versus Western notions of rationality, moderating juridical pronouncements on Jihad, theorizing the rational dimension of Jihad – **approx. 3000 words**
Chapter 4 (title?)	The contested status of Jihad: defensive versus offensive action – different contexts: modernists/traditionalists; believers/unbelievers – **approx. 2500**
Conclusion	**approx. 2500**

USING SUB-HEADINGS EFFECTIVELY

Sub-division headings, which are commonly used to divide up texts, are an important structuring device which, used properly, can help you avoid full rewrites because of structuring problems. Sub-headings:

- Help you to clarify the overall structure or organization of your writing.
- Assist the reader to follow your line of discussion/argument.

In some subject areas the preference is to use different fonts to indicate sub-headings, others favour numbering (for example, 1.1, 1.2, 1.3 and then further breakdown, for example 1.3 into 1.3.1, 1.3.2, etc.).

Avoid using sub-headings as a substitute for careful structuring. This practice can lead to textual incoherence.

Also, the extent to which sub-headings are used tends to vary, with some subject areas approving greater frequency and others insisting on substantial discussion following a sub-heading. Regardless of such differences, sub-headings cannot perform the hard work of structuring – only you can.

CASE STUDY
Example

Box 4.1 Excessive use of sub-headings can cause textual incoherence

A supervisor referred a student to me with a chapter deemed 'incoherent'. The chapter had 29 sub-headings in 34 pages of writing. The separate bits of discussion were disconnected, and the overall composition of the chapter was very fragmented. As there appeared to be no underlying logic in the selection and arrangement of sub-headings, it was impossible to identify a coherent line of discussion throughout the chapter, to detect a unifying point of view. In other words, the sub-headings were distracting rather than helpful to a reader. To address this problem, it was necessary to go back to the planning stage: to rethink the whole structure, to reduce greatly the number of sub-headings, to generate new sub-headings that accurately reflected the focus of the discussion beneath and to review the logical flow of these newly created sub-divisions to ensure they would allow development of a coherent line of discussion. Then came the rewrite.

Do ensure that your sub-headings are meaningful, not merely decorative. To illustrate, where the topic of 'development schemes' is only one of many topics being covered in, say, a research essay on 'environmental degradation', it is not helpful to use this type of sub-heading:

> **Think about what you want to cover, why you want to cover that subject matter and what you want to show, demonstrate, establish or prove.**

Development Schemes

Certain questions immediately arise:

- What is the writer's interest in development schemes as regards the topic of 'environmental degradation'?
- Why is the writer discussing these schemes at all?
- What does the writer hope to demonstrate/show/prove in discussing these schemes?

By indicating the connection between environmental degradation and development schemes, a more precise and informative sub-heading of this type becomes possible:

Increased Pesticide Usage in Development Schemes

A reader can now easily identify that the writer's interest lies in 'increased pesticide usage' in development schemes, see how this focus ties in with the theme of environmental degradation and deduce that part of the argument will turn on this matter of increased pesticide usage.

In undertaking a lengthy discussion of the topic 'development schemes', a more general subheading would suffice, before breaking this down further:

1 *Development Schemes*

1.1 The variety and nature of existing schemes
1.2 The effects of government policy on implementation
1.3 The issue of 'local' knowledge
1.4 Improving overall effectiveness

These headings convey the precise focus of each section of the sub-division.

Developing texts

Once sub-headings are in place as a structuring guide, the next step is the development of text. This brings us to the academic paragraph, which is the basic unit of structure in academic writing. (See also 'Words and phrases for developing discussions', Appendix 1.)

CONTROLLING PARAGRAPH DEVELOPMENT

Understanding the basics of paragraph control and the function of the paragraph in writing is essential for coherent development of your text.

The function of main ideas Typically, the academic paragraph is organized around a *main idea* that takes the form of a general assertion or statement and is then subsequently developed.

> **Ensure that you do have *main ideas* around which to organize your paragraphs by clearly identifying these in your text.**

The main idea can take any sentence position in the paragraph In the more inductive type of paragraph there is a movement from the specific (details) to the general (assertion), in which case the main idea will appear in the last sentence position. With the more deductive paragraph, there is a movement from the general assertion to the specific details, with the topic sentence containing the main idea taking first sentence position, as illustrated below, where the topic sentence is highlighted in bold type:

> ***Two measures could be used to gauge the degree of integration that has occurred between the three Chinese economies since China's open door policy began in the late 1970s.*** *One measure is to calculate the share of 'intra-bloc' trade for the three economies as a percentage of the total exports of the three and look at the trend in these shares over time. Secondly, growth rates for this 'intra-bloc' trade can be calculated and then compared to the growth rates for external trade. Both of these measures could be applied to total trade, manufactured trade, and, at a much more disaggregated level, to selected manufactures.*

A single main idea may take many paragraphs to develop Not every paragraph will contain a main idea. Detailing the nature and causes of a main idea of this type could take many paragraphs, even a page or more of writing:

> *Significant changes had taken place in the geographical landscape during this period.*

There is no set length for a paragraph Paragraphs are often long in academic writing because of the detail needed to develop main ideas. But if the function of the paragraph is to signal the content and structure of a long stretch of writing to follow, the paragraph may be very short, and effectively so. This occurs with the paragraph below, which served as a structuring device, while highlighting the controversial nature of the writer's findings:

> *Previous research has relied on a recessive model that limits available options [references]. The results of this study, however, suggest that there are sound reasons to re-define the accepted boundaries.*

After this paragraph, the writer proceeded to discussion of his results over several pages. This type of strategic use of the short paragraph is not the same as using a single sentence paragraph that contains one bite of information – a single fact or point – which is to be avoided.

Each main idea is used to advance your overall point of view, your position, or your thesis This tight interlocking relationship is illustrated in Figure 4.3.

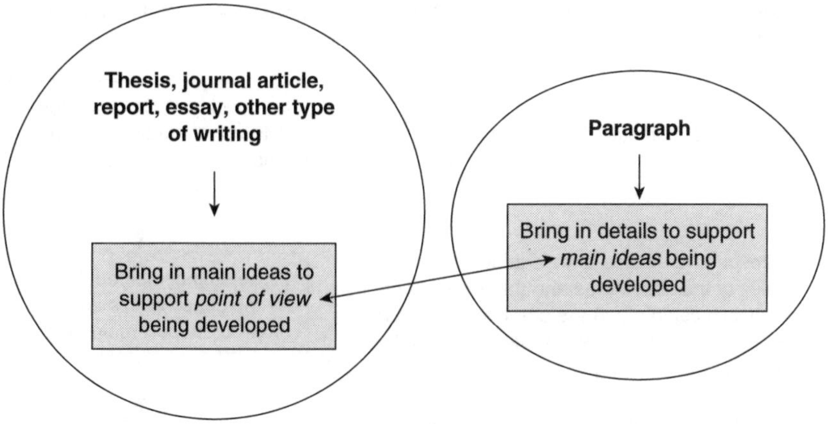

FIGURE 4.3 **The structural relationship between point of view and paragraph development**

Your research theses and essays, or any other type of academic writing, should be organized around a point of view that you are developing. The main ideas you bring forward in your paragraphs should support your point of view – push it along, just as the details you include in developing your paragraphs should support your main ideas.

The sentences in a paragraph should evidence a logical flow Sentences need to hang together, to cohere, so that readers can follow the logical flow of your ideas. Take a close look at the annotated paragraph in Figure 4.4 and you will see what I mean about a logical flow of ideas.

Now look at what happens in this example, where coherence breaks down:

> *Recall bias has been a problem in this investigation. Despite the inconclusive results, the investigation has identified the need for a review of food preparation techniques at this venue. It was not possible to identify clearly the source of contamination.*

As you see, the expected paragraph focus in the first sentence is 'recall bias'. However, the next sentence ruptures this expectation by directing attention to another topic, review of 'food preparation techniques'. There is a further rupture in the third sentence as the reader is directed to yet another topic, the impossibility of identifying the 'source of contamination'. The paragraph is not coherent in terms of the flow of ideas. There are too many ideas presented too quickly, with each idea needing further development.

Paragraph extract: Editorial: 'Treatment bias and clinical judgement', *Age and Ageing*, 31, 2002: 3–4.

The study of potential bias is difficult.	Introducing *main idea* – the difficulty of studying potential bias
Retrospective studies always depend on the quality of the case notes and the accuracy of diagnostic coding, and the one thing that case records usually lack is a comment on what the physician was thinking.	Presenting combined reasons for the cause of this difficulty in order to support main idea
It is difficult enough to keep good records of fact, but writing down thoughts and opinions takes time, and does not lend itself to the abbreviations beloved of the medical profession.	Expanding on previous point to reinforce argument
Prospective data recording for the express purpose of studying bias is equally dangerous, because looking at a process inevitably changes it, so management will not be typical.	Presenting a further reason for the difficulty of studying potential bias in order to support main idea
The study of possible bias therefore has to carry a health warning, but that is no reason why it should not be attempted.	Drawing the implication that such study therefore needs to carry a heath warning, though that is no reason to forgo such study
Of course, once possible bias has been discovered, it is entirely proper to ask why it might have occurred, and whether remediable action is really necessary.	Adding a summary idea that the discovery of bias warrants investigation of cause and consideration of potential action to redress it

FIGURE 4.4 **Illustrating internal paragraph coherence**

STRATEGIES FOR LINKING PARAGRAPHS

Linking is often subtle and sophisticated in writing. Linking may even be unnecessary as, for example, in a methods section, where logic inheres in detailing the sequence of steps taken. Or you may be **mapping the structure in the process of writing** (very common), as illustrated below by this initial sentence of a paragraph:

> *Because of mounting costs, a set of radical strategies was introduced to speed up production.*

This was then followed by about three pages of writing on the radical strategies – of which there were four in all.

In situations where you will be discussing points at length, take care in using the technique of First(ly), Second(ly), Third(ly) to introduce paragraphs, because a reader will have forgotten what you are talking about by the time she/he gets to the fourth point on the third page of writing. Linking phrases of this type would be better:

> One strategy involved …
> Another strategy …
> A third strategy brought into effect because of spiralling costs was … [reminding the reader of what you are discussing]
> Finally, senior management found it necessary to …

Do try to use a range of linking or transition strategies rather than rely on a standard few.

Repeating words/phrases One of the simplest, most common and subtle transitions is the repeated word, phrase or idea:

> **Last sentence of a paragraph:**
> The nature of the ceremonial **rites** performed at this initiation ceremony is particularly important.
>
> **First sentence of the next paragraph:**
> These **rites** are organized around three basic activities, each with its own religious significance.
>
> **Last sentence of a paragraph:**
> Here X postulates two general linguistic notions: the **notion of polarities** and the notion of equivalence.
>
> **First sentence of the next paragraph:**
> The **notion of polarities** derives from X's insight concerning ...

The question-and-answer transition

> **Last sentence of a paragraph:**
> Why did the plan fail?
>
> **First sentence of next paragraph:**
> X, in his analysis, suggests three major reasons.

Do use the rhetorical question with caution, however, as clumsy overuse tends to produce a forced stylistic effect.

The summarizing transition This technique can be illustrated by this example, where the writer has just completed a lengthy comparison of high school and university teaching methods and now wants to move to a new, but related, topic of 'personal responsibility' in learning. His first sentence of the next paragraph is:

> *Because of* ***these differences in teaching methods,*** *universities throw more responsibility on the student.*

He makes the transition by using a summary phrase, 'differences in teaching methods', to refer to the lengthy discussion he has just finished.

The summarizing transition may take even briefer form, with pronouns like *this*, *that*, *these*, *those* or *such* being used to sum up a topic discussed in the preceding paragraph/s. Such pronouns though, like all English pronouns ('it' can be a real problem), carry with them the danger of the **unclear referent.** It is not altogether clear in the following example whether 'these' refers back to 'policies' or 'fiscal arrangements':

> **If English pronouns give you trouble, *name* the referent rather than let a pronoun stand alone.**

> **Last sentence of a paragraph:**
> *The different institutions have produced incoherent policies in terms of the tight fiscal arrangements proposed on introducing the scheme in 1992.*
>
> **First sentence of the next paragraph:**
> ***These*** *have been the subject of vigorous debate in the literature.*

This problem is easily overcome by naming the referent: 'these policies' or 'these fiscal arrangements'.

Using logical connectives Paragraphs can also be linked by words showing logical relationship: *therefore, however, but, consequently, thus, even so, conversely, nevertheless, moreover, in addition*, and many more. Usually though, logical connectives are used to move from one sentence to the next within paragraphs, that is, as internal paragraph transitions.

To illustrate, say a writer has just completed a paragraph summarizing an author's analysis of a documented riot and now wants to move the discussion along. Here are three different logical connectives:

Last sentence of a paragraph:
Brown's analysis provides useful insights into the existing power relations between the army and the government at that time.

Possible first sentences of the next paragraph:

(a) **However,** the power relations embedded in the social structure may be more important in explaining the causes of the riot.

(b) **Even so,** there is no real attempt to grapple with the issue of the government's role in the army's attack on unarmed men, women and children.

(c) **Consequently,** Smith's much-quoted analysis of this same event needs to be reconsidered in view of Brown's findings.

Whatever its form, an inter-paragraph transition should be unobtrusive, shifting readers easily from one topic to the next.

MANIPULATING SENTENCE STRUCTURE

Understanding how to manipulate English sentence structures will allow you to emphasize important ideas and give focus to your writing. It will also help you to avoid monotony in the writing. These basic English sentence structures allow for very sophisticated combinations of simple, compound and complex sentences.

Simple sentence (one main idea):
Trade figures have improved.

Compound sentence (two ideas of equal weight):
Trade figures have improved and so has the economy.

Complex sentence (two ideas of unequal weight):
Although trade figures have improved, the economy remains slow.
or
Although the economy remains slow, trade figures have improved.

Note the shift in emphasis in the turn-around here. In the first sentence the main idea is the 'slow economy'; in the second it is the 'improved trade figures'.

> **Short, sharp, emphatic sentences are best reserved for important ideas or points – simple sentence structure makes them stand out.**

Do vary your sentence structure. If writing consists of a series of simple short sentences strung together it will be monotonous and lack focus. It will be difficult for a reader to discern what *you* consider more or less important about what you are saying. An excess of long sentences has a similar effect. Overloaded sentences that are not well constructed can also cause reader confusion, making it difficult, even impossible, to understand the intended meaning. So do take care with long overloaded sentences, particularly if English is a second language.

Exercise: improving sentence structure

Review sentence structure in several paragraphs of your own writing and compare what you do with the practice of a disciplinary writer you admire. Could you improve?

THE 'DISCARDS' FILE

When developing text, you need to ensure that all ideas you bring forward are directly relevant to the topic under discussion. It is certain that at times you will need to discard material because it just does not fit the context of discussion. This can indeed be hard when it comes to being ruthless about insights and ideas you have developed as beautifully constructed sentences, paragraphs, even longer stretches of writing – pieces of writing to which you remain doggedly attached even though you sense they do not fit. Every writer knows about this dilemma.

Resistant though you may be, do force yourself to discard such material. But never delete it. Cut it and transfer it to a special 'discards' file; give each piece of writing a summary title designating its central import. It is almost equally certain that discarded material of this type will slot perfectly into another context of writing at another time.

Improving overall structure

If you think you have structural problems in a draft you have written, the procedural steps in this exercise should help you to improve it.

Exercise: the coherence test

Step 1

It is now time to become your own reader. Print out a stretch of your writing: either a short text, or a sub-division or two of at least six to seven pages of a longer text. Read quickly through your text with a view to identifying the *main ideas* around which you are building your paragraphs:

- Summarize your main ideas concisely in the margin of your text.
- As you do this note whether:

    (a) Each main idea is being fully developed, or only partially developed so that you seem to be picking up on it in different parts of your text.

    (b) You are repeating yourself (mark 'repeat' on the page), or labouring the point, saying the same thing over and over again in much the same way (note this too).

    (c) You are presenting too many ideas too quickly so that some main ideas are not being developed at all, or seem to be underdeveloped.

Step 2

Type on the computer a sequential list of your main ideas (as noted in the margin of your text), print this out and put it aside.

Step 3

Now consider the overall coherence of your piece of writing:

- Take a highlighter pen and run quickly through your text, looking for evidence of linking – mark any sentences, phrases or words that indicate linking.

Step 4

With your print out of main ideas and other findings:

- Do you think you already have the best order for your main ideas? Or would overall coherence be improved by rearranging them into a new order?
- Do you think there is sufficient linking to ensure the logical flow of your ideas?
- Can you see how your main ideas contribute to the development of a unifying point of view or a thesis, as in argument?

Now you can redraft or simply attend to the parts of the text that need improvement.

Summary Comments

- When structuring at any level of a text (the overall design, sub-divisions or further sections within these), take into account what you are covering, why you are covering that subject, and what you intend to demonstrate/show/establish in doing so. In this way you will be able to embody in your structuring efforts recognition of the overall point of view or argument you wish to develop.
- As the academic paragraph is the basic unit of structure in academic writing, control of the paragraph is essential to the coherent flow of ideas throughout a text.
- Adequate linking within and between paragraphs is needed to ensure overall textual coherence.
- By manipulating English sentence structures effectively, you can draw attention to main ideas or key points while at the same time avoiding monotony and confusion in the writing.

Part Two

Issues Specific to Different Types of Writing, Presentations and Publication Processes

5 Research Essays, Book or Article Reviews and Coursework Exam Papers

Developmental Objectives

By applying the strategies, doing the exercises and following the procedural steps in this chapter, you should be able to:

- Appreciate the different possibilities for essays and what these might mean for your own situation.
- Understand the meaning of academic argument in the context of research essay writing, and how to distinguish ideas from opinions.
- Identify strategies for setting up your own topic or analysing a given topic, developing a position (or thesis) on the topic, compiling an introduction, marshalling evidence, avoiding faulty reasoning and strengthening argument, working up a conclusion, and ensuring clear focus and coherence in your essay.
- Gain insight into the nature of different types of book or article reviews, and develop capacity to focus and structure a review.
- Identify strategies for effective revision and the writing of different types of coursework exam papers.

This chapter considers in some detail prominent types of written assessment in many graduate courses.

Research essays

You should be aware of the unsettled meanings surrounding the term 'essay'.

'ESSAYS' AND THEIR SYNONYMS

Sometimes a **literature review** – reviewing the literature and developing an argument in the process of the review – is referred to by lecturers as a research essay. But then, one course lecturer requested a literature review, when really, as clarified in discussion with him, he wanted a research essay – the development of a line of argument strongly supported by reference to the literature.

You may have to produce a **position paper**. This usually takes the form of a research essay in that a position is adopted and developed by way of argument. However, with a position paper the argument often turns on what *should* be done, so that the argument itself becomes an instrument of change in some context or other (for example, government policy, legal or education reform). But this type of 'should' argument also frequently occurs in what is termed by lecturers a research essay. It may be that there is no difference between a position paper and a research essay in graduate study, but do clarify this if needs be.

Or perhaps you need to write an **exploratory essay**. This seems somewhat like a problem-solving exercise in that the approach tends to conform more to the type of approach laid out under 'Business reports' in Chapter 6 than to development of a formal argument. Some shorter essays, though, explore a topic as an analytical exercise in which no firm conclusion need be reached. Or you may be asked to produce a **synoptic essay**, which usually involves providing a comprehensive overview of a subject or topic, drawing attention to key problems, concerns or issues, and, perhaps, assessing these before presenting a conclusion.

Essays can also be structured along various lines, such as the following, which may or may not be acceptable – you would need to ask:

- Introduction
- Discussion of the 'pros' – points in favour of a question
- Discussion of the 'cons' – points that can be marshalled against a question
- A summary of the writer's own conclusions with supporting evidence (the most demanding part to write).

The variable understandings of the term 'essay' mean you may need to clarify with your lecturer precisely what is expected. I now briefly discuss strategies for dealing with a short essay before proceeding to full discussion of the research essay as formal argument.

THE SHORT ESSAY

Short essays, of say from 600 to 1500 words, can be difficult, particularly if you are expected to read widely in the literature. This puts great pressure on you in terms of selection – what to include for discussion and what to leave out. First, confirm:

1. Whether you are expected to deal with the topic precisely as set.

2. Whether it is permissible to narrow the topic in some way as, for example, if you were to address topic concerns in the context of a particular country, event or situation, or even focus in greater depth on some aspect of the topic.

In the case of (1), it is likely that a broad topic has been designed to test your understanding of what might be significant to discuss and in how much detail (perhaps, for example, certain key issues), with what you select to discuss being important when it comes to assessment. Having identified what you want to cover in the essay, then think about:

- Main ideas you want to bring forward to develop your discussion.
- The best order in which to arrange these ideas.
- Building paragraphs around these main ideas (some may take many paragraphs to develop).

Perhaps you will do the above after writing a first, rough draft.

If (2) applies, you will need to confirm with your lecturer that your revised topic will be acceptable.

I now turn to the research essay as formal argument, which is still a prominent type of assessment in graduate coursework in many disciplines. Argument is also required in many other contexts of academic writing, including some report and thesis writing. Hence, the research essay is given a significant amount of space in this chapter.

The research essay as formal argument

The research essay is characteristically an *argument*, a term that has a special meaning in the academic context.

DECODING THE MEANING OF 'ARGUMENT'

Argument is a type of academic writing, and while argument will be the dominant discourse when you write your research essay, this does not mean that you will not be engaged in other discourse activities. Describing, explaining and informing will all have a place in the process of developing your argument for your reader.

The amount of description or explaining you do, the amount of detail you include, should be controlled by what is needed to ensure your argument is strong.

An argument can be thought of as an *appeal to reason* in which you develop a position, sometimes called a point of view or thesis, on a topic or question. Taking a position involves the exploration of *issues*, though there can be confusion as to what is meant by this term 'issue':

> An **issue** is a topic that sparks controversy within a community of speakers, readers, and writers. More specifically, an issue is a topic that creates a *tension* in the community, a discontent or dissatisfaction with the status quo. (Kaufer et al., 1989: 3) (original emphasis)

Formal argument, then, evidences concern with seminal issues, or sets of related issues, to do with the what, why and how of your research.

Your objective will be to convince your reader, even one unsympathetic to your position, that the position you develop in your essay is indeed *reasonable.* For your argument to be reasonable it needs to be a strong argument. A strong argument depends on the quality of your ideas, which, in turn, depends on the quality of the evidence you include to support those ideas, and the quality of your reasoning. Note that it is not necessarily a matter of whether the argument is true or false, right or wrong, but whether it is strong or weak. All these observations are expanded on in the following discussions.

DISTINGUISHING IDEAS FROM OPINIONS

You may be misled by your lecturer saying: 'I want to know what you think, what your opinion is.' Be careful of this word 'opinion'. What lecturers really want to see from you are *ideas* that can be developed into a strong argument, so that your own point of view – one supported by evidence – emerges in the course of your essay. In Box 5.1 I attempt to clarify the distinction between ideas and opinions by way of a hypothetical example.

Box 5.1 An idea is not the same as an opinion

Take this assertion: **'It is better to live in Cambridge than London'** [Cambridge is a regional city rather than a metropolis like London and other major cities of the world, e.g. Tokyo, Paris, Berlin, Cairo, Sydney or New York].

The above assertion might be an *opinion* expressed by you in conversation with friends. They might agree or disagree, depending on how they feel about the matter, what personal beliefs and attitudes they hold about living in the two cities. No one is likely to require sound evidence for the views expressed, and perhaps people will just agree to disagree if different views prevail.

But say this was a position you wanted to develop in a research essay, and further imagine trying to convince someone who disliked Cambridge and loved London that it was a reasonable position to take. Perhaps your argument would hinge on what is meant by 'better'. Some definition is needed – better quality of life or what? If you were to argue on the basis of a better quality of life, what ideas might you bring forward to support your position? How are you going to convince your protagonist – that London enthusiast?

So you start your research. You uncover sets of comparative statistics showing that pollution levels (traffic, noise, air, industrial, etc.) are much lower in Cambridge than London. You also uncover a recent health survey linking pollution levels to a range of different illnesses.

You now have one *main idea* you can bring forward: *Cambridge has lower levels of pollution, which is known to have negative effects on health.* This one idea could take many paragraphs to develop as you range across the evidence relating to pollution levels and health risks in various contexts (industry, traffic, etc.).

The challenge now of course is to find more ideas to support your position – one won't be enough to convince anyone that it is better to live in Cambridge than London. Nevertheless, the point is made. Regardless of any personal preference for London, a protagonist would have to concede that your idea about pollution and health was *reasonable* because you have evidence to back it up.

BASIC CRITERIA APPLIED IN ASSESSING ESSAYS

When assessing essays, lecturers will apply at least these basic criteria, and possibly others (Clanchy and Ballard, 1997: 4–8). It is expected that your essay:

- Will be clearly focused on the set topic and will deal fully with its central concerns.
- Will be the result of wide and critical reading.
- Will present a reasoned argument.
- Will be competently presented.

I now consider in more detail the different processes involved in producing a research essay as they relate to these criteria.

Topics (or questions)

This discussion of topics recognizes that you may be setting up your own topic or question, have been given a specific topic or question to work on, or have selected one from a list provided by your lecturer.

SETTING UP YOUR OWN TOPIC

If you have been given explicit instructions on how to focus and develop a topic or question of your choice, follow these. Otherwise, consider these questions, because you need to be realistic in setting up a topic, presumably in an area that genuinely interests you:

- What is the word length of your essay?
- How much time do you have available for the essay?
- What is the scope of the literature in the topic area that interests you (too little or too much literature may leave you struggling in different ways)?

Do think about whether your topic will allow you to engage in in-depth analysis.

The real danger is in setting up a topic that is over-ambitious. A topic that is too broad will mean sacrificing in-depth analysis to mere coverage, allowing little opportunity for interesting and subtle insights to emerge.

A useful starting point is to reflect on the nature of topics as set up by your lecturers. Such topics are usually designed to throw you into controversy, to force you to engage the issues with a view to taking a position and developing it. You are likely to be addressing a range of issues in your essay, although a single major issue is a possibility, as the example in Box 5.2 shows.

Box 5.2 A research essay topic can be driven by a single major issue

Subject area: EDUCATION

Central research question: To what extent should tertiary students pay for their own education?

Major issue: 'USER PAYS'

Key questions associated with this issue:

Should *all* students be expected to pay fully for the cost of their higher education – why? why not?

Should *some* students and not others be expected to pay fully for the cost of their higher education – why? why not?

Should *all* students be expected to contribute *in part* to the cost of their higher education – why? why not?

Should this contribution be indexed? If yes, on what bases should it be indexed – socio-economic grouping? cost of producing courses? or what? What are the reasons for your view?

Should other organizations be expected to contribute to the costs of higher education – why? why not?

Which organizations should contribute – public/private? government? industry? business? other?

What criteria might apply in determining which organizations should contribute and under what circumstances?

To what extent should these organizations contribute, in full or in part – why? why not?

What evidence can be brought to bear on the position you wish to take on the topic?

It is also wise to consider whether the issues or controversies that interest you do relate back to your course objectives:

- Review these objectives in your 'Course Guide' (if you have been given one). Browse through lecture and tutorial notes to determine the types of issues being raised by lecturers. Consider also, for example, whether your topic should evidence a strong theoretical focus if theory is an important focus of your particular course.

And a last piece of advice:

- Write your topic out in some detail so that you can have it approved by your lecturer before you begin your research. The more refined it is the more able your lecturer will be to assess its viability in terms of length and time available for research and writing.

ANALYSING A GIVEN TOPIC

Recall the above criterion for assessment: that your essay 'will be clearly focused on the set topic and will deal fully with its central concerns'.

Interpretation of the topic is the first point at which the writing of an essay can go wrong.

Exercise: analysing topics

As already mentioned, most essay topics are designed to force you to engage the issues as you read, and to evaluate different points of view presented in the literature (see 'Treating information critically' in Chapter 2). So bear this in mind as you apply the following Subject/Angle/Process (SAP) method to analysis of your topic. I use a sample topic to illustrate how to go about analysing your own:

Sample topic:
If the arms control enterprise is a child of the Cold War, what use is it now? Should it give way to more radical disarmament efforts or is the arms control disarmament enterprise now irrelevant? Your discussion should take account of theoretical debates of current interest.

Step 1: the subject

Ask yourself:

- What am I being asked to investigate?

With the sample topic it is simple: 'arms control'. But identifying the true subject is not always easy, as topics can be complex and have several parts to them. If you are uncertain about precisely what you should be investigating, get together with fellow students and brainstorm the topic and/or consult with your lecturer – do not proceed to research if you are uncertain.

Step 2: the angle

Now ask yourself:

- Why am I being asked to investigate this subject matter?

At this point you want to ensure that you will deal fully with the central concerns of the topic, all of them. My set of questions after brainstorming the sample topic is very basic; if you were a student in this discipline, you would be able to produce a more refined set:

> **Brainstorm your topic to generate *a set of questions* that can be used to control your reading and ensure you acquire the best and right information.**

> What is meant by arms control? Does it need to be defined or not? (Definitely yes – if there is no settled agreement on its meaning in your discipline.) Is arms control a child of the Cold War – yes or no? Now move to the *central concerns* of the topic:
>
> What does the 'disarmament enterprise' consist in? (Do you know precisely what is meant by this phrase?) *To what extent* does arms control remain relevant – a lot, reasonably so, only minimally or what? In what *precise ways* does it remain relevant, or not? Are there security measures other than arms control that need to be taken into account post Cold War? What are these?
>
> Evaluate the literature and ask yourself: *what is my position on all this?* (Take care to identify the **issues**, the points debated by scholars, and to gather evidence to support the position you will be taking.)

Information providing answers to questions of this type would need to be gathered to deal effectively with the sample topic. By skim reading (see 'Ensuring task-focused information' in Chapter 2), you should be able to avoid wasting time on reading material not directly relevant to your topic.

Step 3: the process

Have you been given specific instructions about how to go about answering the topic? Yes, the sample topic contains a clear directive: 'Your discussion should take account of theoretical debates of current interest', meaning whatever else you do, you must apply the theory.

Commonly used directional words and phrases are:

Discuss
Explore this comment
Analyse
Examine carefully
Evaluate this claim
To what extent ...?
Critically review
Compare and contrast
Do you agree?

Directions of this type always imply the need for argument. Engage the issues, and develop your own position using solid evidence as support.

Compiling an introduction

As the introduction serves only to orient your reader to your discussion, keep it short and to the point, something in the order of a page or so for a 3000 word essay. Short it may be, but the introduction does have an important function.

ESTABLISHING THE CONTEXT

Provide *relevant* background information to establish the context of your discussion. Note how this extract from the introduction to an essay on the sample topic in the previous section is indeed relevant to that topic; it does not stray from the central concerns of the topic:

> *The Cold War and nuclear age were born at about the same time. Seen strictly in this context, the Cold War merely added the nuclear dimension to the arms control enterprise. However, the concern about the devastating nature of nuclear weapons resulted in the greatest media emphasis being placed on nuclear arms control efforts, particularly on the arms race between the two nuclear hegemons,*

the US and the USSR [reference]. Nevertheless, in the same Cold War period, much effort was put into conventional arms control such as Mutual Balance Force Reduction (MBFR) [reference], and areas of chemical and biological weapons as well as confidence building measures (CBMs).

DEFINING IMPORTANT TERMS, PHRASES OR CONCEPTS

If there is no settled agreement on the meaning of a word, term, phrase or concept appearing in your essay topic, acknowledge this, find the common factor, and give a working definition for your essay. Referring to a specialist dictionary or reference work in your discipline is a useful starting point. You can then build a working definition from other scholars' attempts at definition (see the example below under 'Strategies that strengthen argument').

Definition may, however, be a much larger task in an essay, and one not able to be satisfactorily addressed in the introduction. This was the case with the following set question, where definition of the term 'democracy' was itself central to any argument being developed:

> To what extent do the newly industrialized economies of the Southeast Asian region demonstrate a shift to democratic principles of government? Discuss in reference to at least two specific countries. Include in your discussion a review of current debates and theories of democracy.

LAYING OUT A POSITION

Provide a summary statement of the argument you intend to develop in the body of your essay – take care to address all aspects of the topic. If the topic has several parts, then your position should reflect this. Although the topic may appear to be straightforward, topics are in fact rarely so. Consequently, the position taken will often be complex, with several parts (see Box 5.3 below).

Rather than lay out a position, you may be expected to *state the main conclusions* reached in your essay. Or rather than state a position (although it is a good idea to do so), or detail your main conclusions, you will provide *a statement of purposes*, as this writer did after establishing context by way of a brief review of a major debate in the literature:

> *The main purpose of this essay is to provide a critical evaluation of the different positions as outlined above.*

It could be that you find yourself making several of these moves in your introduction.

MAKING A PROCEDURAL STATEMENT

Orient your reader to the structure of your essay, the way in which you intend to organize your discussion in general. Phrases signalling procedure may be of this type:

> Initially, I examine ... This is followed by a review of ... A discussion of the theoretical underpinnings of X is then presented. The fourth section provides a comparative analysis of ... Finally, I draw out recommendations for ...

In many cases though, the procedure is indicated in a more subtle way, as in the hypothetical example given in Box 5.3.

Box 5.3 An introduction should fulfil its reader-orientation function while being tightly focused on the topic

Topic:

'Economic rationalist policies are responsible for the declining economy.' Discuss.

Factors identified as important from the reading:

- Policy-making areas: (car manufacturing, technology, primary exports – foodstuffs)
- Industrial action (national transport and miners strikes)
- Natural disaster: widespread flooding
- Factors in the international political economy

Steps in compiling the introduction:

Step 1: provision of background information *relevant* to the topic (three paragraphs of summary comments (with references) on the economy's decline over the period of interest)

Step 2: definition from the literature of what 'economic rationalist' means

Step 3: *laying out the position and procedure* in a single move as follows (the four-part ordering of the position as expressed below reflected the overall structure of the essay):

(Ist part) Economic rationalist policies of the present government have had a slow-growth effect on three major export industries: car manufacturing, technology and primary exports. Such policies do not, however, account fully for the evident economic decline. **(2nd part)** Industrial strife during the past two years has been particularly disruptive to growth in some sectors. **(3rd part)** The economy has also had to contend with extensive flooding in parts of the country. **(4th part)** As well, there have been specific developments in the world political economy, which need to be addressed in discussing reasons for the economic decline.

This level of generality is usual when laying out a position and signalling procedure. At this stage you are just orienting your reader to the discussion to follow in the body of your essay.

Evidence and reasoning

There are different ways to ensure that an argument is reasonable. Your primary evidence will come from sources you are reading in the literature, and perhaps from raw data that you have generated. In this section, I discuss some key issues in argument development.

ARGUING FROM SOURCES

Arguing from sources means using references, such as direct quotations or paraphrases, book, chapter or page references to marshal support for your position. (See 'Plagiarism and referencing' in Chapter 3). (See also Kaufer et al., 1989; Davis and McKay, 1996: ch. 5 'Cause and effect' and ch. 6 'Argument').

Your essay should reflect familiarity with and understanding of the ideas of other scholars; it should be the result of wide and critical reading. This does not mean merely describing what others have thought and said. Rather, use source material to **advance *your* position,** like so:

> *This is not to say, however, that social cleavage is inevitable. Difference splits communities when it is totalising and rigid, and when it implies inequity. But it can*

be approached in ways that render it less potentially destructive. One way is to recall that while difference is unavoidable, so is similarity. 'Civilisations overlap as much as they compete' [reference], and assertions of total difference between identity groups can be shown to be illusory [reference]. Common ground for negotiation can always be found. Another way is to destabilise power relations by revealing identities as social constructions [reference]. Difference can become a site for respect and delegitimised as a source for chauvinism [reference].

You could, of course, be challenging other scholars in the process of developing your argument, or **neutralizing opposing arguments:**

X [reference] offers sound reasons for the continuing centralisation of services in terms of the economic benefits to government. However, he does not take account of the high costs of maintaining centralisation when determining these benefits.

In developing a position favouring the cost–benefit effects of 'decentralising' services, this writer recognized that X's argument could be used to challenge her own, so she had to neutralize it by showing there was a flaw in that argument: it was too narrow.

Unless you are working with primary source materials (for example, literary texts, archival documents such as letters, diaries, or legal documents, etc.), where it might be appropriate, you should avoid overlong direct quotations. The idea is to *process* the source materials you are reading, so a paraphrase of two or three key points in a long discussion may be sufficient for your purposes. Effective paraphrase demonstrates thorough critical understanding of source materials.

AVOIDING FAULTY REASONING

Solid evidence is a necessary but not a sufficient condition for strong argument. There also needs to be sound reasoning. So do take care with fallacies of the following type, which signal incorrect or faulty reasoning. (For a more in-depth understanding of logical fallacies in argument, see Downes, 2003.)

- **Circular reasoning or arguing in a circle:** For example: 'Penal reform is necessary because of prison corruption, which shows the need for prison reform.'
- **Reasoning that does not follow:** This means that the conclusion does not follow from the premises of the argument you have set up.

- **Black and white thinking:** The tendency here is to go from one extreme to another. For example: 'If teachers cannot fix the problems in schools they should stay out of the debate altogether.' That fact that teachers cannot 'fix' the problem does not mean that they could not contribute greatly to the debate.

- **Assuming that what is true of the part is true of the whole (or vice versa):** For example: making the assumption that drugs are a big problem among 13–16-year-old school students when this age group has been surveyed in only a small sampling of schools.

- **Begging the question:** This occurs when you ask a question that wrongly assumes something to be true. For example: 'Why are men more aggressive than women?' This 'begs the question' of whether men are in fact more aggressive. You must *prove* that men are more aggressive than women, not assume that this is so.

- **Assuming the conclusion:** For example: 'This action is wrong because it is immoral.' You must *prove* that the action is wrong because it is opposed to moral principles, not assume that this is so.

- **Appealing to an unsuitable authority:** This will occur if you draw on an authority who may be a recognized expert in one field, but is not an authority in the subject matter you are discussing.

- **Attributing causality:** It is important to distinguish cause–effect relationships from statistical correlations or coincidences. The data may show a strong correlation between two events, X and Y, but this does not then mean that X (or X alone) *caused* Y.

- **Drawing inferences/conclusions:** Before drawing an inference/conclusion ensure that there is actual 'evidence' to support it. For example, detailing problems in higher education would be an insufficient basis for concluding that policy reform is needed. Such a conclusion could only be drawn from a careful (and convincing) demonstration of the actual link between those problems and current government policy.

STRATEGIES TO STRENGTHEN ARGUMENT

Arguments can be severely weakened by a lack of detail. For your argument to be reasonable, you will need to include sufficient detail to secure it, and you can do this by way of a variety of strategies for developing paragraphs (see also 'Controlling paragraph development' in Chapter 4).

Exercise: strengthening argument

Look closely at the nature of the detail in the following paragraphs and the effects achieved by the different strategies used to secure the argument through paragraph development. Consider too the quality of the reasoning in these paragraphs: does the reasoning seem sound to you? Note as well how the writers draw on their sources to advance *their* arguments.

Definition is used to develop the paragraph below, which is a good example of providing a working definition from the literature in an introduction. The writer defines 'public law' by comparing it with constitutional law, and strengthens his definition by drawing support from other scholars:

Constitutional law is concerned with the ways in which public power is institutionally organised and applied, with the relations between the institutions which exercise public power, and with the relations between these institutions and other social interests [reference]. Public law is a more ambiguous term that refers to the principles governing disputes between the State and its subjects as determined by the courts [reference]. It has been argued [reference] that public law has come to include administrative law, criminal law and even environmental law depending on how the State is conceptualised as a legal actor. For the purposes of this essay, if government action can be defined as the regulation of individual liberty, ***public law can be defined as the regulation of the government's ability to regulate individual liberty*** *(my emphasis). (Further explanatory information was included in a footnote.)*

Comparison is favoured below to demonstrate the difficulties of determining the origins of rugs from their representation in paintings. Note the use of **comparative illustration** at the end, where the writer picks up on details mentioned in the first sentence to strengthen her position:

In trying to identify the origin of a rug, we can use as guiding principles the elements of design, the decorative style and patterning, colours and their combinations, as well as known geographical connections [references]. It may also be possible to physically examine the rug itself – the thickness of the warp and the weft, the types of dyes used, the techniques of application, and so forth.

With a rug in a painting, however, these tools of analysis are either unavailable or less reliable. The medium of painting is an illusion of reality, even if it pretends to be a depiction of the fine details of reality. The rug plays a part in that illusion, and is likely to be shaped by the artist to fit the desired overall composition. ***A rug in a painting may have its pattern altered by the angle of perspective, or a fold in the material may distort the appearance of the pattern; the colours may have been changed for artistic effect, as might the ornamental design and other features*** (my emphasis).

Causal analysis characterizes the development of the next paragraph. Note how the writer develops his general assertion in the first sentence by analysing the causes of technological development in Japan, and strengthens his analysis by drawing on other scholars as support.

Technological development is not a natural process. Social forces lie behind the development of any given technology. In Japan's case, 'economic and technological development have been enshrined as Japanese social goals since the Meiji restoration of 1868' [reference]. It has even been suggested that the 'military class, the samurai, [were] by their own life experience ... able to recognise the benefits and "rationality" of Western technology' [reference]. Be that as it may, the more immediate forces leading to the development of microelectronics and IT in Japan derived from the changes and crises facing Japanese capitalism from the late 1960s onwards [explanatory footnote added]. These included a recognisable slow down in economic growth, and demographic changes causing labour shortages, followed by more recent concerns with an aging population.

Restatement means saying the same thing in a different way, but it is not merely repetition. Restatement is a useful strategy to clarify difficult ideas and/or reinforce their importance. Restatement is sometimes signalled by such phrases as 'That is ...', 'By this I mean ...', 'In other words ...', and often by nothing at all. In the following example, ideas in the restatement, the material emphasized, are much the same as those expressed in sentence 2. The restatement both clarifies the writer's initial statement on orthodox historians, and strengthens it by drawing support from the literature. Comparison is again a favoured method of developing the paragraph as the writer distinguishes the approach of orthodox historians and that of the more radical X:

X's approach to history is considered radical by orthodox historians. Conventional historiographers presuppose that history is a record of 'facts'

> *that, with careful investigation, can be objectively verified.* ***As Y argues, 'orthodox historians adhere to a "discovery" view of the past, holding that the past is there, a field of real entities and forces waiting for the historians to find' [reference].*** *They also view history as a linear sequence of events that is characterised by continuity. X, however, takes an 'archaeological' approach. He is concerned with the discontinuity of events, with 'analogies and differences, hierarchies, complementarities, coincidences, and shifts' [reference], with uncovering the discontinuities themselves in the interstices of time* (my emphasis).

Specification means saying precisely what is meant by a more abstract phrase; in this case, 'the great reform measures'. Failure to specify can weaken your argument because there is no way for a reader to tell if *you* know what you are talking about, as would occur if specification were omitted below:

> *The great reform measures –* ***the reorganisation of parliament, the revision of the penal code and the poor laws, the restrictions placed on child labour, and other industrial reforms*** *– were important factors in establishing English society on a more democratic basis* (my emphasis).

Qualification is needed in this next example, which highlights the problem of using generalizations in argument, something you need to watch:

> *The racist attitudes of opponents of increased immigration are cause for concern.*

It is a poor argument because of oversimplification. The writer implies that *all* opponents of increased immigration have 'racist attitudes', which would be impossible to establish, though this may be true of *some* opponents. Even then, such 'attitudes' cannot be assumed. There would need to be detailed evidence as support, perhaps extracted from the language and rhetoric used by some opponents in their publications or in excerpts from public speeches.

Developing a position

Your essay will need to evidence a coherent line of argument throughout. For this, a coherent structure is essential and the ideas you bring forward must be directly relevant to the topic.

ENSURING STRUCTURAL COHERENCE

By structural coherence I mean the logic of the organization of your discussion, the interconnectedness of ideas, how it hangs together, coheres, as discussed in 'Developing texts' in Chapter 4, to which I refer you. Refer also to 'Words and phrases for developing discussions' in Appendix 1.

> **When structuring a research essay remember: you are not carving up information to cover but sequencing information in an argument.**

Note the following points also. When using sub-divisions to section your essay, work on the premise that you are not merely working out what to cover, but building an argument:

- Why have you arranged your sub-divisions in the order in which you have? Is it the best arrangement?
- What are you trying to show/demonstrate/establish in each sub-division in relation to your overall argument? How will each sub-division serve to advance your argument – what will each contribute to the development of your position/thesis?

In every instance of structuring – whether the whole essay or the sub-divisions – consider this set of key questions, to which I frequently return throughout this book:

- What am I focusing on here? What am I talking about?
- Why am I focusing on this? What are my reasons for talking about this?
- How do I want to develop this discussion? What do I want to discuss and in what order do I want to discuss these topics?
- What/so what? What are the *main ideas* I want to bring forward in developing my argument and what are the *implications* of my discussions? Build your paragraphs around these main ideas. Make sure your reader is not left to comment on your text: 'So what?', meaning that the point of your discussion is lost on that reader.

If there is a need to digress from your main line of argument, signal this as a deliberate digression and give a reason for it, as illustrated:

Before continuing this examination of financial issues to do with setting up the test project, it is helpful to provide a brief overview of a series of political events that caused a departure from the original plan at this time.

DETERMINING RELEVANCE

Relevance refers to the overall focus of your essay. Sometimes lecturers make comments in the margin of an essay such as 'I can't follow the point of all this', 'This seems to be a digression from the main thrust of the argument' or 'How does this relate to topic?' Comments of this type signal that the reader cannot work out the *relevance* of your ideas to the position supposedly being developed.

In the process of ensuring your position is clearly focused on the set topic and deals fully with its central concerns, ensure that all ideas do relate back to your position, as represented graphically in Figure 5.1.

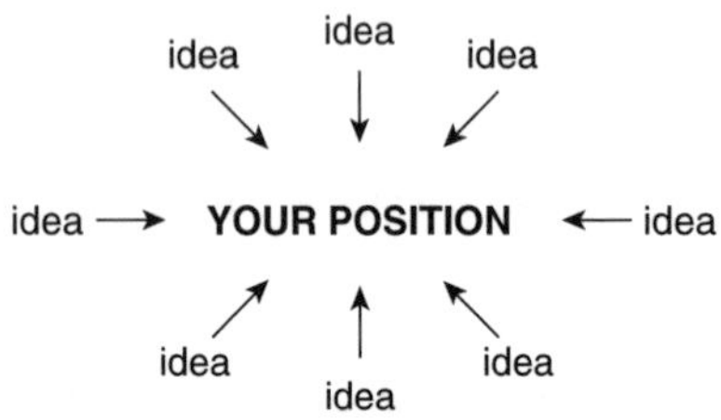

FIGURE 5.1 **Ensuring relevance**

Working up a conclusion

When pressured to submit an essay, it is easy to rush the ending so that there does not appear to be a proper conclusion. Do bring the essay to some resolution, perhaps referring the reader back to the topic for a sense of unity.

Remember, you are drawing together the findings of your essay, so you should not introduce new material that has not been previously discussed in the body of the essay.

In summarizing overall findings, you should avoid mere repetition of the conclusions reached in various parts of the essay. The conclusion is another stage of thinking – a reflection on what has been uncovered during the course of the argument. In effect, try to process your findings for the reader and put these findings into a new set of relationships. Ask yourself questions of this type:

- What do *I* find most interesting or important about my findings in terms of the topic and the position I have developed? And what seems to be of lesser interest or importance?

- Are there any interesting implications of my overall findings? (When answering this last question, you will probably be speculating, so use more tentative language such as: 'perhaps', 'it seems', 'it could be' and so forth, but do ensure your speculations are grounded in findings reached in the body of your essay).

In these ways you let the reader know what you think about your findings, and perhaps leave her/him with something interesting to think about (see also 'The thesis conclusion' in Chapter 7).

Cutting to meet word length

If the essay needs to be cut to meet word length stipulations, do not cut the very detail that strengthens the argument – look elsewhere (see Figure 5.2).

- Introductions are often wordy, over-written and can stand considerable condensing.

- Lengthy arguments or discussions can fall victim to what is sometimes called 'the expository bulge', meaning that there is an unnecessary proliferation of explanatory information, with too much peripheral detail. You need only as much detail as is necessary to secure your argument.

- It is often possible to cut material from the more descriptive or explanatory parts of an essay (for example, historical background), which need to be there but can be condensed.

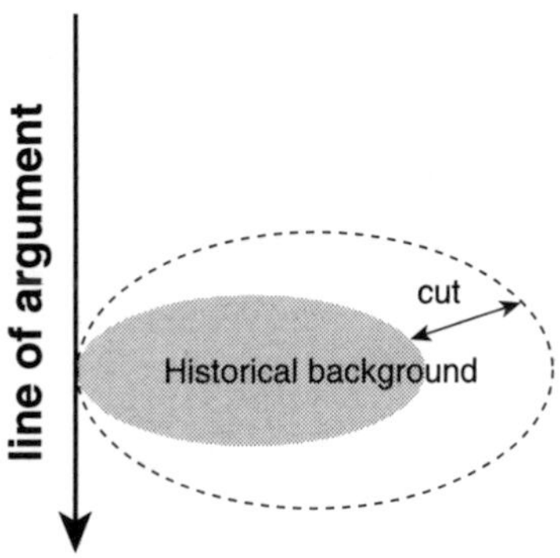

FIGURE 5.2 **Cutting material to meet word length**

Reviewing the essay presentation

The fourth and final criterion mentioned above is that your essay 'will be competently presented':

- Include a separate cover sheet (you may be given one by your lecturer) that includes information of this type: Name (yours); Topic (exact wording); Course details (e.g. AL836); Lecturer (name); Length (as given); Due date of submission.
- Use double spacing or space and a half, and double this between paragraphs or indent them – much easier to read. Leave decent margins so that your lecturer can write comments.
- Do a word count to ensure your essay does meet the designated length where this is stipulated, as there may be penalties (for example, marks deducted) for going over the limit.
- Carefully check the accuracy of direct quotations (these must be exactly as you find them in your source), and also all referencing details. Ensure your writing practices are consistent. Carefully edit and proofread your essay.

All these matters are discussed in 'Reflecting on current practice' in Chapter 3.

Book or article reviews

While my focus here is on book reviewing, it should not be difficult for you to adapt what I say to the journal article context.

THE DIFFERENT TYPES OF REVIEWS

Consider these different scenarios:

1. You have been invited to review a book relevant to your research field for a magazine or journal.
2. As a course requirement, you are expected to produce a book review that emulates professional practice, say, as if for publication in a specific newspaper.

Even in newspapers, reviews can be more or less academic in style. In some daily newspapers, a disproportionate amount of space is given to summary, to telling readers what the book is about, with only minimal critical appraisal. More up-market newspapers are likely to evidence many of the features of the academic review, as discussed below.

3 As part of course assessment, you have been asked to critically review some book or article.

In the case of scenarios 1 and 2, you will need to adopt a style of writing suited to the specific context and audience. You can teach yourself to do any type of writing if you have models to follow. Before drafting, study previously published reviews to orient yourself to the structure, style and treatment of information expected of your review for that particular newspaper or journal – make use of the exercise under 'Mastering (inter)disciplinary writing practices' in Chapter 2.

Scenario 3 is the one I want to address in more detail. In writing an academic review, it is almost certain that you will be expected to engage critically with the book or article (see 'Treating information critically' in Chapter 2). Your review should not therefore be a summary of the content or argument of the book (unless your lecturer specifically requests this). Instead, it should state concisely what the book sets out to do and assess how well the author achieves that goal. Be prepared to give sound reasons for your point of view. These points are elaborated on next.

CONDUCTING AN ACADEMIC REVIEW

Steps laid out in the following exercise should allow you to take a more strategic approach to the conduct of your review.

Exercise: steps in the review process

Step 1

- Look at the title, the table of contents, and read the preface and introduction to gain understanding of the central focus and the coverage of the book.
- Read closely the introduction and/or first chapter. This is to determine the author's purposes or objectives, to identify questions being engaged, hypotheses being examined or issues discussed, and also whether any

limitations have been placed on the scope of the study. Even acknowledged limitations may give cause for critical comment, say, in terms of treatment of material (for example, the author has excluded information essential to a balanced treatment of the subject matter). At this point, identify whether there is any theoretical or methodological framework being used, or even important assumptions of this type, as these will affect the author's approach and interpretations.

- Skim quickly through the whole book first, running your eye over chapter and sub-division headings, opening sentences of paragraphs, and glancing at any tables, illustrations or other graphic materials, as well as indexes and bibliographies. Try to gain a general sense of the argument being developed, as well as the issues being engaged.
- Read closely the final chapter, which should cover the author's conclusions and summarize the main reasons for them.

Step 2

- Now decide on the aspects of the book you consider important to discuss. These aspects will probably cover the strengths and/or weaknesses of the book as *you* see them, in terms of the content and perhaps the style and presentation as well; after all, clarity and conciseness in writing can contribute to a more accessible argument or discussion. Pinpoint the strengths as you see them. Weaknesses may centre on matters of this type: flaws in the general thrust of the argument – weak evidence or flawed reasoning; biases in the methodology, theory or modelling; the uneven treatment of important issues; the current relevance of the ideas put forward or even the whole thrust of the argument (for example, it may be somewhat dated); problems with underlying assumptions about the nature of things; discussions that are too broad or too narrow, etc.

Step 3

- The next step is to read more closely the sections of the book that are relevant to the strengths and weaknesses of the book as you see it. Note the main points you want to make, and identify key quotations or paraphrased material from the book that you can use to support your claims; even just page references will do.

- If you are required to review this book in the context of other studies, then this is the time to read these, after you have a reasonably sound knowledge of the book you are reviewing, not before.
- To situate the review in the context of other studies, ask yourself questions of this type:

  (a) How does the study fit into the broader literature?
  (b) How does the author's position compare with those of other studies I have read?
  (c) In what ways is the argument similar or different?
  (d) What might be the reasons for these differences and similarities?
  (e) What contribution does the book make to scholarship in the research field?
  (f) How useful or not is it? In what precise ways is it useful or not and why?

STRUCTURING A REVIEW

It is up to you how you structure your review, but you could follow this approach if you wish:

- Begin with an initial identification of the book (author, title, date of publication and other details that seem important). Indicate the major aspects of the book you will be discussing in your review – **your focus** in terms of its strengths and weaknesses.

- This could be followed by a *brief* summary of the range, contents and argument(s) of the book, perhaps just a few paragraphs in a shorter review of, say, 1500–2000 words.

- The **core of your review**, the body of the discussion, will be a critical analysis of the aspects you have selected to focus on. Make sure you substantiate what you say by drawing on the book itself as evidence and other scholarly sources if this is appropriate.

- In the conclusion, provide a summary evaluation of the overall contribution made by the book, to the subject area, to your understanding of the topic and to scholarship.

Coursework exams

There are different approaches to exams. Most common are **closed-book exams** into which, as implied, you are not able to take any reference materials at all. This approach contrasts with **open-book exams**, which do allow you to take in certain materials. Your lecturers will tell you which materials are allowed – perhaps notes, books or journal articles for reference. These materials, however, will only prove useful to you if they are well-organized, practised with and thoroughly understood before you go in. Preparation is needed. In the exam there is no time to read these materials, only to find relevant information you know is there because you are already familiar with the content.

With **take-home exams** you will be given an exam paper to complete in a specified time (perhaps a weekend or a week). Take-home exams usually consist of essay questions. As you will have full access to sources (books, articles, etc.) in answering these questions, the opportunity to rework your answers and less restriction on the time you take to write them, lecturers will expect a higher standard than for a regular exam.

Pre-seen exams are somewhat different. Here you will have the opportunity to preview your exam paper beforehand and prepare your answers in the revision period. You might be told that you will have to write on all the questions on the paper; or maybe only some of them will be selected for the examination, though you will not be told which ones. In this case, you will complete your paper under the usual, formal examination conditions. Again, because you have been advantaged in previewing the paper, a higher standard will be expected.

Apart from there being different approaches to examination, exam papers can take different forms, three prominent types being:

- **Essay exams**, which usually allow a choice of topics to write on.
- **Short answer exams**, involving answers of a paragraph or half a page, and sometimes allowing choice.
- **Multiple-choice exams** in which you normally have to answer (tick, circle or nominate an answer for) all questions.

Discussions to follow take account of the different communicative needs of these different types of exam. To communicate effectively in exam papers, you will need to prepare the ground – to revise effectively, which is where I begin.

Setting up a revision plan

The following discussion walks you through three stages of the revision process.

STAGE 1: FOCUSING YOUR PLAN

Grounding revision in course objectives Exams test your knowledge of a particular course within your degree programme, and your ability to apply this knowledge under exam conditions. But it is easy to forget when caught up in details throughout a semester or whole year course, why the course was offered and what lecturers envisioned you might gain from taking it – information that will surely be important in the design of the exam paper. So you first need to identify sources to clarify your understanding of the rationale underlying the course – its scope, aims and objectives, and the probable scope of your exam. So this is where revision should begin.

This information can be gathered from the sources indicated in Figure 5.3, and any other similar sources appropriate in your case.

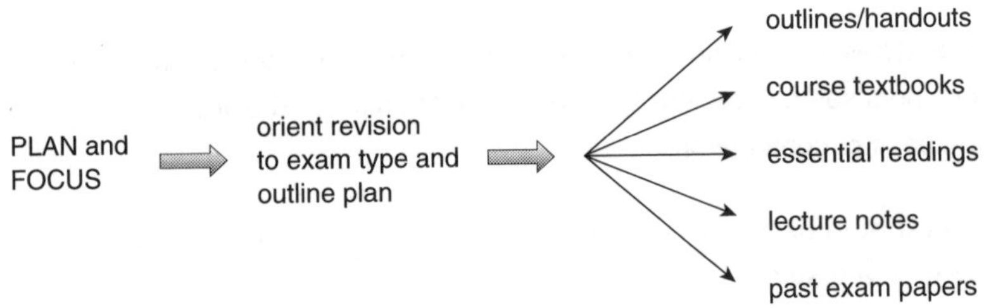

FIGURE 5.3 **Orienting and outlining a revision plan**

From outlines or handouts that detail what will be covered and when, you should be able to see *why* the course was offered – its aims and objectives, and so what your lecturers hope you will learn from it, which will be tested in the examination. Look at the beginning of your course guide if you were given one.

By scanning relevant textbooks, essential readings from seminars or brick materials, as well as lecture notes that cover the whole sweep of your course, you should be able to clarify your understanding of basic content – the main topics covered, how those topics are broken down for discussion (for example, in lectures), key aspects of topic focus, issues of importance and so forth. Doing this should provide a clear overview of the *scope* of knowledge being covered in the course.

Reviewing past exam papers Review past exam papers if these are available (also relevant for take-home exams). But before you do this, make sure that your exam paper will be of the same type as the paper of previous years. You want to avoid putting effort into past papers only to find the lecturer has changed the exam paper from the previous essay format to a short answer paper.

In reviewing past exam papers, you are orienting yourself to what might be expected of you:

- What do the exam paper instructions say?
- Are you expected to answer all questions or to select from a range of questions? Are all questions compulsory in one section but subject to choice in others? Are some questions given different percentage weightings, which is not unusual in short answer papers? If yes, when writing the paper you should give less time to those questions worth less.
- What sort of time schedule would you need to work out if you were to manage your time efficiently in the exam?
- Do you get a sense of the scope of knowledge being tested?
- What *types* of questions are being set and what sort of knowledge do the examiners seem to be testing? Go back to the aims and objectives of your course as a point of comparison.

You should be able to outline your revision plan from notes you have taken during this first stage.

STAGE 2: SYSTEMATIZING YOUR PLAN

With the plan outline from Stage 1, you are now in a position to systematize your plan for intensive revision by using strategies noted in Figure 5.4.

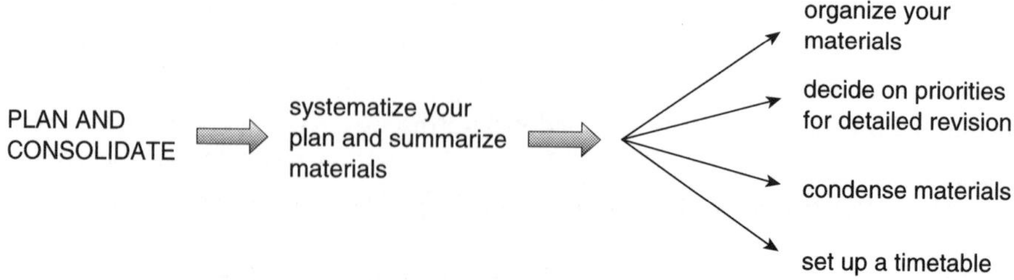

FIGURE 5.4 **Systematizing a revision plan**

The detail of your revision will be different, taking into account different types of exam papers.

Essay type exams Usually in this type of exam it is possible to specialize in revision, focusing on, say, only ten (but not three or four!) out of the 13 or so related topics covered throughout a semester. You will know if you can do this, if in your review of past exam papers you notice that the expectation is for you to select, say, three essay questions from a list of 12.

The essay type exam will not only test your knowledge of the course generally but also your capacity to reason about a topic in the process of producing an argument.

Having identified the set of topics you wish to revise, set priorities, allowing more time for topics you find most difficult; and establish a timetable so that you can monitor your progress in revision.

When condensing materials do not summarize in detail each journal article, essential reading, textbook, or any other source material. Rather, hold your sources in relation. For example, with a theory topic, the revision process might involve taking notes towards understanding of the principles of the theory, developments that have taken place in the theory over time, key figures who featured in these developments, criticisms brought against the theory and why, how advocates of the theory have answered these criticisms and supported their views, the theory's explanatory and/or predictive value, its limitations and strengths and why. To extract this type of essential information, you will need to read across various sources rather than summarize in detail any particular source. This is what I mean by 'holding your sources in relation'.

Use flow charts, diagrams etc. to condense and plot the relatedness of information.

Use your sources to extract the type of essential information that will serve you well regardless of the specific orientation of any particular exam topic or question that is set.

It is also important to understand the relevant issues or sets of issues if you are to produce an argument:

- What are the points on which scholars agree or disagree?
- Are you clear about the reasons for their agreement or disagreement?
- Have you identified important causal relations where necessary – causes and effects of events or actions – their short- or long-term implications.

Be fully analytical in your approach to revision. Decide in the revision process what you think about a subject or topic and why, and what evidence you can use to support your views. There is no time to sort out your position in the exam room – whether you agree or disagree with other scholars' arguments.

With the above approach you should be able to achieve a balance between the depth and breadth of your topic coverage, which is necessary in all exam situations. You want to take to your exam a thoroughly critical, but broad understanding of the course subject matter.

Short answer exams Some of the above advice also applies for short answer papers, though you may not be given a choice of topics to answer or be expected to produce a sustained argument. Still, you will need to establish priorities, set up a timetable for revision monitoring and develop a critical understanding of your material. You would have determined the nature of the questions from your review of past exam papers in Stage 1, the type of knowledge being tested, or the sort of information needed to be able to answer the questions well.

> **Papers of the short answer type often focus on problem-solving, concept or issue definition, modelling, design principles, knowledge application etc.**

> **Condense material along the appropriate lines (e.g. as sets of problems) in flow charts, graphs, tables or diagrams – whatever appeals.**

With problem-solving questions, for example, you will need to practise solving problems in the revision process; it is not enough to know your material thoroughly. First, identify a range of key problems in the revision material on which you need to focus. Then ask yourself as you revise:

- Why is this a problem? (ensures understanding of the distinctive nature of each problem)
- Which strategies (e.g. formulae, techniques, etc.) would enable the best resolutions?
- Is there more than one viable strategy or approach?
- Why do you prefer these strategies/approaches and not others? Be prepared to justify your choices – give reasons for them.

Multiple-choice exams Multiple-choice exam papers are often designed to test how well you are building up basic knowledge of a disciplinary area. It is probably in the area of fine distinctions that the revision will prove most taxing. In the exam, a correct answer may depend on understanding subtle distinctions in the language, so if English is not your first language you will need to practise as much as possible, and perhaps check your answers with a native-speaking friend from your course.

> **Multiple-choice questions test detailed knowledge and understanding, with questions that require recognition of *fine distinctions* in terms of definitions, understanding of basic concepts, models, stages or the sequence of stages in processes, cause and effect relations, comparisons and contrasts, explanations etc.**

When revising, actively look for slight differences, for fine shades of meaning, for paradoxes and uncertainties. As with all exams, however, you are being tested on your general knowledge, so avoid sacrificing breadth of understanding to a detailed but narrow understanding of just a few topics. Prioritize revision tasks along a well-thought-out revision timetable.

The end of Stage 2 should leave you with a condensed set of notes that may include visual materials such as maps or outlines that chart important sets of relations or developments.

STAGE 3: TESTING THE EFFICACY OF YOUR PLAN

It is now time to test the efficacy of your revision plan by way of the strategies suggested in Figure 5.5.

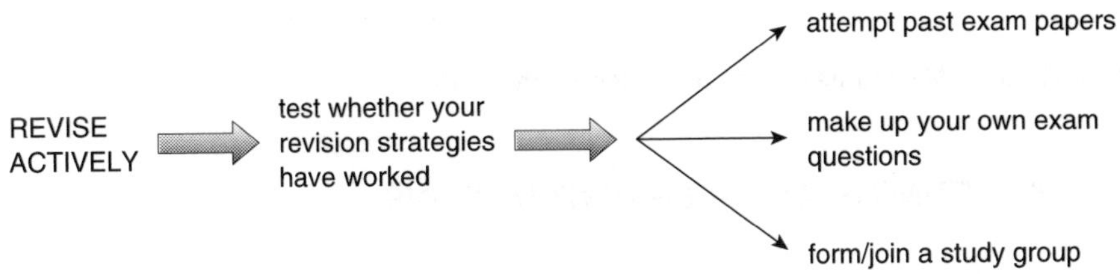

FIGURE 5.5 **Testing the efficacy of a revision plan**

Particularly important in the context of the above set of strategies is the notion of attempting a practice run with an old exam paper if this is possible. At this stage, much of your revision should be complete, so it is then useful to put this knowledge to the test. This is certain to highlight any strengths or weaknesses in your preparedness for the exam:

- Do you know enough to be able to answer the types of questions set?
- Do you think you could complete the paper in the given time?

Your lecturers may be prepared to look over a practice paper to give you feedback on how you are progressing, but if yours is a multiple-choice exam paper that is being recycled from year to year so that you have no access to past papers, then you may have to rely heavily on the strategy of self-questioning. Joining with a few friends in a study group can be useful to question each other, though this might be difficult if you have various other commitments in terms of family and employment, or you are studying off campus.

Exam room strategies

In most exams there is a 'permitted study period', where you will be allowed approximately 10 to 15 minutes to review the paper before the official start of the exam. This is where the next set of strategies, given in Figure 5.6, needs to be activated.

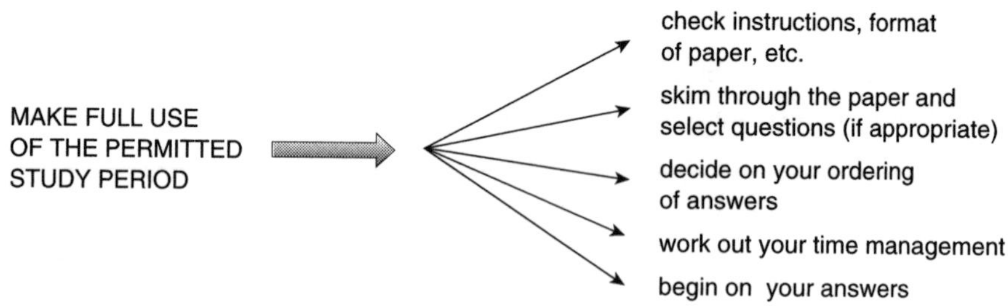

FIGURE 5.6 **Making use of the permitted study period**

INTERPRETING EXAM PAPER INSTRUCTIONS

Do read the exam paper instructions carefully, and follow them rigidly. If you are to select questions, again read carefully the instructions for selection, which could be of the following type in essay exams:

- Select any 4 questions from 5 sets of either/or questions.
- You must answer the compulsory question in section A. Answer 1 question from part B (2 choices), and 1 question from section C (2 choices).
- You are required to select and answer 1 question only from each of the 4 sections.

Work out what each question is testing by highlighting *key words* (take a highlighter pen with you to the exam) – read all questions very carefully. Now make your selection: do not delay with this.

DETERMINING THE ORDER OF YOUR ANSWERS

Decide on the order in which you will answer questions. It may be best simply to begin at the beginning when you have to answer all questions on the paper. But when there is choice, you may feel more confident about some questions than others, and so choose to answer those you know best to see if you can get ahead of time, allowing extra for those questions about which you are less confident.

Indicate on your paper which question you are answering by noting this above your answer (e.g. Question 2 or Topic B3 – use the exact wording from the paper). Doing this is most important if you do change the given order when writing your paper.

WORKING OUT A TIME SCHEDULE

Time needs to be rigorously monitored in the examination room, so wear a watch. Work out your time schedule during this preparatory period: calculate how much time you will give to each question on the basis of how many questions you need to answer and perhaps, too, their percentage weighting. For example:

> 20 short answer questions in a 3 hour paper where each question carries the same weighting means giving about 9 minutes to each question, but where there is a percentage weighting you might decide to give, say, 12 minutes to some questions and only 2 or 3 minutes to others. Or, if you have to write 4 essays over $3\frac{1}{2}$ hours, then you would have about 50 minutes for each essay. If your entire paper were multiple-choice with, say, 120 questions over 2 hours then you would have about a minute for each question.

Consider these strategies:

- Exclude 10 minutes of the allotted exam time in planning your time schedule. This gives you a little spare time at the end of the paper to at least jot down in note form any ideas for answers left incomplete on the way through the paper.
- In answering multiple-choice questions, mark on your exam question paper the halfway mark, preferably with a bright slash so it stands out. This will alert you to how your time is going.

STARTING ON ANSWERS IN THE 'PERMITTED STUDY PERIOD'

If you have any time left, you can begin working on your answers. You could jot down some notes, or, in the case of essay type questions, perhaps begin to outline your first answer in the margins of the *question paper* (not the booklet for writing your answers).

Do not begin writing your answers in the official exam booklet until you are told to do so.

Writing the exam paper

Regardless of your type of exam, make sure you attempt all questions you are required to answer. Also, monitor time regularly throughout the examination – stay with the time schedule set up in the 'permitted study period'. If you are starting to get behind, then move on quickly and see if you can make up time elsewhere in the paper. If you finish early, than read over your answers for a final edit.

ESSAY PAPERS

With essay type questions, it is best to do some planning before writing. Repetition, labouring of points, narrow coverage of topic in too much detail (just a few points being discussed in great detail while other important points are ignored) are all tendencies aggravated by a lack of planning.

What matters is the *quality* of your argument not quantity – how much you write.

If, for example, you had to write three essays in a 3 hour paper, you would have 1 hour for each. Take 10 minutes of the hour for each question to produce a rough essay outline of the type shown in Box 5.4.

Box 5.4 Outlining an exam essay can help you to stay on track with your argument

Introduction: two or three sentences indicating what your argument will be about (your position on the set question), and how you will order your discussion (First I discuss ... I then ... Finally, I ...). Perhaps also, provide any necessary definitions of words, terms, etc. The introduction should be concise and to the point – it is your *argument* that matters.

Body of the essay: jot down *main ideas* or points around which to build your paragraphs – think about the order in which you want to present them:

main idea 1 ...
main idea 2 ...
main idea 3 ...
etc.

Some of these ideas might take several paragraphs to develop. Think about what *evidence* you will use to back up the ideas you want to develop.

Conclusion: summarize the main points made in the course of your argument in three or four sentences – perhaps going back to your set topic or question in the process to round off the discussion – bring in actual words/phrases from the topic.

Remember, you do not need to be writing for every second of the exam. You will not be graded on the number of pages you produce but on the quality of your answers.

SHORT ANSWER PAPERS

With a short answer paper, also allow some time for thinking through your answers before writing – again, you do not need to be writing every second. With short answers there is considerable pressure to be concise – usually you will only have about a paragraph to perhaps half a page or so to write your answer (or maybe you will be asked to draw a model). Distinguish your points clearly (for example, first, second, third), and build paragraphs around main ideas you want to develop (see 'Controlling paragraph development' in Chapter 4).

In your answers use actual words/phrases from the topics. Doing this will keep you attuned to topic requirements.

MULTIPLE-CHOICE PAPERS

If yours is a multiple-choice exam, read each question and all the suggested answers carefully. Note whether or not you are likely to be penalized for a *wrong* answer – as mentioned in the exam paper instructions. Avoid the temptation to pick the first answer that looks correct without reading the others. Some questions may have several correct answers (i.e., 'all of the above'), no correct answer (i.e., 'none of the above'), or a partly correct answer, one of which is more complete or more precise than the others.

Look for **key words** that might affect the meaning of questions – highlight words like conditionals ('if', 'when'), or modals ('might', 'could'), or qualifiers ('never', always', 'sometimes'). If you cannot answer a question, then move on to the next – at the end of the paper you can go back over the questions that remain unanswered, knowing how much time you still have left. As you move through the exam paper, mark clearly (for example with a brightly coloured dot) those left unanswered so as not to waste time searching for them in the end-stage.

Summary comments

- The discourse of argument is a distinctive type of academic writing that tests your capacity to: reason about a subject, exercise your critical judgement, take a position (thesis) on a topic and develop that position in a way that convinces readers that what you have to say is indeed reasonable, that your argument is strong.
- Ensure that your research essay: deals fully with the central concerns of the topic, has a clear thesis (as in argument), backs up ideas with solid evidence, displays sound reasoning and coherent development of the argument.

- As both context and audience have a shaping influence on the style, structure and treatment of information in a book or article review, these aspects require careful consideration in the planning and writing stages.
- Prepare to do well in exams by strategically planning and executing revision around course objectives/aims and exam paper type, by attending closely to exam paper instructions, and by pre-planning and timing the writing of answers.

6 The Literature Review, Reports and Research Proposals

Developmental Objectives

By applying the strategies, doing the exercises and following the procedural steps in this chapter, you should be able to:

- Identify a broad range of strategies useful for scoping a literature review, determining task objectives, ensuring you are writing in review mode while developing sustained argument, distinguishing research/professional orientations in review writing, positioning your research in relation to the literature, critically engaging with the literature and structuring a review.
- Understand the complexities of report writing and appreciate the demands of the audience in some report writing.
- Identify strategies suited to focusing and developing the different types of reports discussed in this chapter.
- Work out what might be required of a proposal given the nature and level of your degree and how far you have progressed in that degree.
- Identify strategies for focusing and structuring a proposal.

This chapter continues the close focus on specific types of writing common in graduate study and research.

The literature review

In canvassing views on the purposes of literature review writing among participants in a workshop I held, one graduate volunteered two striking, related metaphors: *'to case the joint'* and *'to break and enter'*. While these metaphors invoke the criminal activity of staking out and robbing a place, they are nevertheless strangely apt. When you write a literature review, you are in a sense 'casing the joint' in a very thorough way: working out what literature is relevant, undertaking a full critical appraisal of relevant publications and so forth. You should also be thinking about how 'to break and enter', how your research fits in with what has already been done. All research builds on the efforts of scholarly predecessors, as yours will do.

The literature review provides a rationale for your research in terms of what has gone before, a justification of its value and significance.

SCOPING A REVIEW

In terms of 'casing the joint', one taxing issue concerns coverage (except where there is scant literature): that is, what to read and how much to read. While you will certainly have thought about this issue of scoping through the search and reading stages, it may also re-emerge when writing. As a start, think about questions of this type:

- What has been done in my field of research?
- What is relevant in terms of *my* research interests/objectives/questions/hypotheses?
- What do I *need* to cover given the scope of my topic, my level of study and the time I have available to write my text?
- Why might I cover certain bodies of literature and not others?

Of course, the scope of your review will depend on the level of your degree. For a longer thesis, you will need to provide a comprehensive review of all relevant literature, perhaps even an encyclopaedic one. For a shorter thesis or report, you will at least:

- Focus on key writers in the field; you may not be able to survey all writers in the field, so limit your coverage to those key authors/researchers who have contributed significantly to developing the research field.
- Cover the most recent, relevant publications available.

Where there is an extensive literature, the following procedural steps should also help.

Exercise: mapping coverage

Step 1

Categorize the various bodies of literature you are reviewing, as illustrated in Table 6.1, where the research topic was 'Socialization and high school education in China'.

TABLE 6.1 **Categorizing the literature**

Category 1: Methodological literature	**Category 2: Sociological literature on high school education**	**Category 3: Literature on high school education in China**
Identify different possible approaches – evaluate – decide on approach – justify (in China context)	Identify *Issues* in terms of processes/outcomes. Also review and consider variables	Identify 'socialization' issues in Chinese context – compare with those of broader literature

Step 2

- Now apply the strategies outlined under 'Visual mapping of material' in Chapter 4 to each of the categories set up.
- Brainstorm or mind map each category to help you to break down more precisely what needs to be covered.

Working out what to cover and why is rarely easy, but rather an evolutionary process, sometimes difficult and frustrating. You will get there though, even if only through the writing of your literature review, which alerts you to existing gaps in your reading.

A further issue arising in the context of coverage is what to cover in the literature review chapter, and what to cover in other chapters of a thesis. A simple solution is to think in terms of the different purposes you will have in working with the literature (see Table 6.2).

TABLE 6.2 **Working with the literature on different levels**

Literature review chapter	Specific chapter level
The literature review chapter provides a broad-based review of the literature as it applies to overall research objectives	At the level of the chapter, you could undertake detailed discussion of aspects of the literature relevant to the *specific* objectives of the particular chapter you are writing
In the process of the review, it may at times be necessary to signal your intention to reserve more detailed discussion of points or aspects of studies for relevant chapters	Your use of the literature in specific chapters is likely to be integrated throughout your discussion to advance and support points you are developing Mini-literature reviews at the beginning of each chapter might be considered more appropriate

DETERMINING TASK OBJECTIVES

Having worked out what to cover, determine your task objectives. The tasks involved in writing a literature review can be many and varied depending on your research interests and disciplinary practices. You will be doing a number of the following tasks, if not all, and you may also be doing further tasks not mentioned:

- Demonstrating through engagement with the literature that you have a thorough critical understanding of the literature.
- Drawing out key issues essential to your own research.
- Justifying the choice of topic/area of research.
- Critiquing: evaluating strengths and weaknesses of the literature relevant to your own research.
- Pointing out gaps in the literature or identifying problems remaining to be solved.
- Drawing together the main themes and arguments of a particular body of literature.
- Developing an argument in the process of reviewing the literature (see 'Review mode and orientation' below).

- Producing a historical survey. This may be a small part of a literature review and one that is fairly descriptive, as noted in the case study example under 'Critical engagement with the literature' below.

A next step would be consideration of how you might structure your review.

STRUCTURING A REVIEW

The nature and objectives of your research will have a shaping influence on how you structure your review, so do think carefully about these. The following discussion of different options illustrates the interconnection between students' approaches to structuring and their specific research interests.

A **chronological approach** – reviewing the various studies, or groups of studies, in order of their appearance in time – could be appropriate.

CASE STUDY Example

Box 6.1 A student's rationale for choosing the chronological approach

By taking a chronological approach in her theoretical review of the strengths and weaknesses of different models being used in her research field, the student felt she was able to chart advances that had been made while showing what had been lost and gained over time, and what issues had to be addressed, which was where her own research came in.

Or you may wish to organize your review around key themes, concepts, or indeed **key issues or debates,** as this student did:

> *The purpose of this detailed review of the major debates surrounding market reform is to isolate a specific set of issues relating to policy development and implementation, the key focus of this dissertation.*

Or perhaps a **methodological approach** will seem best to you, as in the sample below from literature review chapter of a doctoral thesis that had only four main sub-divisions:

Lead sentence in sub-division 1:
The use of transformations in program development systems is captured by a methodology called the transformational approach [references].

Lead sentence in sub-division 2:
The formal reasoning methods of transformation rules have relied heavily on the formal methods of defining programming languages, which have been available for several decades now (and some are still being developed).

Lead sentence in sub-division 3:
Program transformation has been advocated as a potentially appropriate methodology for program development [references], and regarded as a method in performing program modification and maintenance.

Lead sentence in sub-division 4:
The expected major breakthrough of the PROSPECTRA project lies in its support for 'precise specification of the semantic aspects of interfaces and their form verification' [reference] using algebraic semantics.

Or your structure could be influenced to some extent by the way the **research field itself has developed**, as signalled below:

As these issues are discussed separately in the literature rather than being held in relation, I follow this practice in my Review.

REVIEW MODE AND ORIENTATION

Review mode means moving from review of the literature to points being made in building the discussion, like so:

(**From:** review of literature) —*moving*→ (**To:** points abstracted from the review to develop your discussion)

This movement is illustrated below through eight paragraphs of writing which it is impracticable to reproduce in full (the bold emphasis here is mine):

Paragraph 1: ***Within the literature there are a number of different explanatory models ...***

Paragraph 2: *In the early 1960s X [reference] provided the theoretical explanation for ... In Australia,* ***Y [reference] has pointed out ... She has, however, supported the presence of ....***

Paragraph 3: ***In a 1992 article, Z and X [reference] used*** *the epidemicity index,* ***applied by B and his colleagues*** *to compare …* ***Their hypothesis*** *was that ...The opposite finding would falsify a significant genetic influence.*

Paragraph 4: *No references to the literature in this short paragraph.*

Paragraph 5: ***Their results*** *were not conclusive … They were not able to falsify … Above, I have already considered limitations to the application of …* ***Z and Y [reference] also pointed out*** *the methodological differences limiting comparability of … In fact this last factor probably does not work as they intuitively predict … Longer term admixture probably coincides with … Nonetheless, the result remains that Z and Y's meta-analysis does not resolve the question of ….*

Paragraph 6: ***Others have argued [reference] …***

Paragraph 7: ***Two alternative theories explain …***

Paragraph 8: *The poor in utero nutrition theory, expressed through low birth weight, has not been proposed principally in relation to glucose intolerance.* ***British research correlates [reference] …***

All literature reviews have a strong research orientation in that they engage the relevant research and show how the individual student's research fits in. Your review could have a dual orientation, however: research and practical in which case consider the next point.

Developing arguments is standard practice in literature review writing, but producing a sustained argument throughout is more common in those reviews with a professional orientation.

CASE STUDY
Example

Box 6.2 There can be a strong link between sustained argument and a practical or professional orientation

A student's main objective in her literature review was to decide which policy procedures out of a range of procedures discussed (and contested) extensively in the literature were best and to show why. Strong argument was thus called for. In the writing of her final report, these 'best' procedures, as argued for throughout her literature review chapter, became the underpinning of policy recommendations she put forward for workplace reform in the executive summary.

The literature review chosen to illustrate review mode above (the eight paragraph example) also had a strong practical orientation. Definition and determination of interventions with the 'most beneficial impact' would obviously require sustained argument, as was indeed the case:

> *This paper reviews some of the epidemiological literature on the high prevalence of non-insulin dependent diabetes mellitus (NIDDM) among Aboriginal and Torres Strait Islander People, and on the aetiology of diabetes in these communities. After examining the differing accounts of aetiology these are related to the interventions they suggest. The aim of the paper is* ***to define the kinds of intervention that will have the most beneficial impact.*** *Answers to these questions are sought in accounts of both cause and of action* (my emphasis).

Model yourself on this writer, who managed to avoid the trap of developing a thesis (as in argument) supported *from* the literature (more like a formal argument as discussed under 'Research essays' in Chapter 5). Rather, let your point of view emerge from review of the literature itself – keep the literature in the foreground.

CRITICAL ENGAGEMENT WITH THE LITERATURE

Do engage fully with the literature when writing your review. Avoid becoming the detached observer, presenting a wonderfully complex vision of a world (the literature) which, exciting though it may be, floats free from your own research. This is one problem of the 'interplanetary observer' perspective mentioned in the extract below in the context of advice that is well worth mulling over:

> **'The Nightly News' versus 'Four Corners' or What Makes a Good Review?**
>
> A lot of reviews are just an account of who did what and when and can be as superficial as the six o'clock news [broadcast]. That approach makes a poor review.
>
> In contrast, a good review is more like *Four Corners* [a current affairs programme of in-depth investigative journalism]. It presents the facts, but it also shows their consequences and implications. A good literature review goes behind the facts to show the issues that have been dealt with in the past, the issues that need to be dealt with today, the gaps and ambiguities in the state of our knowledge, and so on.

> Sometimes, researchers think that it is not their place to comment and their role is more like that of some interplanetary observer. Those people usually short-change themselves because the Nightly News approach leaves competence to be inferred from the scope of the review whereas the Four Corners approach makes competence more apparent because the analysis and comment proves understanding of the content and issues. (Brown, 1997: 2)

This stargazer perspective also fails on the level of critical commentary. Full critical evaluation of the relevant literature is a usual requirement, though literature reviews can serve other purposes too.

CASE STUDY
Example

Box 6.3 Disciplinary practices can open up possibilities in writing your review

The initial third of a literature review in a thesis provided a historical survey of a subset of the literature that was descriptive, not evaluative. The writer saw this as a way to provide crucial background information to the study. In the contexts of his research and discipline, 20 pages of non-evaluative material were acceptable. The final two-thirds of this 60-page literature review was thoroughly evaluative. Inclusion in the literature review chapter of context-type material that often appears in introductions accounts for the very broad scope of this particular literature review.

Consider questions of this type when conducting your critique:

- What has been done and how do the various studies or groups of studies relate to each other?
- What is the nature of the contribution made by different studies or groups of studies? What are their strengths and weaknesses?
- What is particularly useful about particular studies or groups of studies being reviewed?
- Are there any limitations in the studies or groups of studies and what are these? Are there any problems – with procedure, techniques, data-gathering and analyses, the theory or methodology being applied, the scope, etc.? Or are there other ways in which certain studies are limited despite having their uses?

- If there are problems needing to be solved or inadequacies in the literature, what are the implications of these for the research field as a whole and your research specifically?

POSITIONING YOUR RESEARCH IN RELATION TO THE LITERATURE

This is the 'breaking and entering' bit. It could be that you are expected to reserve detailed discussion of your own research for a separate section following your literature review. More likely though, you will be expected to hold your research in relation to the literature during the review process. This is a powerful strategy for drawing out key issues or questions you are addressing, while communicating the value of your research and your expected contribution. Indicate at appropriate points how your research ties in with what has already been done in your research field, as in the example highlighted here:

From a Sociology literature review:

To begin with, ***this thesis questions the notion*** *that third generation theories of revolution are necessarily incompatible with some of the second generation theories.*

This thesis will present a more urban-centred model *of modern revolutions.*

Insufficient attention is paid to the mobilisation and organisation of contenders. As the above critique suggests, ***this thesis will attempt to correct this deficiency*** *through greater sensitivity to the politics of mass mobilisation and the struggle between the polity and contenders.*

(Such comments were so skilfully integrated throughout this literature review that it was easy to appreciate the writer's critical standpoint on the different bodies of literature he was reviewing, and the distinctive contribution his research would make in the different contexts of enquiry.)

From a Geology literature review:

However, ***this thesis developed an algorithm*** *for the solution of the PDEs with X's type of boundary condition instead of Y's type which was used by Z [reference].*

From an Economics literature review:

What does this all mean for the model to be analysed here? ***I would like to use the structure of X's model*** *but adapt it to focus on the determination of the capital stock and the real exchange rate, rather than the net foreign asset position and the real exchange rate ....*

By positioning your research in relation to the literature, you will be able to demonstrate the nature and value of your research contribution, which is necessary with a PhD or Professional Doctorate.

AUDIENCE: SIGNALLING YOUR INTENTIONS

Help readers to understand your organizational decision- making in terms of developing your review.

As with all writing, signal to readers, at appropriate points, what you are doing and why you are doing it (see also 'Attending to audience needs' in Chapter 4).

From the start of two different literature reviews:

1. *In the management of any species, an understanding of the species' biology and ecology is essential to develop a management plan. Certain aspects of the species' biology, for example, may be manipulated, aiding the management of the species.* ***This chapter summarises the vast amount of research on the ecology, biology and management of the mouse, highlighting the aspects relevant to the current study*** *(my emphasis).*

2. *Recent advances in numerical and computational technology and the increasing concern about optimal production of hydrocarbon fluids have given rise to an upsurge of interest in reservoir connectivity.* ***Two key problems in the understanding of reservoir connectivity are the inference of the shapes and the interconnectedness of the sedimentary bodies, and the numerical solution of the partial differential equations describing the behaviour of the fluids. These two problems are the main points this dissertation addresses*** *(my emphasis).*

Reports

Reports vary in terms of treatment of information, style and structure, and you may find yourself producing more than one type. There are the more academic reports, such as field, experimental or laboratory reports, progress reports, etc.; the more consultative type, such as option viability reports or cost-effectiveness reports; and reports that emulate workplace practice as, for example, in business, the professions or industry (for example, project management reports). If you are required to write a report:

- read any written instructions carefully, if you are given them; or
- ask your lecturer/supervisor if it is possible to review a model of what is expected, or to clarify what is generally expected in terms of the appropriate style and structure, and the expected length.

POSSIBLE AUDIENCE CONSIDERATIONS

As the nature of the audience can influence the style of a report, questions of this type may need to be addressed at the outset of writing:

- Who is my audience? Lecturers/supervisors? A single organization or industry body? A particular group – for example, farmers or environmentalists? A dual external/academic audience – for example, government ministers and academics? Or members of, say, two different professions – for example, doctors and engineers, or lawyers and business representatives?
- Who is meant to read the report? One person? Different people at different levels of an organization? Varied people from different organizations? Others?
- If the report is to be written as for oral presentation, who is my intended audience? (See Part 2 of Chapter 8, 'General issues in presenting'.
- Given my answers to the above, what factors do I need to take into account when writing? Think along these lines: organizational and other limitations for implementation? Countering anticipated opposition? The assurance of cost-effectiveness? Time or timing considerations? Policy alignment – for example, that the policy proposals are viable in terms of the current government's stated aims? Constraints to action by the intended audience? That the report will address the varied interests of readers from different levels of an organization, or readers from different professional backgrounds? That the report embodies awareness of cross-cultural communication issues? Anything else?
- How logically persuasive will I need to be to convince my audience and what evidence can I use to aid persuasion?

In the following sections I discuss features of prominent types of reports in different contexts. I use these contexts merely to illustrate a range of possible features that may appear in different combinations in a written report. An experimental or technical report, for example, may embody features of a formal report. You will need to adapt the advice here to your specific needs.

Each part of a report should be held in relation to all other parts when writing.

Business reports

Your business report will likely involve analysis of a situation – historical, current or projected – so as to engage problem-solving. As such, it will have a strong practical or workplace orientation.

FOCUSING A BUSINESS REPORT

In orienting business graduates to what was expected in their reports, a lecturer advised them to avoid 'academic argument' (that is, argument of the type discussed under 'Research essays' in Chapter 5) in favour of 'short, crisp reports', which focused the analysis of a 'situation' in sequential terms (see Figure 6.1). This is what I call a *medical discourse model* in view of its obvious relation to the process of diagnosis, prognosis and cure. Superficially, the model looks simple, amounting to not much more than a summary introduction and a dot-point approach to detailing the information covered. But it is far more challenging on a deeper level of analysis, which is what your lecturers will expect.

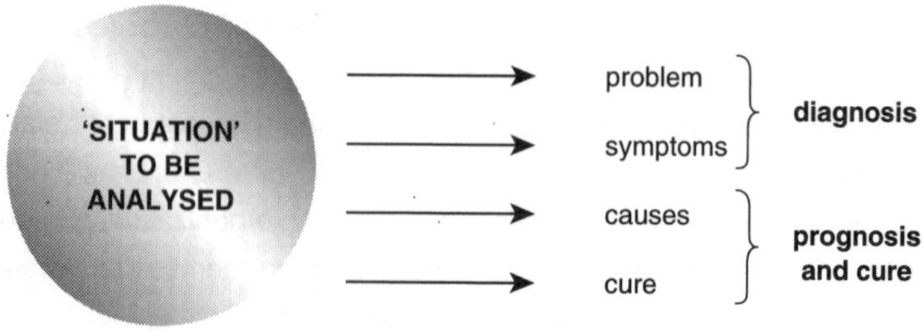

FIGURE 6.1 **A model of a business report**

- **Diagnosis:** Identifying what the problems actually are may be a moot point debated in the literature, a debate in which you would need to critically engage. Also, the symptomatic effects may be contested in the literature, or they may not be fixed but variable over time or context, and so again be difficult to pin down. As for causes, these may require analysis on both surface and deep levels. For example, on the surface the problem may appear to be due to incompetent management, but in probing deeper you find the *real* cause is the flawed structural organization of a company, which, in turn, demands you grapple with difficult organizational issues, perhaps of a theoretical nature.

- **Prognosis:** After identifying the problems, you would then need to assess the probability of these being overcome – this is the prognosis part. This could involve in-depth analysis of a range of alternatives, including close examination of the positives and negatives of each and support for conclusions reached.

- **Cure:** Cure implies the need for recommendations to overcome the problems, perhaps in the form of an executive summary (see 'Formal reports' below), or as a set of proposals. Again you could find that there are various choices needing analysis, perhaps in terms of short- and long-term benefits with further discussion of any projected disadvantages. This could also involve you in analysis of different theoretical perspectives, and perhaps prediction of a speculative nature. It would then be necessary to ensure your speculations arose out of your earlier discussions if they were to have any basis in fact. Throughout this process, you may need to include evaluation of the likelihood of specific proposals having the desired effect – this will be further prognosis.

Experimental or technical reports

Even if you are practised in writing experimental or technical reports, the following discussion could prove a useful refresher. This type of report conforms to the structural model, or some variation of it (and there are many): *Introduction; Materials and Methods; Results; Discussion.* Under disciplinary influences, results and discussion are sometimes combined in one section; sometimes there is a separate conclusion, or the discussion section acts as the conclusion – confirm what applies in your case.

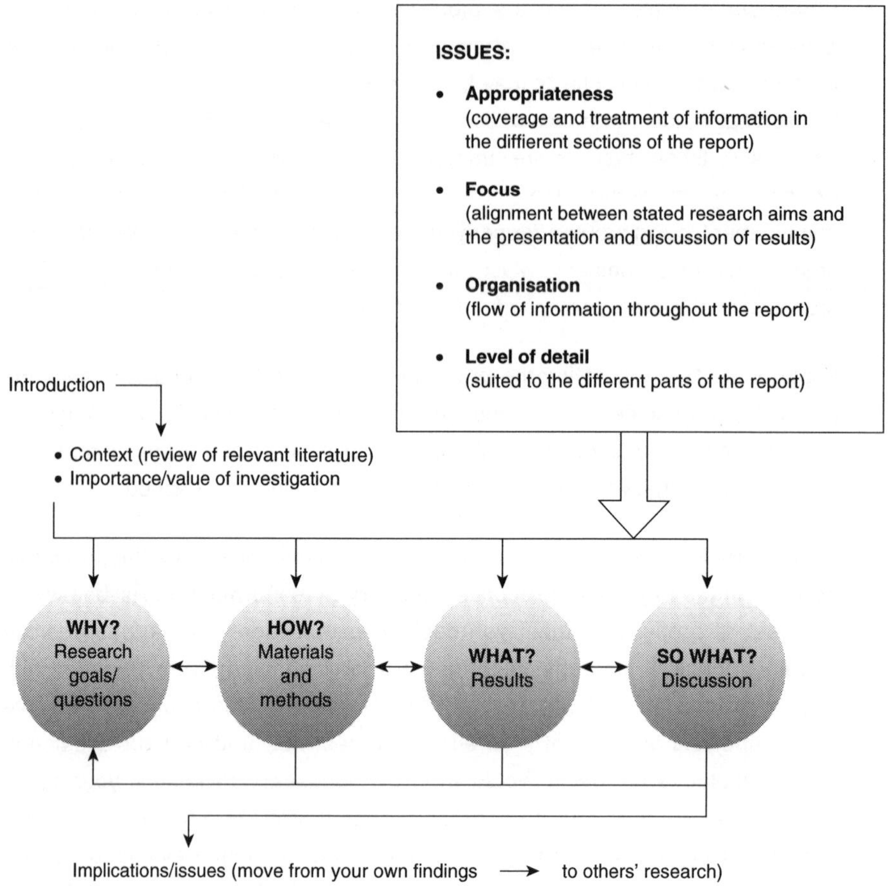

FIGURE 6.2 **Typical parts of an experimental or technical report**

THE INTERLOCKING RELATIONSHIP OF THE STRUCTURAL DIVISIONS

My model in Figure 6.2 is designed to illustrate the tight, interlocking relationship of the structural divisions or parts of this type of report. All parts need to be held in relation at all times, and when writing the results and discussion sections you need to ensure that these line up with your stated research goals/questions, as laid out in your introduction.

The issues I have highighted in the box can be particularly vexing if you are unfamiliar with this type of report writing because of discipline transfer.

- **Appropriateness:** Sometimes discussions read like a repetition of results or like an introduction. Whereas the literature is foregrounded in the introduction as a means of providing 'context' or background to the investigation, in the discussion it is the significance/implications of the results that is focused on, with subsequent references to the literature to show agreement/disagreement with others' findings and reasons for these.

- **Focus:** Sometimes the results presented do not align with the stated research objectives or aims. There is a disjunction between reasons given for undertaking the research and the report of what was found. Every part of the report must relate back to the objectives or aims as set out in the introduction (or perhaps in a separate section).

- **Organization:** Sometimes the ordering of discussions in different parts of a report is such that it is difficult to detect a coherent line of discussion throughout the report.

- **Level of detail:** Sometimes there is insufficient detail to follow what exactly transpired in the conduct of an investigation, with even key details missing. While disciplinary/course practices can influence the level of detail to be included in different parts of a report, there can be unfamiliarity with fairly standard expectations in this regard.

I shall now discuss each of the divisions or parts of a report in more detail, with particular regard to focus.

FOCUSING THE DIFFERENT PARTS OF THE REPORT

Title (separate page) Your title should be specific rather than vague. These examples taken from a handout for a Psychology course make this point: a vague title has been reworded to show precisely what was measured (infants' emotional responses) and what was manipulated (perceived sex):

Vague title:
Observer bias regarding infant behaviour

Focused title:
The effects of perceived sex on observers' ratings of infants' emotional responses

Abstract or summary (separate page and usually just a few paragraphs – provides an inclusive summary) An abstract or summary may or may not be necessary. If it is, do make sure it is self-contained and that:

- It indicates clearly specific experimental objectives, the hypothesis(es) being tested or problems investigated and why – the value of the investigation.
- It provides brief information on how the experiments or tests were done.
- It discusses more fully key findings and their implications in terms of the objectives or hypothesis(es) tested, perhaps in terms of future research and/or theoretical considerations.

Introduction (orients the reader to the aims/objectives and value of your investigation) As the structure of the introduction can vary across disciplines, do clarify expectations. Usually the introduction includes information of this type:

- An initial statement of the topic of investigation and experimental objectives or test purposes, indicating why the investigation was undertaken, and why it was important. Sometimes there is also a scope statement, detailing limitations of the experiment/project.
- Definition of any complex terms or concepts used in the report.
- A succinct review of previous research findings (reference these) for the purpose of detailing what has been done and identifying any gaps, weaknesses or areas of extension leading to the formulation of research questions or objectives. Focus only on information *relevant* to development of your questions; do not be tempted towards broad general discussion.
- A clear statement of the hypothesis(es) in the final paragraph.

From the writing of your introduction, it should be clear what previous research has been done, how your investigation arises out of this research (certifying its value) and what precisely you are investigating or testing, and why.

(Separate theory section?) Sometimes in more technical reports (in Engineering, for example) a separate theory section follows the introduction. This section usually draws out theoretical issues relevant to the research presented in the report or outlines the theoretical model/s or framework/s you are applying in your test/experimental analyses.

Materials and Methods (explains how you went about your investigation or tests) This section is likely to include information of this type:

- Descriptive details of, for example, subjects tested, including the total number, pre-test or selection criteria applied, placement or assignment of subjects, etc; or of the physical environment used, or of the materials, apparatuses, equipment and stimuli used in experiments.

- Explanation of the functional relationship between various devices or instruments used. Focus on only those details relating to your research objectives or the hypothesis(es) you have set out to test.

- A sequential description of the procedure. Consider a chronological, step-by-step description of what you actually did when running the experiment or conducting the test; organize your description around sub-headings if appropriate. It could also be necessary to include some explanatory information on *why* you made the choices you did, as here: *'In order to assess the amount of paint applied to the wood surfaces all specimens were weighed prior to paint application.'*

How much detail you include in this section will depend on whether it is expected that your experiment or test could be replicated from your description. Ask your lecturer whether this applies if you are unsure.

Results (tells what your findings were)

- First consider the best way to group your results for discussion. Create appropriate sub-headings (see 'Using sub-headings effectively' in Chapter 4). Review whether the results you present *do* tie-in with the hypotheses, objectives or research questions laid out in your introduction.

- Next, determine how to order your results for discussion. One way is to direct attention to what is more or less significant about the results in terms of your objectives and/or hypothesis(es) as laid out in the introduction. Or organize discussion of your results around a set of illustrations (graphs, barcharts, tables, figures, diagrams etc.).

- If you do use illustrations, provide adequate explanatory description of them in this section; and draw out what is *significant* about these in your discussion section (unless you are combining results and discussion).

- Appendices can be included if your results are extensive, so that readers can refer to these for more detailed information as they wish.

Discussion (draws out the implications of your findings) This section represents a further stage in the thinking, in which you *process* your results to determine what they really mean. Begin by reviewing yet again your stated aims/objectives/questions/hypotheses as laid out in the introduction. Some compositional moves you could make in this section are:

- Explain what you found in terms of expected or unexpected outcomes, or perhaps conflicting results.

- Determine the importance/significance of your results by situating these in the context of other scholars' findings. In the discussion section always work from *your* findings to *others'* findings.

- Deduce the degree of generality of particular results, whether or not these might apply beyond the particular experiments or tests carried out by you.

- Discuss biases (for example, in the methodology) that may have skewed your results.

- Determine the status of the hypothesis(es) in light of the results obtained compared to those of other studies. You may wish to propose a modified hypothesis.

- Formulate new hypotheses from claims regarding the general applicability of particular results or because results show a need for these.

- Relate your findings to the theory from which your predictions were derived.
- Make recommendations for future research, perhaps by identifying gaps, difficulties and ways of clarifying or extending the present research.

In the process of discussing your findings you can draw attention to your final conclusions, although you may wish to present these in a separate section entitled 'Conclusion'.

Formal reports

A formal research report is often long and comprehensive. As the structure can be influenced by disciplinary preferences, be advised by your lecturer/supervisor as to specific requirements.

TWO PROMINENT STRUCTURES

If you are a science student, your formal report could embody the structural divisions detailed under 'Experimental or technical reports' above. The formal report can also be similar to a mini-thesis in its general structure, in that it often conforms to the structural division of parts shown in Figure 6.3.

DISTINCTIVE FEATURES OF THE FORMAL REPORT

As most of these features are covered in various other sections of the book (see in particular 'Whole text development' in Chapter 4 and 'Dividing up the text' in Chapter 7), here I discuss only those marked with an asterisk in Figure 6.3.

Cover of the report (separate page) If your report is meant to replicate a commission from an outside organization, then the cover page is likely to include this type of sequential information:

- The title.
- For whom the report was prepared.

Items		Part
Cover of the report* Abstract Acknowledgements Lists of tables, figures, plates etc. Table of contents List of acronyms or abbreviations (if necessary) Executive summary and/or Recommendations*	→	**Preliminary matter**
Preface and/or Introduction The main body of the report (divided into parts and/or chapters – one of which might be a literature review – sub-divisions and perhaps sections within these) Conclusion	→	**Body of the report**
Appendix(ces) (if necessary) Bibliography (sometimes annotated)	→	**End matter**

FIGURE 6.3 **Structural outline of a formal report (*see text)**

- The department in which it was prepared.
- The date it was produced.

Otherwise, you may simply have a title page.

Executive summary and/or Recommendations An 'Executive summary' typically contains:

- The major findings.
- Conclusions.
- (Possibly) recommendations.

This summary is often no more than one to three pages, although it can be longer. Or you may be required to include only 'Recommendations', which are then succinctly stated in a few lines, often with sequential numbering as follows (a single recommendation may also be divided into sub-recommendations using (a), (b), etc. to focus specific actions required of the recommendation):

- Recommendation 1 ...
- Recommendation 2 ...
- Recommendation 3 ... (continue with this format)

Recommendations made must arise out of your findings and conclusions, as discussed fully in the body of your report; so substantiation is not needed at this point. Recommendations are usually suggestions for future action to overcome problems investigated in the report.

While positioning of the 'Executive summary' or 'Recommendations' in the report can vary, these sections usually appear just prior to the main body of the report.

Field reports

The requirements for field reports are remarkably varied so it is imperative that you get instructions from your lecturer/supervisor on what is required in compiling yours. In general though, it is necessary to think through what details you should be recording and ask yourself: why these details and not others?

KEEPING PRECISE RECORDS

To illustrate: in collecting samples, it might be necessary to keep records of dates, times of day, season, weather, locations and relevant physical characteristics, selection processes, sample dimensions and other characteristics, techniques of sampling and storage, and so forth. Or, in conducting interviews, there might be a need to record the time of the interview, the characteristics of those interviewed (for example, gender, status, etc.), the communicative content of non-verbal gestures, details of the interview setting, or perhaps indicators of relations among respondents where group interviews are taking place.

> **Carefully record your observations on what occurred, difficulties encountered, unusal occurrences, insights gleaned, emerging themes, etc. Such records will be invaluable when you come to write the report.**

The type of fine detail needed is illustrated in these extracts from a preliminary field epidemiology report, which constitutes one model of this type of writing:

> **Laboratory Investigation:**
> *Rectal swabs, whole stools and blood samples were collected from ill and well passengers and crew members 24–72 hours after the onset of symptoms. Rectal swabs were placed in Cary–Blair transport medium. All specimens were refrigerated and transported to CDC.*

> **Descriptive Epidemiology:**
> *Three hundred and eight (64%) of 482 passengers and 400 (96%) of 418 crew members returned the questionnaire. Fifty-six passengers (18% of the returned questionnaires) and 12 crew members (3% of returned questionnaires) reported illness meeting the case definition [provided earlier in the report]. Symptoms reported by more than 50% of ill passengers included diarrhoea, abdominal cramping, nausea, headache, fever, and myalgia (Table 1). Twenty-four (43%) were confined to their cabin because of illness. The mean duration of illness was 6.2 days. Two passengers were hospitalised after disembarkation.*

Throughout this two-page preliminary report, the writer provided precise, detailed information under the following sub-headings:

- **Background:** concise but detailed discussion of the events that transpired.
- **Method:** detailed coverage of how he went about the epidemiological investigation, vessel sanitation inspection and laboratory investigation.
- **Preliminary results:** in terms of descriptive epidemiology, analytic epidemiological investigation, vessel sanitation inspection and laboratory investigation.
- **Plans for further analysis:** re-entering of questionnaires to verify dataset, completion of data analyses, follow-up of cases to determine the rate of secondary transmission and duration of illness.
- **Plans for writing [the final report]:** including projected completion date.
- **Plans for authorship:** the production of one or more articles for publication.

Progress reports

The purpose of this type of report, as its name suggests, is to report on *how* your research is progressing. Sometimes a (work in) progress report is rather like an updated research proposal, as discussed in the next section, which it could be useful for you to review as well.

THE PURPOSE OF A PROGRESS REPORT

A progress report provides the opportunity to engage fully with the research you have already undertaken in order to:

- Demonstrate what changes your thinking has undergone and why.
- Explain more fully your choices and the direction your research is taking.
- Get the type of feedback that will allow you to continue to progress.
- (Perhaps) provide a timetable for completion.

Your report may include a full literature review (see above), with the length being determined by the level and stage of your degree, and perhaps disciplinary requirements.

Even if there is no formal requirement for you to produce a progress report, it can be immensely useful to do so as a research student. Updating the original proposal to a progress report will assist you to gain better control of your research project.

In preparing to write, ask yourself:

- What have I done in my research so far?
- What difficulties have I encountered along the way?
- What solutions did I employ (if any)?
- How has my research changed in terms of my original research proposal as regards changes of focus, objectives or questions being asked, methodology, issues I want to look at, theoretical questions, experimental or test design and procedures, and so forth?

- Why have these changes occurred and what have been the consequences for my research?

- Do I see any continuing difficulties on which I need feedback? (You could, for example, be trying to make a decision between choices, each of which seems equally viable to you.)

The objective in writing the progress report then is to present an up-to-date account of the status of your research, to detail plans for the completion of the research and to get feedback on all this.

Research proposals

You could be writing research proposals at various points in the course of your degree: prior to enrolment (perhaps as part of an application for a scholarship and/or as an application for entry to study at a particular institution); not long after enrolment in a research degree; at various stages in the first year or so of a research degree; or prior to beginning the research component of a degree that includes both coursework and research.

There are also various synonyms for a 'research proposal' produced during the course of a degree: for example, **position statement** or **statement of intent**.

THE DIFFERENT PURPOSES OF PROPOSALS

The timing of production as well as the level of degree in which you are enrolled will affect the purpose, and therefore both the kind and the extent of coverage in your proposal.

Proposals produced prior to enrolment or in the early stage of your degree may be quite limited and general, perhaps two to three pages. Those produced a year or more after commencement of, say, your PhD may be comprehensive and detailed. If you are producing a proposal to proceed to research after completing the coursework component of your higher degree, your proposal will vary in terms of length and complexity. In certain areas of US study, the research proposal produced on completing coursework constitutes up to the first three chapters of a PhD (introduction, literature review and methodology chapters), as discussed in some detail by Watts (2003). So be advised by your supervisor as to requirements.

Here is what one supervisor had to say about the value of writing a proposal:

> The purposes of preparing a proposal are to plan your investigation and to seek helpful comments and suggestions from other people [in the department] and elsewhere. More importantly, it allows you to show whether the investigation you propose to conduct will provide you with the evidence you need to prove your thesis [as in argument].

The implications of this statement are that the proposal serves to:

- Clarify what you are investigating, and how you want to go about the research.
- Get useful feedback.
- Determine whether the overall thesis design will allow you to establish the argument you want to present (assuming you know what this is).

Another way to see the proposal is as a marketing exercise, its main function being to sell your research. In this perspective, the purposes are: to allow your reader/s to assess the *viability* of your proposed research and to provide useful feedback on this. Your objective is to convince your reader(s) that the following apply:

- The research you propose is worthwhile for the level of the degree, that is to say, the research will warrant the award of that particular degree.
- The scope and quality of your research is suited to the level of the degree; clearly the breadth and depth of research expected will be different for shorter and longer theses.
- The research as outlined is appropriate for the length. Again there is a vast difference between the extent of research required for a shorter thesis of, say, 15,000 words and that appropriate for, say, an 80,000 word PhD.
- The methods you propose to complete the research are appropriate, that is, it will be possible to access the resources needed to complete the research, to conduct the interviews proposed, to carry out field research, to access suitable equipment, etc.
- Your proposed research is viable in terms of time available to complete the degree.

Proposal assessors tend to occupy themselves with these types of issues, so do bear them in mind when writing your proposal.

FOCUSING A PROPOSAL

This section poses questions to think about when focusing your proposal. Again though, which questions are relevant and the amount of detail included in answering them will depend on the degree in which you are enrolled, the nature of your research, the stage you are at in your degree and disciplinary requirements, if any.

What is your field of research or topic of investigation? This question addresses *what* you are setting out to investigate, what it is you want to look at or focus on. This could take the form of identifying the field of research in which you are interested, the general topic area, or a specific topic. These distinctions are chartered in Figure 6.4 by way of an example from Linguistics, but you can adapt it to your own situation.

Field of research:
Second language acquisition

General topic area:
Forms of address in different cultures

Specific topic:
Intercultural problems in teaching forms of address to Thai learners of English as a second language

↓ Scale of refinement

FIGURE 6.4 **Progressive refinement of a topic**

A proposal is just that: what is proposed is not fixed for all time. Do not be overly concerned when proposing a topic that you will have to stay with it, particularly not early in your degree. Topics are sometimes changed or the focus shifts, along with other aspects of the study, during the first phase of a research degree. Do take care though, as a radical change of topic might mean that an appropriate supervisor cannot be found, or that your designated supervisor no longer feels able to supervise your project.

What is the context of your study? It is usual to provide relevant background information so as to contextualize your research. This can be done by way of a mini-literature review, which also allows justification of the foci and interests of the research you are proposing. If you have done little reading, provide general background information by way of topic generalizations. Ask yourself:

- What background information on my topic am I able to provide?
- How does what I want to do fit in with research already done in the field? It may be that you have only a limited, general knowledge of what research has

been done, but that would be sufficient for a proposal accompanying an application.

Your purpose here is to describe the broad context of your study – the *big picture* – and then say which aspects of the research field you want to consider.

What is the primary research objective or central research question? This question addresses *why* you are undertaking your proposed research. There are different language forms you can use to encapsulate the why. To illustrate my point, I again draw on the Linguistics example above:

Language form stating the primary *research aim or objective:*
My aim is to determine the range and nature of the intercultural problems in teaching Thai learners of English as a second language, and the reasons for these.

An alternative language form setting up *the central research question:*
What are the types and causes of intercultural problems in teaching Thai learners of English as a second language?

You may also be testing a **hypothesis** (even more than one), which is defined as 'a proposition put forward merely as a basis for reasoning or argument, without any assumption of its truth' (*New Shorter Oxford English Dictionary*). Or you may be expected to 'lay out a problem' in some detail (see 'Sample of a detailed thesis outline' in Appendix 2).

Having clarified your major aim or central question, break this down into a set of subsidiary aims or questions, like so:

Central question:
How are social identities being constructed by highlands migrants living in the urban areas of X [country named]?

Subsidiary questions:
What conceptions are held by Y migrants about the village and the people who remain there?

What concepts are held about ethnic 'others' who are the neighbours of Y migrants in the urban settlements and how do these conceptions influence multi-ethnic social interactions?

What appeals are made to broader ethnic, class or even national identities and what are these appeals based on (e.g. as highlanders, the poor, as people of X country)?

What do these examples of the practice of identity suggest about processes of nation-making in X?

If yours is an early proposal, there is unlikely to be such clarity about the questions driving your research, so just do your best.

What is the value of your research project? This question needs addressing if you are doing a PhD and perhaps a Master by Research, but not necessarily if you are producing a shorter thesis. A PhD requires an original contribution to the research field (see 'Focusing an "original" contribution' in Chapter 7). Answering this question allows you to convey the nature of your contribution and say why you think it important to conduct the research. The significance of your research project can be conveyed through discussion of the existing literature – its strengths and weaknesses and how your research fits in.

Apart from providing information on the contribution you expect to make to research, it may also be important for you to mention practical or professional value attaching to your proposed research, as might be the case with industry application, commercial uses, reform recommendations, etc.

Do you need to discuss theory or methodology? If theory, modelling or methodology is likely to be a special consideration in your research, provide information to this effect.

- Do you need to, and can you, discuss your theoretical framework or your choice of model?

- Do you need to discuss issues of methodology relevant to your research? It may be appropriate, for example, to discuss your choice of statistical methods for analysing data, issues relating to selecting a sample population for study, the research instruments or measurement devices you will use, experimental procedures, or the different methodologies – their strengths and weaknesses – available for comparative research along with your preference. Give reasons for your choices and decisions.

Methodology should not be confused with procedure (the next point discussed):

> A rationale for the methods used to gather and process data, in what sequence and on what samples, taken together, constitutes a research methodology. This is not a grand term for 'list of methods', but an informed argument for designing research in a particular way. A research methodology needs to be appropriate for

the research problem, and the justification that this is so should form part of a thesis. (Cryer, 1996: 45)

While it is impracticable to include here an entire methodology section/chapter, the extract below points towards Cryer's meaning:

> *When states promote industrial development they assume direct involvement in processes of capital accumulation, even as their effectiveness in this pursuit is strongly determined by the international division of labor. For this reason, X's [reference] suggestion linking states' activities to development outcomes requires, first, taking states as transformative actors in their own right, and second, examining state agencies' transformative activities as they are embedded in definite networks of social relations.* ***To meet these methodological challenges, my study will incorporate a comparative institutional approach [reference], as well as the sectoral approach of Y [reference] and the commodity chains approach of Z [reference]. In addition to their value as theoretical frames of reference, these approaches offer unique methodological insights for procedures of data collection and analysis*** *(my emphasis).*

This is a typical way to present an argument for a particular approach to the exclusion of other possibilities, though your discussion of methodology may be altogether more detailed and comprehensive, even constituting an entire chapter.

How do you intend to proceed with your research? If yours is an early proposal, say something about procedure. This reveals how you intend to go about your research, what activities you will need to carry out and in what order. It might be appropriate, for example, to provide information about general plans for **fieldwork** if this applies (for example, locations, populations targeted, etc.), to discuss experimental or test plans, or to identify primary sources to be accessed (such as archival materials). Of course, in a more comprehensive proposal, all these matters might be covered in a methodology chapter, justifying and validating your approach.

The idea is to give a general overview of what you think needs to be done to complete your research. Include as much information as you can so that a reader can determine any likely problems, unforeseen by you, in carrying out the research (for example, difficulty accessing and using materials or equipment, locating suitable source materials, undertaking fieldwork or anything else). Mention any potential problems you anticipate so as to get feedback.

Is it appropriate to include a substantial review of the literature? The inclusion of a substantial literature review is only likely if you are six months or more into your degree. In an advanced proposal it is likely that the literature review will be detailed and comprehensive.

Do you need to discuss relevant work experience? Where appropriate, give a brief account of any work you have done and are presently doing, putting special emphasis on anything, including courses you might be teaching, relevant to the research you are proposing. Work experience may feature prominently, particularly if this is a key reason for receiving strong support in the proposed research from academic referees, and/or this experience is highly relevant to your type of degree (for example, a Professional Doctorate).

Should you include a timetable for completion of your research? The answer to this is probably yes, if you are at the end of or beyond the first year of research, but no if it is a proposal accompanying an application for entry.

Do you need ethics clearance for your research? Ethics clearance is needed for various types of research using animals and humans, including, at times, conducting interviews and doing surveys on human populations. This will not concern you at the point of applying for candidature, but discuss the matter with your supervisor before writing a proposal when you are on the course.

Are you likely to need special training to undertake your research? It is usual in a research degree to undergo training of various types. But if you are likely to need special training that could impact on time to completion (for example, learning a new language), then mention this.

What other questions do you need to ask? I cannot be comprehensive here but have covered the general questions above. You should think about other questions you might need to ask (and answer) given your research interests.

STRUCTURING A PROPOSAL

How you structure your proposal is up to you. One possibility is to build a general framework around the set of questions What? Why? How? Where? and So what? Many students do find this approach useful, as did the student featured in Box 6.4, who was producing an early proposal as part of an application for a PhD scholarship.

CASE STUDY
Example

Box 6.4 Using the set of questions What? Why? How? So what? can be a useful starting point in drafting an early proposal

Introductory comments:

Nature of the study: cross-disciplinary (Asian Studies/International Relations (IPE)); broad context of investigation; why this topic; context (a little bit about what's been done generally – can do small literature review (page) from past work in area); why I think it is important to research this topic (contribution I expect to make to research)?

Focus of study (the what):
General topic area: investigate the nature of democracy in East Asian countries – (Japan, and others? – to be selected later after further thought, research and discussion).

Objectives of study (the why):
To find out what is 'universal' and what is 'culture specific' about the democracy operating in these countries (define terms). To be considered in the context of IR notion of the 'nation state'. Purpose: challenge existing western approaches. Q: What other questions do I need to ask to meet these objectives? – think about this.

Procedure/methodology (the how):
Examine large-scale socio/eco/political movements that are not confined by the 'nation state' framework (across state boundaries). Need to identify which best for the task (e.g. environmental movements? NGOs? what else)? Why this approach – can I justify it in terms of my objectives? What can these tell us about applying western notions of democracy to the East? About the nation state? Other useful information to be gained? Unusual approach, not tested – likely to cause problems?

Theoretical issues:
A bit about theory – issues I want to grapple with – think about this (prevailing theories/concepts of democracy? the nation state? ? etc.).
What else????? – say something about SCOPE – is this relevant?

The student in the case study example was initially vague about what she wanted to do and why. Using this simple question framework, she said, helped her to clarify her goals as much as she was able. She eventually expanded the above outline into a solid, three-page proposal as part of an application for a PhD scholarship, in which she succeeded.

Summary Comments

- Your literature review should convey to readers that you have a thorough understanding and full critical appreciation of the relevant literature, its strengths and weaknesses – the gaps, ambiguities, problems, issues and questions that need raising, why these are important, what aspects of the literature your research will address and the value for scholarship in doing so.
- Reports are remarkably varied. The style, structure and treatment of information in a report can be strongly influenced by disciplinary practices, and by context and audience (particularly in the case of reports emulating workplace practice), all of which you will need to take into account when writing.
- With a research proposal, you will need to address a range of issues to do with the validity, viability and value of the research being proposed for your level of degree.
- Where the research proposal is to be comprehensive, perhaps comprising several chapters of your thesis, you should range beyond the discussions presented in this chapter; review in particular 'Thesis writing' in Chapter 7.

7 Thesis Writing

Developmental Objectives

By applying the strategies, doing the exercises and following the procedural steps in this chapter, you should be able to:

- Orient yourself to thesis writing in your discipline at your level of degree.
- Manage your project more efficiently by writing early and writing often.
- Avoid unnecessary work by settling typography and formatting decisions early.
- Think through the nature and value of your contribution to research so as to convey this to readers, which is particularly important with a doctorate.
- Understand a broad range of standard academic expectations of thesis writing – both shorter and longer theses – so as to develop more rigour in your writing.
- Identify strategies for dividing up the text and incorporating a thesis statement, structuring chapters in different ways, gaining overall thesis control, and developing the thesis abstract, introduction and conclusion.
- Organize a thesis writing group as a mutual support and learning forum.

Some of the most reasonable questions students ask are the most difficult to answer. Questions like these:

> *'What am I supposed to be doing when I write a PhD?'*
> *'What is so special about thesis writing?'*
> *'What's the difference between a Master by Research and a PhD?'*
> *'What does an* original *contribution mean?'*
> *'Do I have to make an* original *contribution in my Master's thesis?'*
> *'What's required of a shorter thesis?'*
> *'How is a [shorter] thesis different from a long research essay?'*

While there are no simple answers to questions of this type, I hope that the discussions within this chapter will leave you in a better position to provide your own answers.

I consider a shorter thesis as roughly between 10,000 and 25,000 words, and a longer thesis as roughly between 60,000 and 100,000 words. As this division is somewhat arbitrary, scan the chapter to see what might be relevant to you. Where there is no distinction made between shorter and longer theses in the discussion, I mean the advice to apply generally.

Prior considerations

To ease the writing of a thesis, certain preparatory issues need attention early in the degree course rather than later; others are applicable just prior to producing the first *full* draft of your thesis.

SOME INTELLECTUAL PROPERTY ISSUES

With institutions increasingly driven by commercial interests, intellectual property has become a prominent and somewhat complex issue, which may impact on writing and presenting your research:

- Familiarize yourself with your institution's intellectual property policy.
- Seek independent advice from a body in your institution akin to a Legal and Copyright Office if you are uncertain about the implications for your situation, or approach other relevant authorities for advice on how best to proceed.

At a most basic level in terms of communicating your research, these are some situations in which you may need to exercise care:

- If you are to sign any contracts for funding, perhaps industry contracts, take care to protect your intellectual property rights. Know exactly what you are signing away. Who gets the money? Is all of it to go to you, some to your supervisor, or other individuals or institutions? And who owns what in terms of the knowledge you will generate? Are there likely to be any constraints, under the contract, on including in your thesis all knowledge generated by you?

- If you think your research is likely to have commercial value, then investigate up-front how to protect your interests – ask your supervisor or a dean of graduate studies about the appropriate body with which to consult.

- Take care in putting thesis material on the Web without protection. You do not want somebody appropriating your original ideas or data, which has been known to happen.

As a researcher working on a team project, it is unwise to sign away intellectual property rights (for example, on data generated) without careful consideration of benefits and losses to you.

ORIENTATION TO THESIS WRITING

Orient yourself early on to what a thesis looks like in your discipline by reviewing two or three recently passed theses in the degree for which you are now studying. Copies of longer theses could be kept in your department, in one of your institution's libraries, and/or on your institution's website. Even if copies of shorter theses are not kept, your supervisor or some other member of department may have been given personal copies by students which they can loan you. Ask your departmental secretary or supervisor to advise you on how to obtain copies for review, or, as a last resort, key in 'digital theses' or 'digital dissertations' to access online libraries:

- Students in your discipline may be producing different types of theses, such as case studies or topic-based research, so select those that approximate your type of research. Even then you could find that the same types of theses have quite different structures.

- If your thesis is to be a set of published articles, then you may need to review practices for bringing the papers together as a coherent whole, perhaps inclusion of a general introduction, a new literature review and/or methodology chapter, linking between chapters and a general conclusion.

If your thesis is to take the form of a set of published articles, review the whole of Chapter 9.

While every thesis is unique, as yours will be, by reviewing passed theses you can generate ideas about aspects of style and structure, scope of coverage, quality and depth of analyses and so forth. (It is unwise to view these models as *ideal*, however; a pass does not necessarily mean perfection.) You will need to avoid getting caught up in the interesting content (so easy to do). Keep focused on how writers go about the writing – the composition processes. The idea is to get a feel for what constitutes a thesis at your level of study in your discipline.

Exercise: reviewing passed theses

As you review passed theses, engage questions of this type:

- Can you work out from the table of contents page the underlying logic for the structural divisions in the thesis, into parts, chapters or whatever?
- What do writers do in introductions or conclusions? What *types* of information do they include? Do they use sub-headings?
- How do they orient readers to the discussions to come – review the introductions of specific chapters and check between sub-divisions.
- Is there a literature review chapter or not? Or is there a substantial review of the literature in the introduction?
- Does a theoretical or methodology chapter seem to be mandatory or optional?
- What level of analysis, discussion or argument seems to be appropriate at your level of study?
- How much detail seems to be included in the writing of, say, ethnographic or results chapters? Quickly review research objectives and questions in the introduction to see the extent to which the writer has been guided by these in selecting detail for inclusion. You might also take a look at how writers conduct analyses of their data, the level of rigour, sophistication, etc.
- What sort of material is put into appendices (if you think you will need these)?
- How do writers title tables, graphs, figures, photographs, maps, diagrams, etc.? How do they refer to these in their discussions? Do you notice anything special about their preparation in terms of scales, legends, lettering, etc.?
- What do the bibliographies suggest about the coverage of the topic?
- What is the overall presentation like? For example: How wide are the margins? What line spacing is used? What referencing style is used and how are longer direct quotations distinguished in the text?
- Are there any other features of style and structure useful for you to scrutinize?

Having oriented yourself to what a thesis *is*, now activate strategies to ease the path towards that goal, the end product of all your research and writing efforts.

MANAGING THE PROJECT THROUGH WRITING

WRITE EARLY AND WRITE OFTEN.

Writing skills atrophy if unused, which is a definite hazard when writing longer theses. It is not enough to take notes from your reading or to keep lab records, though these activities are indeed important. Do try to ensure that, from as early as possible in your degree, your research efforts issue in written outcomes that are sustained pieces of writing.

Figure 7.1 presents a period breakdown for a 3-year research degree (no coursework), with suggestions on the types of writing possible in each period. Do what suits you best though. For example, it might be more appropriate to write a methods section of an experiment early on, or perhaps write up test results produced early, or attempt thematic analysis of a literary text being used in your research.

Analytical reading reports Like all students, you will be reading the literature – and sometimes there is an enormous amount to be read. Consider writing analytical reading reports (a few pages or so) when you complete a particular block of reading for your thesis. You can begin writing these very early on in your research.

Your purpose in producing these reports is to fully assess the strengths and weaknesses of the small body of literature, perhaps only three or four articles, you have just finished reading, just as you would in a full literature review (see 'The literature review' in Chapter 6). These reports should be written as properly developed analytical writings, with clear paragraph structure and a coherent line of discussion (see 'Developing texts' in Chapter 4). The advantages of doing these reports are several:

- They ensure you practise your writing.
- They help you to sort out what you think about the reading, force you to process carefully the material being read. The act of writing is a counter to vagueness in terms of understanding both your sources and the ideas you are developing from them.

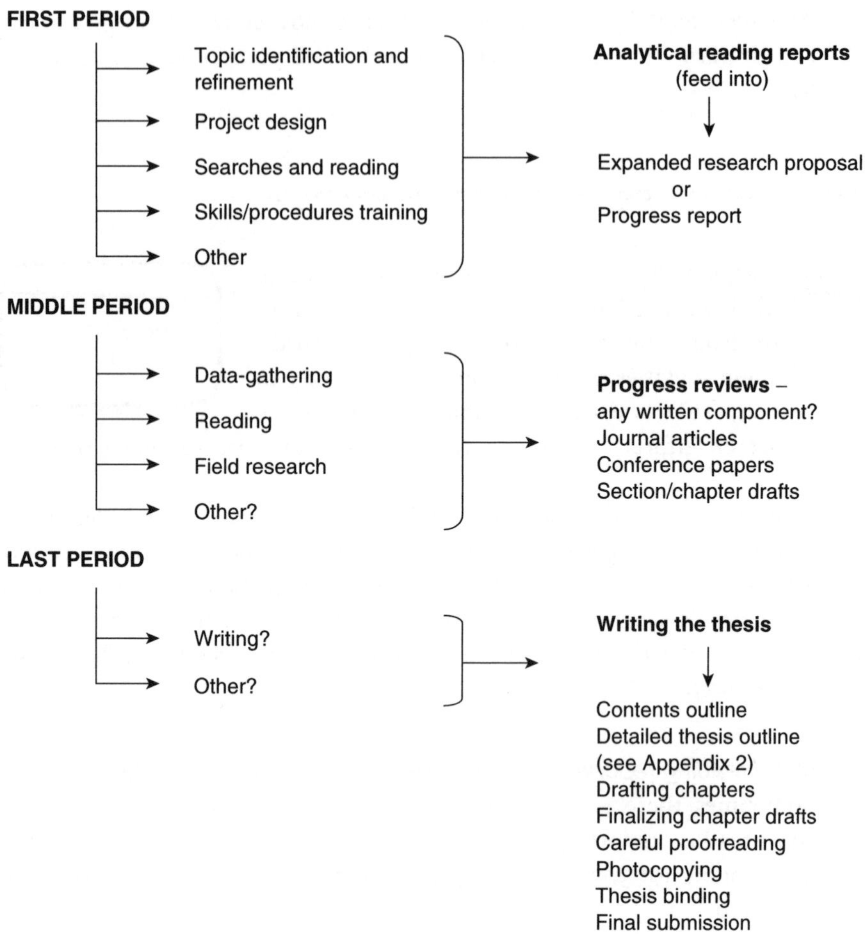

FIGURE 7.1 **Managing the project through writing**

- They can feed into the writing of a substantial literature review if this is required.
- They are a useful base from which to discuss with a supervisor your progress, your ideas, and any uncertainties or difficulties you are experiencing in your research.
- They can minimize the (sometimes) daunting effects of beginning the writing of a thesis.
- They are especially useful if English is not your first language, as they allow supervisors and academic skills or writing staff to identify early what you need to work on to improve English language and writing in your course/disciplinary context.

SETTING UP A THESIS WRITING SCHEDULE

When you begin to write a first *full* draft of your thesis, set up a detailed writing schedule that includes time available for reworking chapters in the process of, or subsequent to, producing the first draft.

Exercise: setting up a writing schedule

Step 1

Set up a time line that demarcates months to submission and includes an actual submission date, as below (based on 8 months to submission):

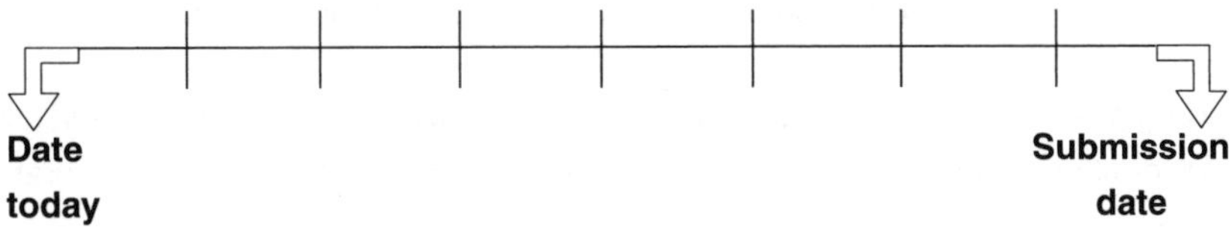

Step 2

Now work backwards from the submission date allotting time segments to the different writing tasks (for example, chapter drafts) and activities, as I do with the last month below:

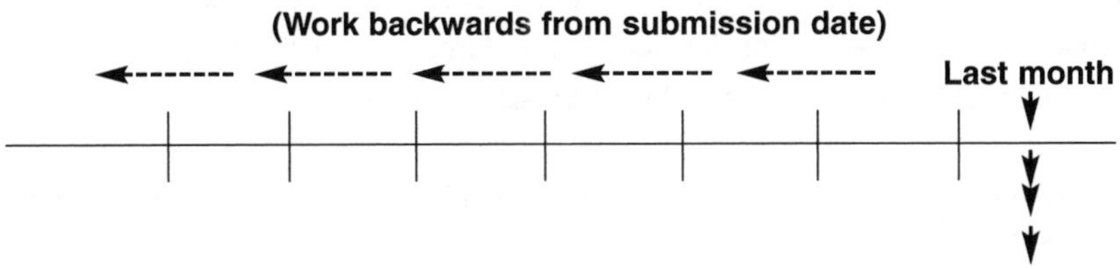

- Proofreading and editing
- Checking references and bibliography
- Polishing style and presentation
- Photocopying
- Binding
- Submission

Step 3

Set up a schedule that details dates for submission and return of drafts, revision of the whole thesis, etc. – everything you have to do to complete the thesis. Discuss the viability of your schedule with your supervisor to negotiate any changes needed to accommodate the supervisor's commitments.

SETTLING ON TYPOGRAPHY AND FORMATTING

Again at the point of beginning your first *full* draft, clarify institutional/departmental formatting expectations if you have not already done so. The few strategies suggested below complement the discussion on 'The mechanics of academic writing' in Chapter 3, which you might review.

- First, find out if there is an institutional document covering the following features for your level of degree: content standard, formatting, presentation, typing and typesetting, font sizes, photocopying, binding and so forth. Or your department may have standardized requirements that your supervisor will know about.

- Margins need to be able to accommodate binding needs. Decide on these in a first full draft as re-setting margins at a late draft can throw out figures, tables, graphs, photographs, etc. that you have incorporated in your thesis.

- Decide on spacing (for example, space and a half or double spacing). Follow usual practices in your discipline. Again, deciding to change line spacing at a late stage can be a nuisance in that figurative illustrations can be thrown out.

- As regards art work, photographs, maps, figures, graphs, tables, etc., check formatting of legends, professional standards of production, appropriate placement of these in the body of your thesis and so forth.

Keep a record of practices settled on (and approved by your supervisor) in a first chapter so that you can refer to this for later chapters; or perhaps you can set up a style template on your computer – ask for help from your local IT support.

Expectations of theses

While your supervisor will advise you as to more specific expectations, there are standard expectations that apply generally across disciplines at any level of thesis writing.

STANDARD EXPECTATIONS

Your final draft will need to evidence at least the following:

- Coherent development of the thesis overall (see 'Whole text development' in Chapter 4).
- Adequate signalling of intentions and embodiment of audience needs (see the next section).
- Evidence that the relevant literature has been thoroughly worked and understood. You may need to write a literature review (see Chapter 6) and/or integrate the material you have read into your own discussions throughout the thesis.
- Logical rigour and sound reasoning in terms of analyses, discussions or arguments (see relevant parts of 'The research essay as formal argument' in Chapter 5).
- (Perhaps) demonstrated knowledge and full critical appreciation of experimental or test procedures, relevant theories, models or methodologies (see 'Treating information critically' in Chapter 3).
- Competent presentation of material. Do make sure the thesis is a scholarly presentation. Use appropriate citation and bibliographic formats as discussed under 'Plagiarism and referencing' in Chapter 3. Proofread very carefully; ensure that references are correct in the text and the bibliography – cross-check these. Check the consistency of legends for tables, figures, graphs, etc. and that these are correct. Check that there is a table of contents page, an abstract and whatever else is required at the beginning, perhaps a list of abbreviations or acronyms if there are a large number in the thesis.

BRINGING EXAMINERS INTO VIEW

It is useful to write with examiners in mind, whether you know who these will be or not.

Taking care of audience needs is a further standard expectation, and one that can prove something of a challenge for thesis writers. Difficult as it can be to think beyond the sometimes obsessive intellectual processing that is thesis writing, bear in mind that your thesis is a communication with the scholars who will assess it (see also 'Attending to audience needs' in Chapter 3 and 'Engaging the reader' in Chapter 9):

- Never forget that you are writing for examiners.

- Think positively about examiners – they are not out to get you. But they will be close critical readers concerned to maintain high standards in the research field.

- Regardless of their subject expertise, write as if examiners know nothing about what you are doing and why you are doing it – it is important to demonstrate that *you* have complete control and critical understanding of any subject matter under discussion in your thesis.

- Always respect examiners' needs by signalling your intentions at appropriate points throughout your thesis.

- It may also be necessary to contextualize your discussions at times to put examiners in the picture, just as the writer in this example does in his lead-in into a lengthy sub-division:

  By the late 1970s, two major problems had become apparent in the forest management sector: tremendous forest destruction and increasing poverty among the local people, including the migrant and native people occupying the forest lands. During this period, there was a growing acceptance that the punitive actions adopted by the national government were ineffective in keeping the marginal communities away from the forest lands. ***Consequently, social forestry programs were introduced; these subsequently evolved into community forestry programs, as discussed in the succeeding sections*** *(my emphasis).*

By the time you approach writing the final draft of your thesis, you have certainly earned the right to a display of confidence:

- During different stages of your research you may have found yourself in awe of your supervisor and other scholars with whom you have worked. It is now time to let that awe settle into collegial respect. As you write, respect *your* knowledge and trust your own judgement.

- Over-familiarity with your research may lead you to feel at this final stage of writing that all you have to say is fairly obvious (students often feel this). But of course, it was once not obvious to you, and the research you present will certainly not be obvious to your examiners.

- You are in control of the writing, and in being so you have the power to guide your examiners towards the understandings or meanings you wish them to take up as you move through your discussions. After all, at this stage you have become something of an expert, perhaps even *the* expert, on your topic.

Longer theses

Identify any institutional and/or departmental guidelines or policy papers that relate to the writing of your thesis – ask your supervisor, other students, a dean of graduate studies or other appropriate authority about these. Such documents might be guidelines of a type that address general issues of style, formatting and standard expectations, and perhaps also more substantive issues in terms of focusing and structuring your thesis.

FOCUSING AN 'ORIGINAL' CONTRIBUTION

> To make an *original* contribution, you need to uncover new knowledge in order to advance knowledge in your field of research.

The PhD needs to be seen realistically, particularly if you are researching in a climate that allows only 3-year scholarships, if, indeed, you have scholarship funding at all. So do not make the mistake of pondering too much over the great work you feel you have to produce or the revolutionary contribution you need to make. The requirement is for an *original* contribution, and part of the difficulty lies in that word itself. It is a word that mystifies more than it clarifies, and so needs to be unpacked.

Exercise: determining the nature of your contribution

I list below a number of activities that involve making an original contribution to research, to advancing knowledge. Identify which of these activities apply to your research so that you can communicate clearly the nature of your contribution, probably in the thesis introduction. Perhaps you are doing not just one but several of these activities, or making contributions of a type I have not mentioned, in which case, add these to the list:

- Filling a significant gap in the research (could be almost anything).
- Challenging prevailing methodologies, theories or test procedures.
- Continuing an on-going line of enquiry (common in the experimental sciences).
- Developing new experimental procedures or perhaps a model.
- Developing new products, software or technology, perhaps for industry.
- Using established techniques or approaches in a new context (common in area studies).
- Providing extensive new data (common in field research).
- Producing a portfolio of creative work with a shorter accompanying thesis.
- Presenting studio work or performance presentations, as in some arts.
- Writing a biography, as perhaps in History or English.
- Setting up a comprehensive practical study for professional development purposes.
- Doing a comprehensive analysis that issues in new, and important, policy proposals.
- Documenting a language, as perhaps in Linguistics.
- What else?

Now think through the value of your research – why was it important to take up your line of investigation?

WHAT PHD EXAMINERS SAY IN THEIR REPORTS

Although I am focusing on PhD examiners' reports, much of the discussion in this section should be useful for theses other than doctoral dissertations as it opens up the whole topic of expectations of theses. It should also prove useful if your thesis is to be examined by way of a viva or oral. Rigorous practices in research and writing of the type now discussed will aid you in defence of your thesis (see Murray 2003).

The information in this section is taken from examiners' reports (to which I had access) used in a pilot study done by Brigid Ballard (1995). The study analysed examiners' reports for 62 PhD theses. Each thesis had three external examiners, who were both national and international. The study covered reports from six disciplines – English and History in the humanities; Anthropology and Political Science in the social sciences; and Botany and Zoology in the life sciences.

While this study was a small one, it clearly has generic value also. I am certain that the examiners' comments will echo your supervisor's advice on what to do and what not to do in writing your dissertation. Below I summarize some of the main categories of examiners' commentary.

Overall quality and contribution to scholarship Among thesis qualities most commonly valued was the capacity to **contribute innovatively.** In the life sciences this was often communicated along the lines of an incremental advance on a commonly recognized problem, with summary comments like the following:

> 'Pioneering work' – 'stimulating' – 'breaks new ground' – 'important and valuable contribution to knowledge' – 'major piece of original research' – 'offers significant and useful insights' – 'advances scientific knowledge' – 'tackled problems difficult though intriguing to scientists'

Similar comments appear for theses in the humanities and social sciences:

> '... develops diverse and original methods which should exert an influence on other scholarship in the field.'
> 'This is a major piece of original research.'
> '... a major contribution both to ethnography and to social theory.'
> 'This thesis is an important contribution to the history of the domestic economy in X [country named], to women's history and to the agricultural history of X.'
> 'This thesis breaks new ground that will, I think, prove to be significant to the scholarship in the area.'
> 'As an original contribution to knowledge ... this thesis qualifies twice over.'

In assessing the nature of the contribution, examiners also considered 'justification' for the research undertaken, the importance of the 'questions' being addressed and 'issues' canvassed; the capacity to relate research concerns to those of the broader discipline; and the grounding of the research in the relevant scholarship.

Whether there was a formal review of the literature or not, thorough knowledge and **critical understanding of the relevant literature** was extremely important to examiners, engendering such comments as:

> 'Takes account of all relevant literature' – 'close critical review of others' investigations' – 'relates findings fully and forcefully to extant literature' – 'judicious use of a wide range of sources'

But, more critically:

> 'failure to review and take up relevant literature across disciplines' – 'appears not to be fully conversant with the literature'

Evidence of publication in quality journals was highly regarded by examiners in the life sciences in assessing the overall quality of a thesis. Examiners in the humanities and social sciences also considered, and provided advice on publication, either as journal articles or as monographs, but did not attribute the same importance to there being existing publications from the thesis in assessing overall quality.

Scope, viability of topic, breadth and depth of study Examiners were also concerned about the **appropriateness of the chosen topic** for the level of a PhD and the time frame:

> 'To tackle such a topic is clearly to undertake a task "involving a comprehensive study of a scope and size that could normally be expected to be completed in the equivalent of 3 years full-time study".' [This latter quote is taken directly from the university instructions sent to examiners.]
>
> 'The candidate has identified a viable topic, researched it with appropriate techniques and methodology, and reached results with care and clarity rarely accomplished by a doctoral candidate.'
>
> '... although "viable", the topic is also extremely difficult to address.'

Some topics were clearly thought beyond the scope of a PhD, and others not viable:

> 'Neither the supervisor nor the student seem to recognize that they were tackling a major problem that was probably too difficult.'
>
> 'This is a monumental thesis involving, in my view, too much effort for the degree of Doctor of Philosophy.'
>
> 'Undoubtedly, the thesis adds an appreciable amount of detail to what is already known ... Yet it is doubtful whether the material is significant enough to warrant a reference to the thesis in any future publication ... It may be that this is not the

candidate's fault. Assiduous though the research has been, it is possible that material of the desired significance is simply not there to be found.'

Examiners also took account of the breadth and depth appropriate for a PhD, sometimes commenting on the scope and quality of the **bibliography** or **list of references** in the process of determination. In one case, a thesis considered inappropriate for the level of the degree did gain a 'pass' recommendation:

> 'In short, this thesis seems more in the nature of a Master's than a PhD dissertation. But its limits are inherent in its conception, in terms of which it is complete and adequate, and would therefore not be removed by rewriting, however substantial. And since I would be reluctant to fail such a competent piece of work I recommend that on the basis of it the candidate be admitted to the degree of Doctor of Philosophy.'

Research techniques and methodologies, results, discussions, analyses and arguments The importance attributed by examiners in the life sciences to **competence in research techniques** and procedures is evident in the following summary remarks:

> 'Has mastered a diversity of procedures' – 'high technical expertise' – 'displays competence in the variety of techniques' – 'demonstrates acquisition of the art and techniques of research science' – 'maturity of scientific approach' – 'employed intelligently a wide range of current techniques' – 'used a range of experimental techniques with great effectiveness' – 'data analysed by appropriate statistical methods' – 'well designed piece of research'

But also this:

> 'Each of the other topics investigated in the thesis are at a low level of technical expertise and not carried through to conclusions.'

Many examiners from the life sciences complimented students on the quality of their data and the **logical rigour** of their discussions. For example:

> 'Good solid empirical data' – 'data suggests careful observation' – 'careful selection of data for presentation' – 'the logical rigour of the discussions is extremely impressive' – 'logical and systematic throughout'

The more negative comments tended to be of this type:

> '... too often prepared to reach firm conclusions in the light of insufficient data.'
> '... there are observations in the Discussion that were not mentioned in the Results.'
> '... gets caught up in the minutiae of the results and has failed to highlight the significance of many of his findings.'

These reports suggest you need to be realistic about the importance of your results – grand speculations were not appreciated. You will also need to draw out the *significance* of the results in the discussion section, and their *implications*, as doing this was thought essential by examiners.

Examiners of theses in the humanities and social sciences were no less careful in their scrutiny of analyses and arguments, with many praising and detailing evidence of **'critical thought'** (or remarking on the lack thereof). One noted 'the subtlety and brilliance of analysis' in a thesis; others commented as follows:

> 'The whole thesis is vigorously argued. It is one of the strengths of this work that it repeatedly provokes argument and, indeed, invites debate throughout the text.'
> 'The structuring of the argument is, indeed, one of the most reassuring and impressive aspects of the thesis.'
> 'The quality of the analysis is excellent throughout – the present work represents a well researched, well argued study.'
> 'The author almost always appears aware of alternative explanations and [the] reasoning is frequently ingenious.'

But also:

> 'The first two models are in danger of functioning as straw men in the argument ...'

There was also this type of comment, which highlights the value examiners attributed to **overall coherence**:

> 'The connecting discussion throughout the thesis is almost always clear and intelligent.'
> 'The weakness of the thesis lies in its inability to maintain a common thread of argument throughout what is a very long and detailed piece of work.'

Where **theory** was an important consideration, this too was carefully assessed. One examiner praised the candidate's awareness of 'alternative theories and explanations'; another, the 'theoretical sophistication' of the study; and yet another, the 'creative' and 'rigorous' use of theory in the thesis under examination.

The importance of 'sound' **methodology** and its careful application in context was another vital consideration for many theses, as was 'clear definition of concepts' – one examiner displaying considerable annoyance because of a student's failure to define seminal concepts.

Academic style and presentation Details of style and presentation were consistently referred to in the commentary, with examiners in the life sciences being particularly meticulous about these aspects. Examiners were enthusiastic about 'clarity and simplicity', 'conciseness', a 'succinct' thesis, 'consistency of style', impressive 'flow and cohesion' of discussions, with further comments like this:

> 'The physical presentation of the material, the quality of the line drawings, charts, and illustrations are of outstanding quality.'
>
> 'Let me observe in conclusion that this thesis is not only full of original insights and judicious syntheses but also impeccably written and presented as a material object, which makes the task of reading much more pleasurable.'

There was strong disapproval of 'discursive and unfocused' writing, a 'journalistic style', 'long-windedness', 'frequent repetition' (on several occasions), and labouring the point:

> 'There is a tendency to "overkill". When the candidate proves a point [the candidate] continues to prove it again and again.'

Some examiners were clearly irritated by excessive numbers of typographic errors and spelling mistakes, many of them meticulously listing these for future correction. Careful proofreading is indeed important.

SUMMARY OBSERVATIONS ON EXAMINERS' REPORTS

- All examiners took careful account of the instructions for examination sent to them in making their judgements, often framing comments regarding assessment in terms of the phraseology of that university's instructions. Do find out what is sent to examiners by your institution if your thesis is to be examined externally.

- Examiners were keen to pass students, and felt bad, and sometimes angry, when struggling to find positive comments to make about a thesis. They did not expect perfection, and sometimes easily accommodated both high praise and strong criticism of aspects of a single thesis. On occasion, more serious criticisms were tempered by examiners making allowances for probable causes of perceived weaknesses in a thesis. Generally, they seemed to see the candidate as an 'apprentice' at the beginning of a career in research, not at an end. (This is despite the fact that many of you will not actually continue with research careers). Mostly, these reports show considerable encouragement and support for doctoral candidates.

- Examiners perceived the role of the supervisor(s) as extremely important, congratulating both student and supervisor on an excellent thesis, and often including the supervisor in criticisms of a problematic thesis:

  'The candidate has made use of a broad range of archival and secondary materials, and handled them with a skill and sensitivity which reflect well upon her and the supervision she has received.'

  'These matters could have been resolved during the writing stage had the candidate responded to strong supervisory direction. The finished work shows little evidence of pressure upon [the candidate] to condense [the] work through judicious selection of exemplary material … How far this may be judged to be a failure in the supervision and how far a failing in the candidate (in refusing to respond to guidance) is impossible for an external examiner to assess.'

  'More to the point, has a supervisor ever put such questions about [the] work to this very evidently assiduous candidate? Did the supervisor ever challenge [the candidate] to explain …? The candidate seems in desperate need of challenging discussion of the work.'

- Some examiners thought they were not the best person to examine, or had insufficient knowledge to do so, which highlights the importance of choosing external examiners carefully:

  (a) 'After reading [this] thesis, I can only wonder why you or the candidate or whoever wanted me to read it as an outside examiner. I say this because I am in such disagreement with the whole thrust of the analysis.'

  (b) 'As far as I am able to judge the matter – since I am not myself a [member of the candidate's discipline] – the candidate's approach has been thoroughly professional ….'

- Coverage of the thesis being examined was, in all instances, comprehensive. The 186-plus reports (there were extras because of resubmissions) show that all examiners were diligent and detailed in their assessment of the research and writing on both the levels of the overall thesis and individual chapters. It would seem from these reports at least, that very little escapes their eye.

Shorter theses

Shorter theses can have distinctive topic orientations, which, in turn, will affect expectations of your thesis.

DIFFERENT TOPIC ORIENTATIONS

The issue-driven topic One dominant orientation across many disciplines is the issue-driven topic. In this context, engaging key issues of interest to scholars in your discipline will be central to the development of the discussions/ arguments presented in your thesis.

The data-driven topic Or perhaps yours is a data-driven topic, where the accumulation and presentation of new data (for example, through fieldwork, local surveys, interviews, the generation of statistics, participant or non-participant observation, conducting trials or tests) is paramount.

CASE STUDY
Example

Box 7.1 The data-driven topic will entail critical engagement with relevant issues

A French student is studying linguistics. For her research project, she undertakes a comparative survey of a small group of British students, who are studying French at university while receiving private tuition from her. Her central research question is: *What are the effects of dual contexts of learning on second language acquisition?* The presentation of new data will be fundamentally important in the writing of her thesis. Still, analysis of the data will also involve critically engaging relevant issues.

It could also be that your interest has led you to improve, even marginally, on an existing model or product by way of a series of practical tests. Data generated by way of these tests might then be used in your thesis to critique that model or product.

The literature review orientation Orienting the topic to a review of the literature also seems to be an attractive option for many shorter projects. In the example below, the writer, signals this orientation in the thesis introduction.

> **Thesis title:**
> *Community participation: A key element in mother and child primary health care activities*
>
> **Extract from the introduction:**
> *This literature review aims to present, in the context of health care, a synthesis of the major themes and arguments relating to the concept of community participation and PHC [Primary Health Care] and MCH [Maternal and Child Health Care]. It is acknowledged that there is a wealth of literature on the general concept of community participation; however, this review will be confined to community participation as it relates to MCH/PHC. First, literature on the different theories, practices and approaches to community participation will be reviewed in the PHC context, along with the debate on the vertical/horizontal approaches to PHC. Second, current issues relating to MCH and its correlation with women's participation and health will be reviewed. Third, a framework for further research will be formulated. This will be followed by a summary of the major themes and future directions for research.*

There may have been other possibilities available to you. Or it may be that your orientation was decided for you by way of disciplinary expectations. Note though, that regardless of your topic orientation, treating information critically is paramount (see Chapter 3).

ORIENTATION AND PRACTICE

Regardless of the orientation of your thesis, it will need to evidence internal coherence in terms of:

- The focus of the study, your precise topic of investigation, and the topics discussed throughout.
- The objectives, questions or hypotheses that govern the investigation and the discussions presented in the body of the thesis.

It is important to carry through what you say you are setting out to do in your introduction. So ask yourself:

- Does the body of my thesis actually do what I say I will do in my introduction?
- Do the discussions in the body of the text actually meet the research objectives or answer the research questions or engage the hypotheses set up in my introduction?
- Have I justified my choice of methodology (if appropriate), presented a sustained and convincing argument for my approach?
- Does my thesis evidence a coherent line of discussion/argument throughout?
- Have I provided sufficient evidence, and the right kind of evidence, to support discussions and arguments in the body of my text?

A shorter thesis should also be a critical, but not necessarily an exhaustive investigation of a topic. The scope of the study is likely to be limited along the following lines:

- The review of literature will be selective, perhaps confined to essential readings and recent research only that allows you to position your study in the research context.
- Data-gathering is likely to be small-scale and localized. You will probably be working with easily accessible subjects, conducting interviews or tests, doing short surveys, or carrying out manageable experiments.
- Arguments and discussions will necessarily be limited, though logically sound, so that generalizing from findings to other contexts is not likely to be an aim, though speculating about these findings might be warranted.

Structuring a thesis

Structuring or organizing vast amounts of information on the scale of a thesis can certainly stretch you. Strategies presented in the remainder of this chapter are designed to help you with macro-structuring: dividing up the text, overall structuring, structuring thesis chapters, gaining control of the thesis as a whole, and structuring individual parts of the thesis: the abstract, the thesis introduction and the thesis conclusion. (Review also 'Whole text development' in Chapter 4.)

DIVIDING UP THE TEXT

The thesis text is usually divided along the lines of Figure 7.2, although variations do occur and shorter theses are unlikely to require a statement of originality.

Here I shall discuss briefly the features in Figure 7.2 marked with an asterisk, as these are not covered elsewhere in this book.

Cover of the thesis* Statement of originality* Acknowledgements* Abstract Table of contents* Lists of tables, figures, plates, etc. (optional) List of acronyms or abbreviations (optional)*	→ **Preliminary matter**
Introduction The main body of the thesis (divided into partsand/or chapters, sub-divisions and sections) Conclusion	→ **Body of the thesis**
Appendix(ces) (optional) Bibliography or List of references	→ **End matter**

FIGURE 7.2 **Basic divisions of a thesis (*see text)**

Cover of the thesis The first page of your thesis should provide sequential information of this type:

> **The ordering of preliminary information and wording is likely to be standardized in your institution, so do check.**

- The thesis title
- your name in full and
- the month and year of submission

which is followed by a statement to this effect:

> A thesis submitted for the degree of ... (fill in your degree, e.g. Doctor of Philosophy) at ... (fill in the full title of your institution).

or

> A thesis submitted in partial fulfilment of ... (where your thesis is only one component of a degree that includes coursework; then continue as above).

Statement of originality As a doctoral student, you will probably need to include a signed statement indicating the extent to which the thesis is your original work: perhaps entirely, or in the case of investigations carried out jointly with others, perhaps largely but not entirely.

Acknowledgements It is usual to thank all those who assisted you in the production of the thesis. Some students also take this opportunity to thank family members and friends for their support.

Table of contents

- On the table of contents pages indicate the page number of the start of each chapter, and perhaps those of sub-divisions or sections within these – practice varies. Include the Appendices and Bibliography.

- Pages of the preliminary matter are usually numbered with roman numerals (i ii iii iv v vi vii, etc.). On occasion though, I have seen pages in the preliminary matter left unnumbered, so review theses in your discipline.

- Consecutive page numbering in arabic numerals (1 2 3 4 5 6 7, etc.) is used for the body of the thesis, from the first page of the introduction to the last page of the thesis.

List of acronyms or abbreviations If there are a substantial number of acronyms or abbreviations in your thesis, then it is useful to include an alphabetical listing of these in the preliminary matter. Regardless of how well known an acronym is in your field, the usual academic practice when introducing it into the text for the first time is to give the name in full, with the abbreviation or acronym in brackets, thus: North Atlantic Treaty Organization (NATO). Subsequent references in the text can then be to the acronym, NATO. Examiners are unlikely to read longer theses in one sitting, and may forget the meaning of an acronym. If there is no list of acronyms at the beginning of your thesis, on *first usage* in a chapter, write in full even those acronyms you have previously used.

KEY STRUCTURING STRATEGIES

Strategy 1: Capitalize on word length As you approach structuring, first think about word length. Approximately how many words will you need for each chapter, given designated word length? Your sense of this might be rough but thinking about it may prevent overwriting. If you are inclined to overwrite, work from a lower word length in allotting the number of words to chapters. Work on, say, 70,000 for a PhD with an upper limit of 80,000, or 10,000 for a shorter thesis with an upper limit of 15,000. Examiners generally seem to appreciate tighter theses.

Strategy 2: Apply this set of core questions The vitally important set of questions below should inform your research from the outset of your degree, as your answers to such questions are likely to evolve over time. When structuring, activate the set of questions in Table 7.1 at different levels of the writing (for example, the general introduction, individual chapters, long sub-divisions) in order to guide your readers to an understanding of what you are doing and why.

> **Pause frequently when writing to consider that critical question: 'so what?' Keep asking yourself as you write: what are the *implications* of my arguments/discussions?**

Answering the what/so what questions in Table 7.1 feeds into the development of a thesis statement, as elaborated on next.

PROVIDING A THESIS STATEMENT

Pinning down your thesis can be like trying to hit a moving target – difficult. Perhaps it will help to think about it in different ways:

> **A thesis (the physical product) should have a *thesis* (the overall argument advanced in the thesis).**

- What do I think my overall argument actually is?
- What is the big message I want to communicate to readers?

TABLE 7.1 **Core questions for structuring at any level of the text**

WHAT? (Research focus)	**WHY? (Research purpose)**	**HOW? (Research method or procedure)**	**WHAT/SO WHAT? (Implications of your research)**
What is your 'topic of investigation'? What will you be discussing? What are you going to *cover* in the thesis? What are the boundaries of your coverage? If you are placing limitations on your coverage there may need to be a special section on **scope of the study**, which details the nature of these limitations and reasons for them. Now try to identify manageable topics or sub-topics suited to chapter or sub-division headings respectively. Ask yourself: How do these topics or sub-topics relate to each other in terms of my overall research focus? (This would seem to be the easiest question to answer, but it can be hard. For example, imagine how your focus and structuring of sub-divisions within a chapter would vary depending on which of these topics you chose to focus on: *The* politics *of the **debate** on logging rainforests in Brazil or The politics of the **economic debate** on logging rainforests in Brazil.*)	Why are you covering this topic? What precisely is your major research objective, or the 'big question' driving your research project? If you are setting up hypotheses, how do these relate to your overall research objectives? Or your intention may be to solve a particular problem, so that you need to produce a *Problem statement* (see Appendix 2). What are the subsidiary objectives or questions that arise out of your overall objective? Can you identify these clearly? Try listing them for your own clarification? These might prove a useful basis for chapter structuring. Chapter level: What are the specific objectives of individual chapters and how do these relate to your overall thesis objectives? What are the *relations* between your overall research objectives and those specific to chapters? And do these seem to form a *coherent* set of objectives?	How are you going to order discussion of your topics? What precisely are you going to do and in what *order* are you going to do these things? Why? This would involve considering chapter titles and the *logic* of their ordering within the thesis; at the level of the chapter, sub-division headings and the logic of their ordering within a chapter; at the level of the sub-division, the logic of the ordering of topics for discussion.	What are the **main ideas/points** you want to make in developing your discussions or arguments? (See 'Developing texts' in Chapter 4). You may be uncertain about these ideas/points until you write a first draft. But, if you are clear about some, jot them down now when structuring. Answering the 'so what? is also vitally important when writing. Remember to draw out the *implications* of your discussions. Your reader should not be left thinking: 'Well I take your point, and this is all very interesting (e.g. a piece of analysis with good critical insights) but, so what? Why is it important for you to be telling me all this?'

- What is the overall point I am trying to make that underpins what I say throughout my thesis?
- Why should somebody want to read my thesis? What is different/important about it?

Your thesis is your answer to that big question driving your research, or to the problem at the heart of your research. Even a rough, working thesis can help guide your early structuring efforts. Confine your thesis statement to a single short sentence, no more than two or three lines. Pin the statement above your work desk and/or place it permanently on your computer so that you see it every time.

> **Put a *working thesis* into a header so that it turns up at the top of each page of your draft. This is a useful way to refine it as you write and remind yourself that each chapter should somehow be contributing to development of a thesis.**

MY THESIS is that: ....
(This always takes the form of a big general assertion – a statement)

The example below constitutes a thesis statement, in this case as laid out in the introduction:

I will argue that X's [country named] poor record of environmental law enforcement and compliance by industries cannot be explained solely by reference to specific aspects of environmental law, but rather, is a result of the very nature of X's social, political and legal system.

Everything done in this shorter thesis (the product) was meant to advance the above thesis (the argument).

Chapter structuring options

Often PhDs have as many as eight or nine chapters; a shorter thesis might have about four. Word length will affect the number of your chapters, but so too can the principle of structuring used, the type of research and so forth. There are many different approaches to structuring chapters, four of which I include here for discussion.

It could be that there is a preferred basic structure in your discipline, which should take precedence over anything I have to say in this section. Or perhaps your supervisor will refer you to one of the useful resources that target structuring and writing theses in cognate disciplines, such as that by Perry (2004) on marketing and related fields.

A SCIENCE MODEL

If you are researching in the experimental sciences, you will likely use some variation of the following model in structuring core chapters: *Introduction*, *Materials and Methods*, *Results*, *Discussion*. The model also suits other research contexts, for example if you were conducting tests or reporting on investigations or tests, collating data and presenting findings, and then drawing out the implications of your findings.

Review 'Experimental or technical reports' in Chapter 6, where I discuss in some detail expectations of the different sections of this type of structural framework.

This might be called a science model of structuring, though certainly not all science theses evidence this modelling, and disciplines other than those in science use the structure.

THE ILLUSTRATIONS-BASED MODEL

Some students have reported the value of taking this particular approach to structuring, which might be just the model for you. First they process their data, producing different sets of illustrations (for example, tables, graphs, photographs, figures, bar or pie charts, etc.) for each chapter. They then consider the order in which they want to present the illustrations in a chapter, and structure accordingly.

This is a model in which a great deal of intellectual effort is expended before the writing of each chapter begins. Some research that is heavily data-based will certainly lend itself well to this type of structuring.

A 'PHOTOGRAPHIC' MODEL

Another approach to structuring chapters is what I call the '*Photographic* model'. Figure 7.3 presents a table of contents outline with the structure figured at right to illustrate this approach.

Introduction

Chapter 1: Theurgy and Orthodoxy in the Western Tradition
I. Yeats and Magic
II. Eliot and Orthodoxy
III. Levelled Consciousness, Mysticism, and Conceptual Methods

Chapter 2: Critical Constructs: Identity and Contrast
I. Theosophy, Philosophical Rationalism, and the Art of Imagination
II. Occultism and the Celtic World of the Poet-Magician Yeats
III. Yeats's Method of Conception: the Dionysiac and the Appolonic
IV. Absolute Idealism and Eliot's Early Method of Conception
V. Catholicism, Hulme's Imagism, and Eliot's Art of Criticism
VI. French Symbolism, Modernism and the Sceptical Outlook

Chapter 3: Masterful Images
Crossways (1889)
The Rose (1893)
The Wind Among the Reeds (1899)
In the Seven Woods (1904)
From The Green Helmet and Other Poems (1910)

Chapter 4: Sensation and Thought
Poems Written in Early Youth
Prufrock and Other Observations (1917)

Conclusion

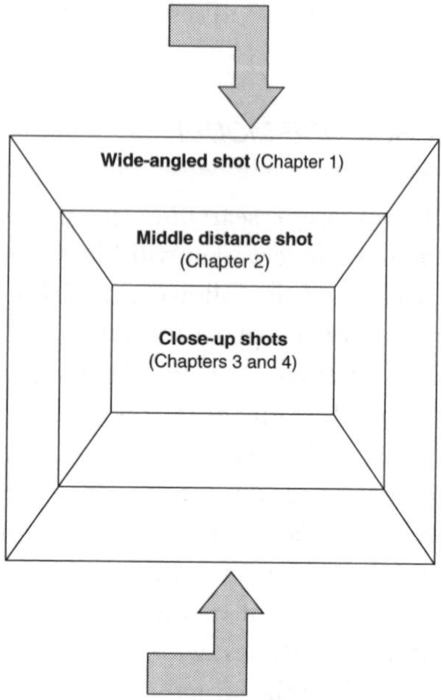

FIGURE 7.3 **A Photographic model of structure**

Chapter 1 provided a broad overview (*wide-angled shot)* of the two distinct traditions of Western supernaturalism to which the two poets inclined, and the conceptual implications of their different preferences. There was then a move in Chapter 2 to a *middle distance shot* of the conceptual tie-in of these two traditions with other areas of the Western metaphysical tradition, which in turn were linked to the literary movements attracting the two poets as well as the types of literary criticism they espoused.

Chapters 3 and 4 then zoomed in for *close-up shots*, detailed analyses of the early poetry to show how each poet's conceptual framing of reality was influenced by the different traditions of Western supernaturalism to which they held.

The Conclusion then built on these four chapters to show how changes in the poetic output of each poet mirrored progressively changing attitudes to their preferred forms of Western supernaturalism.

A SEQUENTIAL MODEL

Your research might be of the type that easily lends itself to the sequential model of structuring chapters, where there is an underlying logic to the sequencing of chapters. In Figure 7.4 historical chronology – moving successively from landmark changes pre-contact through landmark changes occasioned by European contact to the present – is the underlying principle of a structure that has both parts and chapters, as well as sub-divisions, which I have omitted from the Figure for reasons of space.

Table of Contents

Introduction

PART I. THE PRE-CONTACT PERIOD
(C. 1200BC TO 1770)

Chapter 1. The Formation of Tongan Society:
Development of the Ancient Modes of Production

Chapter 2. The Emergence of Centralised Power:
The Transition to a Feudal Model of Production

PART II. THE EUROPEAN CONTACT PERIOD
(1770–present)

Chapter 3. Taufa-ahau's Land Reform:
The Creation of an Independent Class of
Small Land Holders

Chapter 4: Capitalist Penetration: The Transition
to Mixed Modes of Production

Chapter 5: 'Internationalisation': The Transition
to a Dependent Capitalist Mode of Production

Conclusion

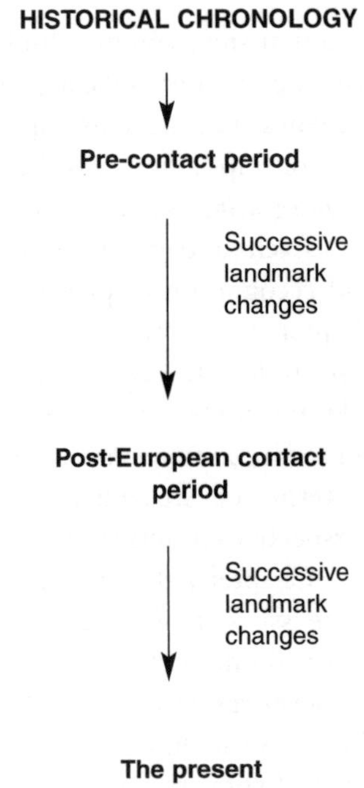

FIGURE 7.4 **A sequential model of structuring**

If there are no disciplinary requirements for thesis structuring, be creative and experiment, perhaps coming up with more than one likely structure to discuss with your supervisor. Let your research objectives determine the best structure for your thesis. It could be that your chapter structure will evolve from central themes covered in your research, or the seminal issues you need to engage, as happened in the example discussed in the following section under 'Visually mapping core chapters', which was a case study type thesis.

Gaining overall thesis control

Different strategies are now suggested for gaining control of the overall structure and development of the thesis.

VISUALLY MAPPING CORE CHAPTERS

As a first step, you may find it useful to visually map core chapters on paper, or with a computer. Take a little time to study Figure 7.5, which is an example of a student's successful attempt at doing this as he set out to determine the logical relationships among his thesis chapters. His topic was: *The legal/policy framework for integrating indigenous peoples in protected area management in X [country named].*

Each fundamental issue in the central triangle – governance, sustainable use and recognition of property rights – was covered independently in successive chapters (Chapters 4, 5 and 6). These were the chapters analysing data from the case studies. In each case, there was analysis of the dichotomies pictured in the relevant circles: the balancing of property rights preservation and biodiversity conservation in terms of 'Governance;' the compromise of practices and policies in terms of 'Sustainable use;' and the reconciliation of national and local perspectives in terms of the 'Recognition of property rights.'

Chapter 7 then provided a comparative analysis of the implications of these three issues and Chapter 8 expanded the discussion to determine an appropriate policy framework that would allow for (a) Sustainable Livelihood, (b) Secure property rights and (c) Effective Governance. (The first three chapters of the thesis, not included in the above model, covered the introduction, theory and methodology, respectively.)

BRAINSTORMING THE TABLE OF CONTENTS

Do attempt a solid table of contents outline before writing your first *full* draft, even though it will need some reworking on completion of the writing. A table

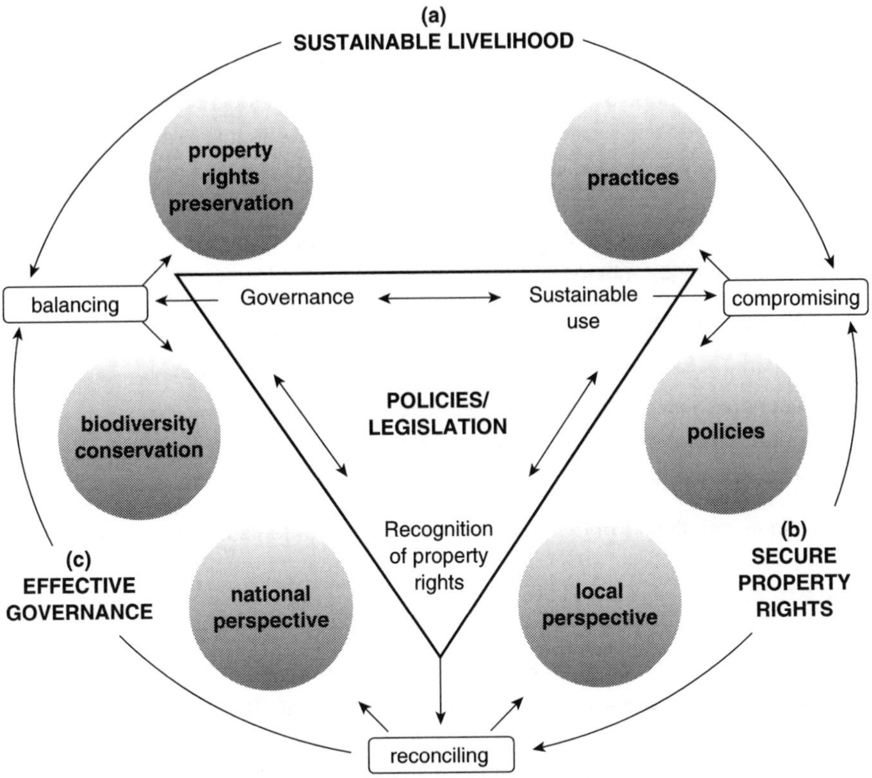

FIGURE 7.5 **Computer modelling of thesis chapters**

of contents outline is a useful guide as you move through the writing of different chapters, which you may not necessarily want to write in sequence.

Exercise: building a table of contents

The purpose of doing this exercise is to determine the *logical* relations among the different parts of the thesis, not just to work out what you want to cover (see also 'Sequential outlining' in Chapter 4).

Step 1

First, start to build your table of contents outline as follows, while taking into account thesis word length:

Introduction:

What is your topic of investigation? What problem are you tackling, what are your research objectives or questions? Why is it an important topic of investigation? What contribution do you expect to make to the field of research (if relevant)? What sub-divisions do *you* need in your introduction? (Mock up titles of these if you can.) You do need to be able to answer these questions as clearly as you can. Some supervisors require that their students produce a full, rough draft of the introduction; others are happy with these questions being answered in dot point form.

Chapter 1 (title?):

First sub-division (number and/or title?)
Second sub-division (number and/or title?)
Further sections within the sub-divisions
(numbers and or titles?)

Any ideas you want to jot down while drafting?

(Continue with this format throughout the table of contents outline)

Step 2

Now apply the set of core questions – What? Why? How? What/So what? discussed above – to determine the *logic of relations* among the parts. This will show:

- How the foci and objectives of the different chapters fit in with your overall research focus and objectives as laid out in your thesis introduction.
- Whether the order in which you have placed your chapters, and sub-divisions (and further sections) within different chapters, is best after all – whether they evidence a logical flow.
- Whether *main ideas* (if you know them) you wish to bring forward in the different chapters are likely to contribute to the coherent development of a thesis or unifying point of view.

Discuss your outline with your supervisor. Make any suggested adjustments, and then move on quickly to the writing itself; spend no more than two or three weeks on this task.

PRODUCING A DETAILED THESIS OUTLINE

Some students and supervisors do not find that a table of contents provides enough detail or sufficient information to assess the overall coherence of a thesis. In that case, you could produce a more detailed thesis outline. While students find doing this difficult (a lot of hard thinking is involved), they consider it well worth while.

CASE STUDY
Example

Box 7.2 Students report many benefits from producing a detailed thesis outline

One group of research students approaching the thesis write up were encouraged to produce a detailed thesis outline. Doing this, they said, had *'reduced anxiety'* and *'increased confidence'*:

- This was because they now had a stronger sense of *'how the whole thing hung together'*, to quote one.
- Or as another student commented: *'The best thing about the detailed thesis outline exercise for me was that I was able to concentrate totally on the bits [of the thesis] I was writing because I sort of knew how everything fitted in.'*
- And another had this to say: *'My table of contents was pretty good but I still didn't know where I was really going with the argument until I did the detailed thesis outline. It helped me sort out my argument – what I really wanted to do with my chapters. It was great.'*

Appendix 2 contains an example of such an outline. This outline was produced by a doctoral student who already had a rough full draft of the thesis (approximately 90,000 words). However, I have done the exercise often with students beginning to write their first full draft or with those who have come unstuck in the middle of writing a draft.

The purpose of this exercise is to communicate, as best you can, *what* you are doing, *why* you are doing it, *how* you will go about this, and the argument you wish to present:

- at the level of the whole thesis and
- at the level of individual chapters.

While the writing is rather formulaic, it is meant to be. You can shape introductions to chapters more creatively when you come to write them, while still communicating clearly foci, objectives and procedure, and parts of your argument.

Writing specific parts

This section looks specifically at the writing of the abstract, the thesis introduction and the thesis conclusion.

Developing the abstract

For longer theses, the abstract is usually around one to three pages in length and for shorter theses, about a page, though do be advised by your supervisor. The abstract usually covers:

- What you did in your research.
- Why you did it – your objectives or aims.
- How you approached your topic, your methodology and/or theoretical framework if relevant.
- What your findings were and reasons for them.

Practices in writing abstracts can vary, though. I have noticed, for example, that abstracts for PhD theses in Mathematics tend to focus solely on main findings, as typified below:

> *There are two main results contained in this dissertation. The first result is a description of an algorithm for the computation of polycyclic presentations for nilpotent factor groups of a given finitely presented group. This algorithm is a generalisation of the methods employed in the p-quotient algorithm [reference] to possibly infinite nilpotent groups. The second is a method for the computation of the Schur multiplicator of a group given by a polycyclic presentation and a method for the classification of the isomorphism types of Schur covering groups for finite soluble groups. Both Algorithms can be treated in a similar context, namely forming central downward extensions of polycyclic groups.*

The abstract, often left to the last minute to dash off, is actually important in that it is used by other researchers to decide whether or not they will take the trouble to view your thesis in full, which might be the only avenue for accessing your research if you do not publish. Avoid a poorly constructed PhD abstract, which is also there for everyone to see in such international directories as

About $\frac{1}{3}$ of space ←

Why was it important to undertake the study? (And for PhDs: what does it contribute to scholarship in your field?)
What is the scope of your enquiry? Were any limitations placed on the study? (While you will undoubtedly point this out in your introduction, it is also helpful to restate this concisely in the abstract.)
What did you actually do?
What were your research objectives/questions/hypotheses?
What approach did you take? (If you need to, discuss your methodology, how you went about fulfilling your objectives, what models, or theories, etc. you used.)

About $\frac{2}{3}$ of space ←

What were your findings? Set out clearly the main conclusions reached and provide some discussion of how you arrived at these. Also draw out their implications. Mention too any inconclusive findings, giving reasons for them.

FIGURE 7.6 **Core questions for structuring an abstract**

Dissertation Abstracts. Consider the set of core questions offered in Figure 7.6 and take up what is appropriate for you.

Often about one-half to two-thirds of the abstract is reserved for discussion of findings/conclusions and their implications for past and future research, though again, confirm usual practice in your discipline.

The thesis introduction

The purpose of your introduction is to introduce readers to the research presented and discussed in the body of your thesis: to the foci and parameters of your research, justifications for choices made, thesis procedure and so forth. While considering the following issues, bear in mind that the introduction is functionally significant in shaping reader-expectations of what they will find on reading your thesis.

Align what you say you will do in the introduction with what you actually do in the body of your thesis.

THE ISSUE OF LENGTH

Length may not be an issue for you. Still it may be wise to discuss length with your supervisor before writing the introduction.

CASE STUDY
Example

Box 7.3 Supervisors can have definite ideas about the shaping of a thesis introduction

One supervisor rejected his PhD student's introduction of 30-plus pages, saying an introduction should be about 'eight pages and should cover context, issues and method in that order'. So the student re-wrote to those instructions. He initially established the context of his research by providing dense background information; he then identified the key issues in the process of defining his research objectives; finally he provided a conventional chapter-by-chapter description of the thesis procedure.

TIMING THE WRITING OF AN INTRODUCTION

If you have produced a well thought-through table of contents or detailed thesis outline, it should not matter when you write your introduction. Still, supervisors frequently recommend that students write an introduction prior to producing a first full draft, even though this will eventually need to be re-written, or tidied up, in order to accommodate changes made during the writing process.

FOCUSING AN INTRODUCTION

Deciding what information to include in the thesis introduction and what to include in the introductory sections of individual chapters can prove challenging. This is primarily a matter of scale, as shown in Table 7.2.

Your overall thesis objectives (or questions), which can be distinguished from the specific objectives you have in particular chapters, should be broad enough to embody the latter.

The set of questions below is designed to help you further focus your introduction. (Engage those relevant for your type and length of thesis, and include additional ones if needs be).

- What is your topic of investigation, your research focus?
- What questions are you asking? Or what are your hypotheses, objectives or aims? Can you formulate these clearly? Do you need to provide a problem statement as well (see 'Sample of a detailed thesis outline' in Appendix 2)?

TABLE 7.2 **Information scale for the general and chapter introductions**

Thesis introduction	Chapter introductions
• The purpose of the thesis introduction is to orient the reader to the research presented in the body of your thesis • The introduction should include all information necessary to prepare the reader, to put the reader in the picture as regards the specifics of your research project: what the thesis focuses on, the context of the study, the research questions or objectives driving the investigation, the methodology applied, the argument you intend to present, etc. • It may be necessary at times to reserve more detailed discussion of issues etc. for specific chapters and signal where these will be discussed in greater depth	• Chapter introductions perform a similar orientation function in that they introduce the reader to the foci, aims, procedure and argument of *each* specific chapter, and provide any other necessary reader information for that chapter

- What is your *thesis*, that is, the underlying argument connecting all the parts? Can you state this clearly?

- Do you need to justify the *scope* of your study? You may need to tell your reader precisely what you are covering and what you are not covering and why, perhaps to offset potential criticism for not having done something you never intended to do.

- Why is the research you have undertaken important? Can you demonstrate its centrality? Or how is your study different from others done in the research field? What contribution will *your* research make to knowledge? (This may be conveyed through context, the next point.)

- How much context, background information, should you provide (this can be extensive in some theses, even up to 20 or more pages)? What might you include here, and why? Consider the *relevance* of what to cover in terms of your research objectives, your thesis aims.

- Should there be a formal literature review in the introduction (sometimes used to provide context), or elsewhere, or not at all?

- Do you need to explain your methodology or experimental procedure, or provide a discussion of the theoretical framework of your thesis here or in a separate chapter, or not at all?
- Should you include a chapter-by-chapter outline of your thesis? If not, what other method might you use to convey the procedure of your thesis? How will you indicate what you are going to do and in what order you will do these things?
- Are there any other questions relevant to *your* research or disciplinary needs that you want to add?

The thesis conclusion

Conclusions have varying degrees of importance in the overall structural scheme of individual theses. Some theses do not have formal conclusions because the final chapter proves a natural point of closure, given the structural design. Most do, however, and many supervisors and examiners consider it imperative that there be one.

Your conclusion may be fairly short and straightforward, as much discussion of findings has taken place in the individual chapters. Or it may be long and complicated, and very demanding to write in drawing out conclusions of individual chapters and providing detailed discussion of these.

It is not usual to introduce new material into your conclusion. The student in this example did consider it appropriate to do this, but only for the purpose of bringing the reader up to date:

> *A model of the middle-ground which integrates the research findings introduces a conceptual framework to consolidate the study. This chapter then summarises the research findings and reflects on the process of the research through an analysis of each of the study's aims. Lastly, I metaphorically 're-visit' each case study* ***in order to bring the reader up to date with news and events that have occurred since completing fieldwork at each site*** (my emphasis).

Now consider the following points. (If your conclusion is to take the form of a general discussion that draws the whole study together, also review the strategies for writing a discussion in 'Experimental or technical reports' in Chapter 6.)

> **Fix this idea firmly in your mind: my reader wants to know what *I* think about my findings.**

PROCESSING FINDINGS

Merely listing or repeating your findings from various chapters – Chapter 1 shows, Chapter 2 shows, etc. – gives no insight into the meanings you attach to these findings. Not only do you need to draw together all findings into a coherent whole, you need to think about the weight and significance you attach to specific findings in terms of your research objectives or questions. When drafting your conclusion, refresh your memory by returning to those objectives/questions, as laid out in your introduction.

Not all findings will be equally important, so think about them in terms of a scale of significance. Ask yourself:

- What do I consider most important about my findings in general and why?
- Which findings seem to be of greater or lesser significance and why?
- Are there any specific findings to which I want to draw particular attention and why?
- Is there anything unusual about any of my findings needing special mention and why?
- Has my methodology or anything else affected my interpretation of findings and is this something that needs to be discussed (for example, biases inbuilt into the research design)?

By processing thesis findings in this way, you are bringing them into a new set of relations. You might also want to explain what you have found in terms of expected or unexpected outcomes in the process of attributing significance.

DRAWING OUT IMPLICATIONS

Draw out the implications of your findings. In longer theses, it is usual to situate findings in the contexts of past and future research. Ask yourself:

- To what extent do my findings align with those of other scholars, in what precise ways, and if not why not?
- If certain findings suggest a need for further research, what might this consist in and how might such research extend or improve the current state of knowledge in my field?

As a writer of a shorter thesis you may not be in a position to suggest future research, but this does not mean you should avoid thoughtful discussion of implications.

CASE STUDY
Example

Box 7.4 Drawing out the implications of your findings can add zest to a conclusion

A shorter thesis examined the fall of a democratically elected government to determine whether the key actors participating in the downfall had acted within the framework of that country's constitution. The student concluded that they had done so. But in her view, a major *implication* of her findings was that there was perhaps a need for review of the constitution itself in the context of early twenty-first century society. This she aired in the conclusion, giving thought-provoking reasons why she believed such a review might be warranted.

GROUNDING SPECULATIONS

Use the more tentative language (e.g. it seems, perhaps, maybe or it could be, possibly/possible, it is likely/unlikely, etc.) suited to speculative uncertainty.

The implications of your research project may be complex and variable, leading you into the realm of speculation. Some findings, for example, might appear to have application beyond the parameters of your research, and they may do. But judicious judgement is called for. Ensure that such speculations are contained within the boundaries of the arguments and discussions developed in the body of your thesis. Keep your speculations grounded; do not let them float free from these boundaries so that they appear wildly improbable or even questionable.

Organizing a thesis writing group

Your fellow graduates can be a great personal and academic resource when writing your thesis. A thesis writing group:

- Is a fruitful learning forum providing opportunity for reflection on the complexities of structuring and developing a thesis, and the sharing of ideas and helpful feedback from peers on your drafts.
- Is a motivational stimulus in providing regular opportunities to share your grievances, frustrations, challenges and, of course, your triumphs with fellow research students.
- Reduces the sense of isolation that you and fellow students may be experiencing.

If there is no existing group of this type in your research environment and you feel it would be useful to form one, follow these procedural steps.

Exercise: organizing a thesis writing group

Step 1

First approach an appropriate authority (for example, a graduate coordinator) to see if you can get hold of an email distribution list for research students in your group. Then send out a friendly email to determine level of interest. To work well such groups do need commitment from those involved.

Step 2

Having determined a sufficient level of interest, then organize a first meeting to sort out conduct of the group. Consider matters of this type:

- Whether you want it to be a students only group in which you will read each other's outlines and drafts, meet regularly to provide feedback on these, and to discuss strategies to address writing challenges, and so forth.
- Whether you want to reserve the possibility of inviting writing experts or scholars to address your group on occasion.
- How often you want to hold meetings, venue for meetings, length of meetings, prior distribution of materials for meetings, whether refreshments will be provided or not, and so forth.
- What organizational protocols you will follow. Usually the organization of such groups is democratic, with members opting to take charge of their own sessions by distributing copies of their draft to fellow students, identifying what specifically they would like feedback on given the stage they have

reached in the writing, and perhaps organizing the procedure for their session. People also like to chat and have a bit of fun.

While you and other students may initially be tentative about critically evaluating each other's work, well-intentioned criticisms will always be welcome, as will more positive comments on a draft.

Summary Comments

- By closely reviewing recently passed theses in your discipline at your level of study, you should gain a strong sense of the standards required of the end product – your completed thesis.
- The hallmark of thesis writing is rigour: rigour in foregrounding and developing a thesis, in attending to audience needs, in treating the literature critically, in referencing source material, in using theory and justifying methodology, in conducting tests or experiments, in analyses, argument and discussions, in the way you present illustrations, and in the overall style and presentation.
- Structuring and developing writing on the scale of a thesis is intellectually hard work. So do try to produce bits of writing regularly throughout your degree that will feed into the thesis.
- Producing a *detailed thesis outline* before proceeding to the writing of a first full draft can alleviate the anxiety and stress associated with writing parts of a thesis without knowing how all the parts relate to each other as a coherent whole.

8 Oral and Visual Presentations

Developmental Objectives

By applying the strategies, doing the exercises and following the procedural steps in this chapter, you should be able to:

Part 1: The different types of presentations

- Understand and distinguish key expectations of tutorial and seminar presentations.
- Identify strategies for generating funding for a conference, locating appropriate conferences and getting a paper accepted.
- Identify key factors influencing poster design and develop capacity to design your own posters.

Part 2: General issues in presenting

- Identify practices influential in successful planning (analysing audience, finding the right language, assessing venue needs and building 'time' into a plan).
- Understand how to make the best of formatting options available to you in different situations of presenting.
- Avoid some of the technical problems in using illustrative material (for example, slides or transparencies).
- Identify strategies for orienting an audience to your talk, attracting and holding audience interest, canvassing audience questions, managing venue, dealing with the unexpected and managing nervousness.

This chapter covers common types of presentations: tutorial, seminar, conference and poster presentations. While I do take account of the different needs of coursework and research students, the presenting situations of the two groups can overlap. Because of this overlap, I have structured the chapter in two parts. I advise you first to read the section referring to your particular type of presentation in Part 1, and then the general advice contained in Part 2.

The nature of oral presentations

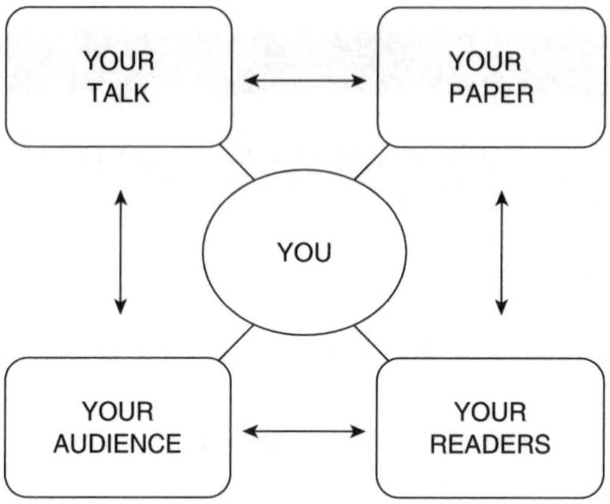

FIGURE 8.1 **The basic elements of an oral presentation**

The oral presentation is an interactive mode of communication that has a variety of functions. Its basic elements are configured in Figure 8.1 so as to convey the set of relations common to situations in which you will be presenting.

A presentation is often accompanied by a paper to be submitted to lecturers/supervisors, or circulated at a conference you are attending or published in the conference proceedings. Nevertheless, what you present orally is likely to be different from what you write in an accompanying paper, which is why the two are kept separate in the Figure.

DISTINCTIVE FEATURES OF PRESENTING

In presenting, you will need to:

- (Possibly) handle the demands of multi-media presentations.
- Design your talk to fit the time available to you.
- Tailor your language and organize your talk to suit a listening audience.
- Control the presentation of your work and interaction with an audience.

- Employ strategies to attract and hold audience interest.
- Develop the ability to 'think on your feet' when responding to questions or feedback from the audience.
- Manage nervousness, which often accompanies speaking to an audience.

Note the repeated mention of an audience in these points, a dimension given much emphasis in this chapter. Having a live audience both constrains and opens up your possibilities.

Part 1: The different types of presentations

Tutorial and seminar presentations

Tutorials and seminars are the two prominent types of presentation within graduate coursework and research.

DISTINGUISHING THESE TWO TYPES

The distinctions between tutorial and seminar presentations set out in Table 8.1 are at best approximate; *your* tutorial might well seem more like a seminar, or vice versa.

Coursework and research students will not necessarily have the same objectives or interests in presenting their work. Nevertheless, there are some commonalities to consider whether, as a coursework student, you are giving a talk in a tutorial group, or, as a research student, presenting a more formal seminar paper to departmental and/or other students and staff of your institution.

CLARIFYING EXPECTATIONS

Prepare in advance of your tutorial or seminar by clarifying expectations.

Identifying formatting requirements Clarify with your lecturer/supervisor whether there are special requirements for the format of your presentation. For example:

TABLE 8.1 **Distinguishing features of tutorials and seminars**

	Tutorial presentation	Seminar presentation
Presenters	Usually coursework students	Usually research students
Audience	Fellow students studying your particular course and the lecturer taking that course	Likely to be more mixed, with staff and students coming from across the department/school and perhaps from external areas
Basis of presentation	Discussion of course topics	Discussion of student's research
Level of formality	Usually less formal	Usually more formal
Purpose	Often part of assessment	Often part of a review process

- You may be asked to write a short paper, read it and hand it in immediately after a tutorial meeting.
- You may be expected to produce a substantial paper as part of a review process, and to speak for up to an hour on your paper.
- You may be asked to speak from notes and hand these in or write a substantial paper on the basis of them, or you may not have to submit a written version at all.
- You may be expected, or choose, to use multi-media formatting (for example, a combination of slides, overheads, whiteboard, scripted notes) or give a PowerPoint presentation.
- There may be no formal expectations.

Requirements for your oral presentation may be set out in course guides; or they may be formalized in departmental/centre guidelines. In other situations your lecturers will simply tell you what is expected. It is also possible you may be given no information at all but left to your own devices, in which case:

- Generate ideas/strategies by reflecting on what impresses you about other speakers and their presentations (take some notes to this effect).

Determining assessment procedures Clarify the criteria by which your presentation (and paper?) will be assessed. In **coursework** you may be asked to submit a paper, either before or after your talk, as part of the assessment:

- There may be different criteria for assessment of your presentation and your paper.
- Lecturers may give different weight to various aspects of your presentation (for example, ability to initiate group discussion of important ideas; evidence of clear understanding of key issues, procedures or theories; clarity of structure and delivery of the talk) and of the accompanying paper (for example, breadth and depth of reading; the quality of the argument; methodological soundness, etc.).

As a **research student** you are likely to be presenting as part of a progress review in order to gain useful feedback from peers and other colleagues.

FORESTALLING CRITICISM IN PROGRESS REVIEW SEMINARS

Research students often report a fear of undue criticism in progress review seminars, and unfortunately such fear is occasionally borne out, which is why this subject is treated separately from hints on managing nervousness at the end of this chapter.

> **You cannot be expected to have all the answers with research that is still in progress.**

If your research is still in progress, there will be uncertainties, perhaps incomplete developments or gaps in your research of which you are aware:

- Remind your audience at the outset that it *is* work in progress in order to elicit their understanding and forestall criticism of the type that assumes you are already the expert.

Also:

- Assign the audience a useful role. Tell them on which aspects of your project you would particularly like feedback so that you can benefit fully from their expertise.

Positioning the audience to respond in this way will give them something specific to think about during the course of your seminar. Assigning the audience a role can help forestall undue criticism and provide you with valuable feedback, just the feedback you want.

Furthermore:

- If you have concerns that the nature of your coverage or the structure of your talk might invite criticism, again tell the audience why you are covering that material, and why you have structured the presentation in the way you have. Others will not always see the sense of what you have done.

Conference presentations

This section provides extra information for if you are to present at a conference.

GENERATING FUNDING

If you are a doctoral student, your research area may reserve funding for you to attend and present at conferences, either yearly or at some time during your candidature; this is less likely if you are a coursework student. Funding usually covers cost of registration and return air fares and reasonable accommodation. For the most part, conferences attended are either local or national. Whether there is funding to present at an international conference may depend on the financial situation and policy of the area in which you are located and, possibly, on your field of specialization.

A conference budget may also be included in your scholarship funding (as with some government and industry scholarships for example). If, however, all these avenues are closed to you, consider the following sources.

External funding agencies You may be able to generate funds from industry, government or business organizations, particularly if your research has direct relevance; and also from private foundations. Your supervisor or other colleagues could advise you on appropriate outlets. Some institutions also have centres or offices concerned primarily with grants and funding. Review websites of your own and other institutions via the Internet, and use these services to identify possible sources of funding.

In applying to private funding agencies, do take care with the following:

- When you apply, be rigorous in conforming to the application guidelines.
- When you write your application, keep it concise and to the point. These bodies receive many applications, and will not want to be tangled up in unnecessary

complexity and detail when determining whether or not you are a worthy applicant.

- Embody in your writing of the application *actual wording* from the agency's materials describing their objectives, interests, criteria for funding, etc. Doing this will help you to align what you expect to achieve through your research with the agency's purposes in setting up the fund, and so make it easy for the agency to appreciate the fit.
- In attempting to convince the funding agency that you *are* a worthy applicant and an appropriate candidate for funding, give some thought to the aspect of persuasion in writing the application – sell the value of your research.

LOCATING APPROPRIATE CONFERENCES

Consider a range of avenues to locate conferences:

- Supervisors are a great resource, and will know about national conferences relevant to your research area.
- Online discussion groups and forums are a useful resource as fellow researchers and professionals often post up-coming conferences to the group list.
- Journals being used in your research will mention conferences, and you can build up a list of those relevant to you.
- Graduate student notice boards are another place to locate conference announcements.
- Professional organizations that you can join supply information on up-coming conferences through print or electronic newsletters.
- The departmental grapevine can be useful for finding out about conferences – so ask around.
- If your research is interdisciplinary, keep in contact with researchers in all involved disciplines for information on conferences relevant to you.

GETTING A PAPER ACCEPTED

The degree of difficulty you will experience in getting a paper accepted for a conference is hard to predict. It certainly helps that you are at the cutting edge of research, although this does not guarantee acceptance of a paper.

The abstract Papers are mostly, but not always, accepted on the basis of abstracts, which are called for by conference convenors, usually by a set date. As your abstract will compete with all others – perhaps with those of senior academics as well as, in some cases, senior people from many other areas of endeavour – you need to give thought to its composition.

Where there is a **conference theme** it is usually expected that an abstract addresses the theme, and any other requirements (for example, length of abstract) as specified by the conference convenors. Demonstrate the link between your subject and the conference theme by building the theme wording into your abstract. But is this enough?

One study suggests not. While the specifics of this study may not seem relevant, it does have interesting general implications. Berkenkotter and Huckin (1995) report on gate-keeping at a particular academic convention, the large annual conference of the professional US organization called College Composition and Communication. The main activity of the conference is the presentation of scholarly papers, and in 1993 approximately 4000 proposals (one-page abstracts) were submitted from which about 1000 were accepted for presentation. Initially, a pilot study (of 96 abstracts) was conducted to isolate distinguishing features of successful abstracts as opposed to general features evidenced in most abstracts received. A later extended study issued these results (1995: 102):

1 The high-rated abstracts all addressed topics of current interest to active, experienced members of the rhetoric and composition community; the low-rated abstracts often did not.

2 Almost all of the high-rated abstracts clearly defined a problem; the low-rated abstracts often did not.

3 The high-rated abstracts all discussed this problem in a way that would be seen by experienced insiders as novel and therefore interesting, whereas virtually none of the low-rated abstracts did.

4 The high-rated abstracts usually projected more of an insider ethos through the use of terminology, special topoi [traditional themes; rhetorical or literary

formulas], and/or explicit or implicit references to the scholarly literature of the field than did the low-rated abstracts.

As detailed in Table 8.2, there are at least three important implications that can be drawn from the two studies that may have general application in many areas of research.

TABLE 8.2 **Implications for focusing a conference abstract**

Implication 1	Implication 2	Implication 3
• It will help to review abstracts from previous sessions of the conference at which you will present, if these have been published • Try grouping their *distinguishing* features (see exercise below)	• You should be on top of what is going on in your research field: know the literature well, the shifts in research directions, the *hot* topics and issues • Demonstrate your knowledge of all this in your use of the disciplinary language and by way of scholarly references	• It is important to lay out a problem clearly and propose to treat it in a new or different way that is likely to prove exciting (or at least, attractive) to experienced researchers in the field, and manageable within the time allowed for presentation

Exercise: workshopping the abstract

Before writing your abstract, examine abstracts from relevant, published conference proceedings and consider questions of this type:

- Why might these abstracts be of interest to the audience targeted?
- Does the writer make an effort to situate his/her audience by providing appropriate background information or context? (The extent of background information given will depend on the nature of the audience – the more general the audience, the more context needed.)
- Does the writer convey explicitly or implicitly the value/significance of the research being reported on in the paper?
- How are the abstracts organized? Review two or three and break them down into moves like so: first, s/he does this, second, s/he does this, third,

s/he does this, etc. Also, consider the level of detail provided with the different moves.

- What do you learn from the abstracts? Why the research was carried out? How it was done? Findings or conclusions reached? The implications of these? Anything different?
- Do you consider that these are confident writers on top of the research field or subject matter under discussion? How is this confidence conveyed in the writing?
- Do all abstracts make a strong impact on you? Or do some impress more than others? How would you rate the better abstracts, say, on a scale of 1 to 10?

Poster presentations

Poster presentations are increasing in popularity at conferences. You could consult professional graphic designers to advise you (some institutions have such people) or get help from those experienced in poster design in your department; or, like most students, you could design your own. Some students use computer software such as Photoshop or Illustrator, and many simply use word processors.

Find out if there is a graphics area or technology support centre on your campus, which might give advice and allow you free or cheap access to such equipment as a colour printer and photocopier, lamination facilities and so on. You can achieve a striking and attractive poster with some care and thought.

FACTORS THAT MIGHT INFLUENCE DESIGN

As external factors might impinge on your design, do some prior research:

- Find out if there will be a large display of posters, where yours might be one of a hundred, or just a small display.

- Enquire whether the exhibition of posters will stand alone, or whether you will be expected to stand beside your poster to give additional information and talk with interested people.

- Find out what space will be available to hang your poster if you don't already know. You will need to know both approximate dimensions and the orientation. (i.e. □ or ▭)

- Find out what you will need to hang it with – Velcro fasteners or what. You can be caught out by not taking your own!

- Consider whether the poster you have in mind will be portable if you have to carry it long distances, say, for an international conference.

DESIGN PRINCIPLES

Above all, a poster is a visual composition, or as some prefer, a 'visual grammar', your key concern being how to utilize the graphics to aid comprehension. Bear in mind the *golden rule* – simplicity, clarity, brevity – as you embark on the process of design.

> **The golden rule: simplicity, clarity, brevity – less material rather than more is best.**

Exercise: designing posters

Step 1

- Before you begin design, think back to posters you may have seen and found attractive. Can you pinpoint striking features that you could draw on?
- Decide on what type of poster you want. Do you want a poster that is a large single entity (most popular) or one that consists of various bits? If a single entity, what size is the poster to be? What backing do you want to use? Your choice of material, its type and thickness, may be affected by whether or not you want lamination – matt is better than gloss.

Step 2

- Decide on the ratio of graphics to written text which you need to fill, but not crowd, an A4 sheet of paper.
- Decide on what to include in the written text, perhaps a title, sub-headings, dot-points and/or continuous text. Consider a short, pithy title. Strip all text

ruthlessly so that only the most essential information is conveyed. The written text should complement the graphics.

- Reproduce the separate bits of text for your poster in appropriate type fonts, sizes and variations as discussed below under 'Technicalities of using illustrations'.
- Decide on what graphics you will use (for example, pictures, photographs, graphs, diagrams, tables, maps, figures).
- At this point ask yourself: how readable will my text and graphics be from a distance of, say, 15 or 20 feet? Look at the difference between READABLE and **Readable**. Enlarged fonts vary in the space they take up and in their readability depending on the style chosen. BLOCK letters are not a good idea, as they do not allow for the definition afforded by a mix of upper and lower case letters, which is easier on the eye. Also, what size should your graphics be?

Step 3

- Assemble the separate bits (the title, sub-headings, blocks of information, graphics, etc.) in an imaginative and creative way, experimenting with design proportions of space, graphics and text. Or you might want to do this exercise on the computer. Try not to get stuck in the groove of 'linear' arrangements. Another possibility is to carve up the poster using sweeping curved lines or circles of information, which can be most effective.
- Now play around with the positioning of texts, graphics and space to produce a scale model of the overall design on a piece of A4 paper. At this point be prepared to go back to the drawing board to rewrite text, alter graphics, or find substitute ones if necessary. Leave a substantial amount of blank space or your poster will look too crowded; about one-third of the total space available should be blank.
- People's gaze tends to move from left to right, and often gravitates towards the centre of a design. But I have also seen effective posters that avoid centring, so that the poster can be read in more than one direction.
- Consider what mix of colours you want: as background; to give emphasis to key points; to ensure communicative consistency in the overall composition (for example, the same colour/tone being used to highlight all key points or for headings). Experiment with the colour spectrum on your computer; try strong contrasts (for example, bright yellow on blue or purple on green) or

sharp tonal variations in a single colour. Consider two or three colours with tonal variations, as an overuse of colour can distract from rather than help communication. Colours can change from computer monitor to colour printer, so do a test print.

- Get a colour printout of your assembled A4 poster before you blow it up. A4 to A2 is equal to double the enlargement in text height, and A4 to A0 is equal to four times the enlargement in text height.
- Move back from your display to try to gauge the overall communicative effect – ask a colleague's opinion. Are there changes you could make to improve communication? Is it easy to read from a distance? Do the graphics increase or detract from the overall communicative effectiveness?
- Leave it for a few days and return for another look.

Step 4

- Scrutinize every detail of your poster. Edit ruthlessly and proofread very carefully, as you want to avoid errors appearing at the enlargement stage.
- Now that you are sure all is in order, proceed with the enlargement.

Part 2: General issues in presenting

This part of the chapter contains general advice intended for students making a presentation of any kind.

Planning for success

Design of a presentation should always begin with a thorough analysis of the audience.

AUDIENCE ANALYSIS

If you are presenting in a course, you will know your audience – fellow students and your course lecturer. As a seminar presenter you could have a mixed audience: staff and students from your discipline and possibly from other disciplines, and perhaps invited public guests, such as practitioners in the field. Determining audience make-up could be challenging if you are presenting at a conference. You may be able to deduce this from the nature of the conference itself or from materials sent to you on registration, but if not, ask the conference convenors about the likely audience composition. You may also be taking courses that require you to develop skills for presentations in your future professional life. A psychology graduate, for example, had to organize a presentation with an audience of young children in mind.

Exercise: audience profiling

The idea here is to generate as much knowledge about your audience as possible prior to preparing your presentation.

Step 1

Use this set of questions to profile details of the audience for each of your presentations (not all questions will prove equally relevant on each occasion):

- Audience size?
- Cultural background? (e.g. English-/non-English-speaking background; other cross-cultural sensitivities to note)
- Gender balance?
- Age make-up?
- Education level? (e.g. university, higher level degree, technical, school leaving certificate, mixed)
- Make-up of the group? (e.g. disciplinary or interdisciplinary academics/graduate students, disciplinary area specialists, university administrative staff, professionals, practitioners, business people, government representatives, mixed group)

Step 2

With your profile before you, now consider the following questions, the purpose being to determine whether your particular audience will really want to hear what you wish to present:

- What three assumptions can you make about the likely interests of your audience in general? jot these down.
- At what three points might your research interests and knowledge converge with those of your audience? jot these down too. (Exercise your creativity with a mixed audience – you may be surprised at what you uncover.)

LANGUAGE APPROPRIATENESS

With an audience profile in hand, consider adjustments you may need to make to the language of your presentation in order to accommodate your audience:

- All disciplines have specialist languages, specialist terminologies, special ways of speaking and communicating, which is fine for initiates but not for a mixed audience with varying levels of knowledge and expertise. If, for example, you are working in a highly theoretical or technical field, modify your use of terminology to accommodate all members of a mixed audience.

- If your audience is likely to be from different language backgrounds, embody respect for this in your language choices, and in your delivery by enunciating clearly, slowing down and speaking up.

- A lower level of formality is better suited to oral communication. Keep the language clear, simple and concise, less formal. First (I) and second (you) person usage is common in presentations. As you are interacting with an audience, remember to speak *to* that audience, certainly not as casually as you would with friends, but informally, which does not mean that you cannot also sound competent and professional.

VENUE NEEDS

Also give brief consideration to venue in terms of what you may wish to do with your audience (I will return to the subject of venue later):

- Will the setting and room layout be suitable for your type of presentation? (for example, you may want your audience seated at tables for workshop activities, or if you wish to have the audience engage in group discussions a formal theatre with fixed chairs would be unsuitable.

BUILDING 'TIME' INTO A PLAN

A demanding feature of all oral presentations is staying within the allotted time. You need to take full account of the time you have to speak (be it 10 or 20 minutes, an hour or more) in developing your talk if you are to manage time effectively:

- It takes longer to speak to a paper than to read it through at your desk.
- Illustrative material on overheads also takes extra time to explain, as do PowerPoint slides; and time is taken up moving between media, putting up illustrations, running through slides, and using audio, video or computer equipment.

In short, make special allowances for the fact that you are presenting to a listening audience, and using multi-media if that is what you are doing.

The example in Box 8.1 is one student's time-outline for a 50 minute (mainly) PowerPoint presentation for a progress review seminar.

CASE STUDY
Example

Box 8.1 It is best to build 'time' into a talk at the planning stage

PARTS OF THE TALK

1: about 10 minutes

- introduce self; purpose of seminar (work-in-progress/want lots of feedback – identify where in particular) (4)
- show slides on area of field research to orient audience – interest them (6)

2: about 3 minutes

- focus of research (the topic)
- central research question (other related questions and issues)

3: about 25 minutes or so

- the importance of the study (2)
- background of study (what's been done – **read from the paper**) (8)

– the emergence of New Religious Movements (NRMs) (5)
– factors contributing to their emergence (5)

} **important points about each**

- definition of key terms, phrases, acronyms used in thesis (5)

4: about 10 minutes

- Outline of methodology and procedure – why this approach is best (**get feedback**)

Formatting options

Where there is choice, canvass a range of formatting options before making a final decision on how to organize your presentation.

USING SCRIPTED NOTES

If your talk is to be fairly short, say 10–15 minutes, you may decide to speak from scripted notes. This situation is akin to having to write a 1000 word essay; it might seem easy, but it is actually quite difficult.

With a short talk, try to *uncover* what is significant about your topic rather than cover the topic.

Having a short time to speak exerts considerable pressure on *selection*, deciding what is most significant to include in your talk. Begin with these questions:

- What is significant/important about my subject?
- What is new about it and what might be particularly interesting for my particular audience (return to your audience profile)?

All your effort will be directed to this matter of selection, after which you may decide on an outline of main ideas or key points around which to build your short talk. Or you may decide to develop the talk around a set of illustrations (for example, tables, figures, charts, etc.), or as a PowerPoint presentation (note comments below under 'Technicalities of using illustrations').

READING A PAPER AS A PRESENTATION

If you are presenting a formal, longer paper and speaking for, say, 50 minutes, you may feel too insecure to work from scripted notes and prefer to read your paper. Or it may be that you are expected to read your paper, word for word.

Coursework students In a course, you may be asked to read, in a 40–60 minute time slot, a written paper of, say 1000–2500 words, to be submitted at the end of the session for assessment, or reworked after feedback from the presentation. Usually, this type of presentation occurs in a tutorial where your audience is homogeneous – fellow students and the lecturer. There is then little to be said in terms of formatting, except to stress:

- Structure the paper in a way that it will not be too difficult for the audience to follow – you still need to take account of audience needs.

Also, review strategies discussed below under 'Fine-tuning and rehearsal' (outlining papers, making objectives clear, building in repetition, summarizing key points for emphasis, pausing for effect, projecting voice and varying modulation, etc.).

Research students You could be asked to produce a substantial written paper as part of a progress review and give a presentation. Some aspects that may concern you about this situation are:

> **Clarify the requirements of your presentation in terms of the nature of the coverage, length of the paper and time allotted to present.**

- Trying to reduce a lengthy paper, sometimes 40–50 pages or more, to fit your presentation time.
- Addressing an audience of mixed disciplinary/academic interests, which may include other research students and departmental staff as well as staff and students from outside your department and/or invited guests, or even audiences with a more complex make-up.
- Handling questions and criticisms from the audience.
- Managing nervousness.

All these challenges are discussed in the remainder of this chapter. Seek advice too from your supervisors and lecturers, other staff members and more advanced students. Many of them will be experienced speakers who have had to work through similar concerns.

REWORKING A LENGTHY PAPER TO PRESENT

Some graduates feel they have neither the time nor the inclination to rewrite a lengthy paper to accommodate reading for a specified time, and so decide to highlight certain parts of the paper to read and leave it at that. You may adopt this approach, or you may prefer to rework the paper somewhat. As it is impracticable here to include an example of a reworked paper, I pass on these few strategies for condensing.

Condensing the material of your paper Making your full paper available to the audience prior to a presentation will leave you in the enviable position of not having to provide detailed support for all that you say. So cut excessive detail, the very thing that can make the reading of a paper tedious, however imperative it is that such detail be included in the writing. While you can take liberties with evidence, referring the audience to your paper if more detail is requested, do be prepared to refer them to precisely where in your paper that detail can be found.

So that you are not reading throughout the presentation, use these strategies:

- **Condense** – for example, summarize a lengthy argument as key points on an overhead or slide, or isolate and list key issues to discuss.
- **Outline** – for example, model or picture the framework of your argument, theoretical discussion, experimental procedure, methodology, etc.
- **Use illustrations** – for example, tables, graphs, figures, drawings, etc., to convey information succinctly.

While you may want to read sections of your paper in detail, break up the reading by using some of these strategies. A more varied presentation can be more interesting anyway.

POWERPOINT PRESENTATIONS

PowerPoint presentations are very popular. They may even be a standard requirement in your area, so you will need to be familiar with this technology. Well-done PowerPoint presentations are visually aesthetic and exude an aura of sophisticated professionalism. Used by an audience-sensitive presenter, such presentations can be exciting and powerful. But not all is golden in this slideware realm; presentations can also be boring for audiences, a complaint one hears too often. Yale Professor Edward Tufte, who has published on the cognitive style of PowerPoint, notes (2003: 3):

> At a minimum, a presentation format should do no harm. Yet the PowerPoint style routinely disrupts, dominates, and trivialises content. Thus PowerPoint presentations too often resemble a school play – very loud, very slow, and very simple ... PowerPoint is a competent slide manager and projector. But rather than supplementing a presentation, it has become a substitute for it. Such misuse ignores the most important rule of speaking: respect your audience.

A peculiar effect of this audience/content neglect is a type of memory stasis – the audience fails to remember anything much about the presentation ten minutes later, which defeats the point of giving the presentation in the first place. Full critical appreciation of audience interests/ needs as discussed at different points in this chapter is as vital as it is with other presentation formats. Where choice does exist, considering possibilities inherent in other formats covered above, or multi-media formatting as discussed next, should help you to decide whether PowerPoint formatting is the best option given the specifics of your presentation situation. You should be sure to study the next section as it contains many considerations that are applicable to presenting using PowerPoint.

> **Mastery of the PowerPoint medium does not equate with successful presentation.**

MULTI-MEDIA FORMATTING

Using multi-media formatting, some combination of transparencies (overheads), whiteboard, posters, audio or video tapes, computer slides, scripted notes, etc. can certainly spice up a talk. But do take care with illustrative material.

Technicalities of using illustrations Watch that you do not fall into the trap of using illustrations as a substitute for thoughtful content selection and structuring of your talk. What happens then is that speakers fail to make the critical connections, or include too much information for audience comfort, or zoom through illustrative material too fast (all of which can also happen with PowerPoint). It is frustrating for audiences to have a presenter show a complex table or figure that is loaded with information only to have it whipped away before it can be read; or for the audience to realize that the print is too small to read; or for them to find that there is too much information to process and the speaker cannot manage this either; or to have a single table conveyed in ten slow-moving slides or bites of information so that the audience loses sight of the overall point.

> **Another golden rule: simple uncluttered illustrations are best.**

Also, take into account the following points:

- When using overheads/computer slides, try to **fill the frame**.
- In using colour, consider combining opposite colours on the colour spectrum for best effect. Do take care with reds and greens together as this combination might confound colour-blind people.
- Work towards **consistency** of design – for example, repeating colour and font sizes for different level and types of information – in a set of overheads. Your audience will soon tune in to the communicative meanings thus embodied.
- Experiment with fonts, as some are better than others. I used Courier New in the example below because it gives better definition, and I wanted to avoid upper case letters, which are hard to read. It is important that people *will* be able to read your visuals:

Headings (about 34–36 point)

Sub-headings (about 28–32 point)

Text of visual (no smaller than 20 point)

- Consider no more than about **five points** for the text of a transparency or slide. Condense information in each point so that the point itself consists of no more than 10–12 words.
- Ensure graphs, tables, figures, diagrams, maps, etc. contain only essential information. If these are necessarily complex, be prepared to draw out in a concise way what is significant about them.
- Use abbreviations where your audience will understand these – this saves space.
- Number your transparencies before you present to ensure they are in the correct order and position (the right way up).
- Do try not to turn from the audience when speaking to illustrative material (a big problem with PowerPoint). A pointer could be useful, but work out beforehand how you will handle this somewhat unwieldy device as you move between your transparencies and the audience. A laser pointer might be available, but could be distracting if it is left to wander randomly as you glance up from your computer at the audience. Or, with transparencies, you could work from the projector itself rather than the screen. While facing the audience, use your finger or a pen to make points on the overhead projector rather than the screen.
- If you are presenting in a large venue, check beforehand that people at the back of the audience will be able to see the screen. It sometimes happens that they cannot, and it may be quite easy to prop up the screen.
- If you are doing a PowerPoint presentation, take with you a set of transparencies just in case you need to revert to an overhead projector because something has gone wrong with your computer and/or the outlet (for example, the network goes down).

Fine-tuning and rehearsal

Once again, ensure audience is to the fore as you fine-tune your presentation.

ENCODING AUDIENCE MANAGEMENT

Essential to a successful presentation is effective audience management. Strategies for addressing the key aspects noted in Figure 8.2 can be encoded in your presentation.

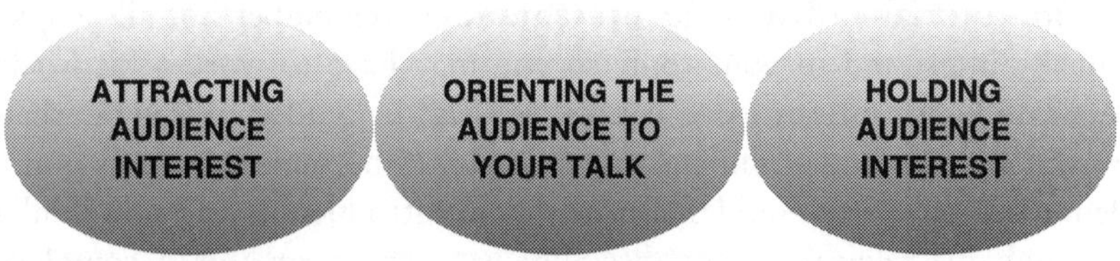

FIGURE 8.2 **Key aspects of audience management**

Attracting audience interest In all situations of presenting, avoid seeming unenthusiastic about your topic (perhaps as an unfortunate effect of nervousness).

Do try to convey enthusiasm for your topic.

- Enthusiasm is very catching, as illustrated in this academic's opening comments to a broad general audience:

> Science is sometimes mysterious, sometimes impenetrable, sometimes frustrating, usually hard work, and often hard work for little result. But science is always exciting. Fascinating and exciting.

- Humour, too, is a great device. If it seems appropriate, and if you feel comfortable with it, build some into your talk. For example, an academic presenting to a broad academic audience began her talk by silently putting up an overhead of a humorous newspaper cartoon on a highly topical issue of the time regarding academic salaries (generating much laughter), and then said: 'I know you would all rather talk about this, but I'm going to talk about …' She certainly caught the interest of her audience, and there was substance to follow.

- Use everyday analogies and metaphors (easy for the audience to relate to), like the Engineer who began his rather technical talk by humorously detailing the types of structural mismanagement that would ensure collapse of the family home.

- Another strategy is to link your conference paper to those presented prior to your own; even a few casual references in passing can be a useful way to engage, and re-engage throughout, the audience. This is particularly impressive where there is a conference theme, as it helps give a sense of continuity to on-going presentations.

With **tutorial and seminar presentations**, remember not all people will be equally interested in your topic so you may have to work a bit harder to generate audience interest. In a course, you will be guided in this by what you think will interest and stimulate students taking the same course as you. As a student researcher, you could mention in your introduction how you think your paper might be relevant to the discipline as a whole, or how it complements work being done in other areas of the discipline. Ask yourself:

- Why might the advances I am making in my research interest members of the wider discipline? (You can assume that 'outsiders' have come precisely because they are interested in your topic.)

Orienting the audience to your talk Start by thinking about these questions:

- What is my talk about?
- Why am I talking about this topic to this particular audience (return to your audience profile)?
- How will I approach the talk?

Build into your talk an overview of the paper you intend to present; keep it simple and clear. Remember that your audience is listening, not reading. Audience members are not able to backtrack, but instead rely on you to make the information easy to understand and follow.

There are different ways in which you can orient the audience to what you want to say:

- Use an overhead/slide to outline or model the talk before you begin.
- Give the audience a written outline before you begin; keep this tight and compact.
- Circulate your paper the day before your presentation so that people have an opportunity to read it before your presentation. (Circulating a paper at the beginning of a presentation is not a good idea. People then tend to read the paper instead of listening to your talk, distracting both them and you. Sometimes, unfortunately, conference convenors request distribution of the paper at this point.)

Holding audience interest Your audience is alert and listening – they know what your talk is about. Now, how will you hold their attention? In the main, try to remain sensitive to audience reactions, and consider the following strategies:

- Let your eyes roam across the audience. Make eye contact with many, not just one or two.

- Modulate your voice, change pace sometimes and pause for effect. Presenters often speak too fast. For a mixed audience of English and second-language speakers you should deliberately slow down, which is a good idea anyway. Speaking too fast can be a side-effect of nervousness, which needs to be managed.

- Do speak up. Make an effort to project your voice, particularly where there is no microphone. Audiences tend not to be forgiving of the softly spoken.

- Alter the pitch of your voice to avoid tonal monotony, which can be soporific or an incitement to daydream. Sometimes audiences do need a wake-up reminder and a change of pitch can achieve this.

- Pause frequently. Give the audience time to absorb your ideas, to have these implanted.

- Summarize and recap – look backwards and forwards – help the audience to follow. While redundancy or repetition is a negative in writing, it is a positive in presentations.

- If you notice someone snoring in the audience, do not let this put you off. Not all members will stay with you all of the time (particularly not those who have had a heavy night out!), but some may be completely engaged and listening intently.

- Make reminder notes to yourself about all these matters, on your paper or on prompt cards.

THE VALUE OF PRIOR REHEARSAL

The value of a full rehearsal prior to presentation cannot be over-emphasized. To manage time effectively, you will need to practise the delivery of your talk, preferably in front of an audience:

- The best option is to get together with fellow students and borrow a room at your institution with the requisite equipment and other venue needs. Ask your lecturer/supervisor about this; it is usually possible for short periods. Fellow students can be very helpful in providing useful feedback before the official presentation takes place – remember to inform them about the nature of your audience if needs be. A trial run can be relaxing and fun, alert you to the necessity for last-minute changes, help quell nervousness and increase confidence.

- Family or friends might be willing audiences, but if you will be using equipment unavailable at home you could be misled as to the effectiveness of your time management.

- As a last resort, you could record yourself speaking your paper, and play it back so as to act as your own critic. But this is unlikely to give you a secure sense of how long it will take to deliver your paper, particularly if you will be moving between written text and visuals.

On the day: issues of delivery

By this stage you should be well prepared, rehearsed and brimming with confidence. But other issues may arise in relation to delivery.

THE PRESENTING VENUE

Whenever possible, visit in advance your venue for presentation. Look over the equipment and consider matters of this type:

- How big is the room? Will all audience members be able to hear if there is no microphone (do you need to get one?). Is the screen for visuals positioned so that those in the back row will be able to see it or does it need some adjustment?

- Will all your equipment needs be met and can you operate the equipment? Test equipment beforehand. It can throw your timing out if you have to fiddle with equipment to get it to work, and this can cause anxiety, though the audience is bound to be sympathetic. All equipment in the room may be operated from a complex panel, and there are differences in such panels. It will be disconcerting if the panel is one with which you are unfamiliar.

- Identify that there *are* computer outlets if you are doing a PowerPoint presentation.

- Note also whether you will need assistance in presenting, as you would if an overhead projector were not within reach of where you are to stand. If you do, ask a friend, or the conference convenors to help you locate someone to assist you.

WHAT TO DO WITH YOURSELF WHILE PRESENTING

Whether you sit down, walk around or stand at a lectern to deliver your talk can depend on how nervous you are, the size and seating of the audience, the formality of the presentation, or whether the equipment you need to use glues you to a certain spot, such as with a fixed microphone over a lectern, or sitting at a computer. Often it is just a matter of personal preference. If your choices are open, do what makes you feel most comfortable.

DEALING WITH THE UNEXPECTED

Anything can go wrong with a presentation, and it often does:

- The equipment breaks down. Or the room you are scheduled to speak in is changed at the last minute and you find it has no computer outlet for your PowerPoint presentation.
- You realize you are running out of time and you have far from finished your talk. Or a speaker on your panel has run way over time so your talk needs to be cut short on the spot. Or the format of your panel session has been changed and you suddenly find you have less time to speak (it never seems to be more!). These types of things often occur.

As regards this last point, one useful strategy is:

- Always think through beforehand how you might cut your paper short if you were to discover your speaking time had unexpectedly shrunk – actually mark out what you could cut without disturbing the overall coherence of your talk.

You may have to make quick adjustments to cope with a new situation, but most presenters have had to confront the unexpected at some time, and are likely to feel sympathetic if this should happen. Draw your audience into your dilemma; make the best of the situation, and do not let it throw you off balance.

CANVASSING AUDIENCE QUESTIONS

Question time often makes students nervous. It is easy to feel such relief at having finished your presentation that it is hard then to concentrate on questions. But do try to listen carefully because question time can be complex, as indicated by the situations mentioned below.

The belligerent or antagonistic question Often the reasons behind aggressive questioning go beyond the scope of a paper, perhaps to a preferred ideology, theory or methodology, and there is little you can do except to respond if you can and move on quickly. Avoid engaging in argument in question time. Or, if your interest is aroused, offer to continue the conversation in a coffee or lunch break.

Uncertainty about what is being asked Sometimes questioners are themselves uncertain about what it is they are really asking and so tend to be circuitous in putting questions. If you think there *are* questions being asked but you remain confused, ask politely for a rewording of the question(s), or for just one question at a time.

When you don't know the answer You may be presenting work in progress that is incomplete, so you may not have all the answers. That aside, no one is infallible and it is easy to be caught out on occasion. You should admit you had not thought of that point and thank the questioner for drawing your attention to it. But be sure that the question is not simply irrelevant.

An irrelevant question Some questions might be outside the scope of your paper, in which case just say so in your response. Or the question might imply the need for further research, beyond your scope, and you could say that. Or, if the question is more in the nature of a comment or observation of little relevance, then say so, or perhaps smile, nod and move on.

When there is not actually a 'question' There can be a tendency for audience members to want to share their views and ideas rather than ask specific questions; others want to have their say. That is fine and can be interesting. But overlong, rambling speeches from audience members can be a problem too, unless there is a good Chair. When this happens, it might help to glance at a Chair who is not intervening, or you might have to politely intercede yourself to end the one-way 'conversation'.

Managing nervousness

Take charge of your audience – lead them towards appreciation of your paper.

Many presenters (students and academics alike) experience nervousness. Some nervousness is good – it keeps you alert and focused. But excessive nervousness can be terrible; all your careful preparation can collapse under a feeling of enormous strain:

- Be realistic. Try not to place impossible expectations on yourself. It really does not matter if your presentation is not perfect, if all does not go quite according to plan. Presentations rarely do.
- Avoid engaging in self-sabotaging 'inner talk' of the type that predicts difficulties and failure – for example, 'I've never been any good at presentations', or 'They're going to hate my paper'. Of course they won't.
- Think positively. Visualize your past successes and triumphs, your many past achievements – focus on a specific academic achievement that made you feel great.
- Remember that the conference convenors found your paper interesting enough to include. You do know a lot about your particular subject, and the audience can be persuaded that they want to hear what you want to tell them.
- Keep your presentation in perspective. It is not the whole of your life, just a part of your overall academic endeavours at this time.

One useful strategy to help control nervousness is:

- Learn your opening remarks by heart – not merely the polite or funny bits, but the intellectual lead-in. Do the same with your concluding remarks. A rambling conclusion or no conclusion because you are out of time can increase anxiety. Be able to cut straight to the conclusion if you run out of time.

Nervousness usually decreases with further experience. But if you think the problem serious enough to warrant help, take steps to control it by contacting your counselling centre for professional advice.

Summary Comments

- Invest 90 per cent of your energy in planning, preparation and rehearsal and 10 per cent in delivery to improve the likelihood of a successful presentation – make it a triumphant occasion.
- Always put yourself in the picture. If you are presenting in a tutorial, a seminar or at a conference, clarify expectations in terms of any specific requirements as to coverage and structure, the length of your paper, time to speak, time for questions and so forth.
- A key factor in the success of any presentation, including poster presentations, is meeting audience expectations in terms of their interests, so give this matter close attention in both the design and delivery stages.
- Try not to place impossible demands on yourself. Prepare well, do a practice run of your talk with fellow students if possible (help each other out), think positively, try to enjoy the opportunity to present, and do not be too concerned if everything does not go perfectly on the day – it rarely does.

9 Journal Article and Book Publication

Developmental Objectives

By applying the strategies, doing the exercises and following the procedural steps in this chapter, you should be able to:

- Understand some of the pros and cons of publishing while producing a thesis (where the thesis is not expected to be a set of published articles).
- Take a constructive approach to the (at times) sensitive issue of co-authorship with supervisors.
- Identify strategies for targeting an appropriate journal and shaping a paper (including converting an existing text) for publication.
- Understand what goes on in the peer review process and possible outcomes, and identify strategies for dealing with calls for substantial revision, or rejection of your manuscript.
- Identify strategies for contacting book publishers and focusing a book proposal.
- Decide whether electronic publishing might be the way to go.
- Form a publication syndicate with fellow students in your research group as a mutual support and learning forum.

As a graduate, publishing may be a new endeavour for you. This chapter engages a broad range of issues related to journal article and book publication.

Publishing while producing a thesis

Different attitudes prevail on the value of publishing while working on your thesis. This practice is common in the sciences, but less so in the humanities, where the preference may be for a book after the thesis has been examined and passed. Attitudes can also vary from supervisor to supervisor in areas where publication is not viewed as mandatory.

THE PROS AND CONS OF PUBLISHING

If you remain undecided, consider the following points:

- Published articles or even those accepted but not yet published (in press) impress when applying for jobs. This is also one way to get known, particularly if you hope for a post-doctoral fellowship or academic position.
- Publishing during the degree may force you to formulate your ideas clearly in writing, earlier than you might otherwise do.
- If your research is of the type that lends itself easily to papers fitted to particular chapters (for example, separate tests, experiments or case studies), then little time will be lost on thesis production if you publish.
- If you hope to publish a book from your thesis, articles published during the degree allow potential publishers to more easily gauge the quality of your work, and so might spur a quicker response (hopefully a book contract).
- If your thesis has a more holistic structure, extracting papers for publication could mean considerable reworking of thesis material, causing delays in thesis production.
- If the rules of your institution do not allow a set of published articles to stand alone as a thesis, you will need to consider how much and what type of work will have to be done to turn your articles into a coherent thesis.
- A book may be much more impressive in some disciplines, but keep in mind that there can be several years' time-lag in the publication of something as long as a book worked up from a thesis.
- Rather than publish during thesis production, some students put aside articles to work on while their thesis is undergoing examination.

Co-authorship and thesis requirements

You may have concerns about the issue of co-authorship if you do decide to publish. Many graduates find this troubling. By co-authorship I mean the practice of including supervisors, and perhaps other staff members, as co-publishers of articles derived from work being done on your dissertation. In some areas, co-authorship is a common practice. Also, there can be reflected prestige in publishing with a supervisor who is a well-respected scholar, nationally and internationally. However, many students can feel pressured to include supervisors' names on their publications. So how can you assess whether it is reasonable for supervisors to expect inclusion?

INCLUDING SUPERVISORS AS CO-AUTHORS

This is often a particular issue for science students, so I draw here on a student publication that issued from a survey of students and supervisors in one science area. However, the observations should be useful regardless of your discipline.

The authors observe:

> ...students and supervisors [in the survey] agreed on the basis for co-authorship of publications. Most students and supervisors thought that co-authorship was appropriate only when the supervisors had contributed both intellectual input and had written sections of the manuscript. (Christian et al., 1997: 30)

> **If the issue of co-authorship is worrying you and others in your research group, meet and decide on strategies to resolve the situation.**

They suggest discussing this issue with supervisors early in the research to avoid conflict, and include a useful guide (see Table 9.1) to assess a supervisor's contribution. As the authors point out: 'In this hypothetical example, the supervisor had minor involvement in planning, analysing, interpreting and writing, and no involvement in carrying out the experiment (executing). This adds up to a score of 20 and consequently does not warrant authorship' (1997: 30). Some supervisors have suggested, however, that provision of funds and/or resources to conduct the research should also be taken into account where the supervisor has been directly responsible for obtaining these.

TABLE 9.1 **Determining a supervisor's contribution**

Activity	Contribution	Score	Student A	Supervisor X
Planning	None	0		
	Minor	5		√
	Moderate	10	√	
	Major	20		
Executing	None	0		√
	Minor	5		
	Moderate	10		
	Major	20	√	
Analysing	None	0		
	Minor	5		√
	Moderate	10		
	Major	20	√	
Interpreting	None	0		
	Minor	5		√
	Moderate	10		
	Major	20	√	
Writing	None	0		
	Minor	5		√
	Moderate	10		
	Major	20	√	
Total		**Max 100**	**90**	**20**

Source: Galindo-Leal, cited in Christian et al., 1997: 30

Where there is co-authorship, a further issue turns on whose name should go first on the publication – presumably yours if you have done most of the work. While co-authored publications from thesis work are unlikely to negatively affect the requirement of originality, you may want to discuss this with your supervisor.

Targeting an appropriate journal

Although rejections are part of the business of publishing, you can minimize the possibility of rejection by avoiding inappropriate journals. Before you act, consult with your supervisor about suitable journals for publication of your material.

PROFILING THE TARGETED JOURNAL

To determine the fit between your paper and the targeted journal, you will need to produce a profile of that journal. Doing this will also aid the writing process if you are first author on a joint publication.

Exercise: building a journal profile

Consider carefully the following questions and take some notes on your findings:

- How often is the journal published? Might time delay in publishing, say yearly, affect the relevance of your paper (in fast-moving research areas material becomes dated quickly)?
- What appears to be the reach of the journal's audience – broad general interest? inter-or cross-disciplinary interest? disciplinary interest or a specialist audience within your discipline? Would your paper have the right appeal? Can you see why editors (and reviewers) thought articles already published did have the right appeal?
- What quality indicators or scholarly attributes can you isolate to help determine the status of the journal?
- Is the status of the journal appropriate for your needs? If the journal seems to publish mainly high-profile scholars in your field, would it be better to consider another one if you are as yet unknown? Some of the best journals also have high rejection rates because of the volume of submissions. Do not be deterred, however. If yours is a high-quality paper, perhaps co-authored with your supervisor, you have reason to be confident.
- What are the scope and aims of the journal? If this information is not given (look at the inside covers of journals), then quickly review abstracts and/or introductions to see what types of content seem to be favoured. Does your content seem to fit the journal's profile (for example, a theoretical versus a practical focus, or a preference for more multi-disciplinary-type articles)?
- Do the style, formatting and length of printed articles fit with your needs? Or will you have to compromise here?
- Are there any prohibitive conditions? For example, do you have to pay to publish (usually estimated on the number of pages)?

Shaping a paper for publication

In shaping your article:

- Take into account all editorial instructions.
- Probe more deeply the fit between your article and publications in the selected journal by taking up the exercise under 'Mastering (inter)disciplinary writing practices' in Chapter 2.
- Applying that exercise will also prove insightful if you are converting an existing text (for example, a research essay, a report, a chapter of your thesis) to an article for publication. You need to work out what rewriting you will need to do to meet the expectations of journal editors, and the best way to do this is to study the style and structure of articles published in the journal you are targeting.

FOLLOWING EDITORIAL INSTRUCTIONS

Having identified an appropriate journal:

- Obtain instructions to authors for publication. These are sometimes printed at the back of journals, or you may need to write for them or download them from the Internet if there is a site for that journal.
- Follow these instructions meticulously. Make sure your paper conforms in all respects before forwarding it to the publishers.

These instructions are highly prescriptive and cannot be negotiated. They may consist of several pages covering many details of preferred style (for example, formatting, font styles for headings, referencing and bibliographic style, focusing a title, preparation of illustrations, nomenclature, numbering, notation, spelling, use of abbreviations and contractions, etc.).

FOCUSING THE ABSTRACT

Convey the value or significance of your research to journal readers.

Give the aspect of persuasion some thought when writing the abstract (or the introduction if an abstract is not required), particularly if you are still unknown and not publishing jointly with a well-known scholar. Ask yourself

- What potential body of readers of this journal might be interested in my article, or aspects of it, and why?
- How can I convey to those readers what is innovative, different, important or exciting about the research presented in my paper?

Do think carefully about this. The idea is to attract as many potential readers as possible. Review and compare what authors published in your journal of interest have done by applying the exercise on 'Mastering (inter)disciplinary writing practices' in Chapter 2.

REVIEWING PRACTICES IN PUBLISHED ARTICLES

To further reinforce the value of taking up this exercise, I refer to one particularly illuminating study. In his substantial investigation of the introductions of published articles in mainly science disciplines, John Swales proposed the CARS (Creating a Research Space) model of journal article introductions (Figure 9.1). The arrows on the right indicate the declining persuasive effort required by a writer in moving from the point of convincing a reader of the significance, value or importance of the research, to explicit statements on the nature of the research presented in the paper.

Compare this CARS model with introductions of articles in the journal you have selected. Not all science articles evidence these types of successive moves in their introductions, but many do. Many of the moves indicated also appear in the introductions of articles in areas other than science, and in many theses too. The CARS model is at least a fine example of how to go about uncovering composition or organizational strategies being applied in the writing of journal articles (not just the introduction), or any other type of writing for that matter.

ENGAGING THE READER

Ken Hyland, a noted linguist and scholar, has studied different aspects of what I think of as the *insider* ethos of writing papers, which you could find useful to follow up (see, for example, Hyland (1999) on writer stance in disciplinary discourses, and Hyland (2000) on social interactions in academic writing). It is his study of reader engagement (2001) that I want to consider here. Hyland

Move 1	**Establishing a territory**	
Step 1	Claiming centrality [of the research being presented] and/or	↓
Step 2	Making topic generalization(s) and/or	declining rhetorical effort
Step 3	Reviewing items of previous research	
Move 2	**Establishing a niche**	
Step 1A	Counter-claiming or	
Step 1B	Indicating a gap or	
Step 1C	Question-raising or	↓
Step 1D	Continuing a tradition	Weakening knowledge claims
Move 3	**Occupying the niche**	
Step 1A	Outlining purposes or	
Step 1B	Announcing present research	
Step 2	Announcing principal findings	↓
Step 3	Indicating RA [research article] structure	Increasing explicitness

FIGURE 9.1 **Creating a Research Space – the CARS model of journal introductions (Swales, 1990: 141)**

points out: 'Writers construct an audience by drawing on their knowledge of earlier texts and relying on readers' abilities to recognize intertextuality between texts' (2001: 551). (By intertextuality, he simply means the way in which the same practices recur in different disciplinary texts, and sometimes more generally in academic texts.)

Constructing an audience involves varied aims, including positioning the reader to respond to the text. Again I draw on Hyland (2001), summarizing these aims in paraphrase:

- Soliciting reader solidarity, trying to encourage particular reactions, securing reader agreement, inviting reader collusion, manoeuvring readers to see things in the same way as you do, positioning readers as fellow-travellers, appealing to collective understandings, predicting and responding to possible objections and alternative interpretations, and so forth.

So what strategies can be used to achieve these ends? From a corpus of research articles (240) and interviews with academics from the same disciplines, Hyland identified strategies illustrating how academic writers engage their readers. Table 9.2 is a tabulation of his characterization of reader engagement. It is the use of strategies of this type that demonstrates the extent to which all communication, including academic writing, is indeed a 'social process' (Bazerman, 1988: 251), or, more precisely, a social practice.

Exercise: identifying disciplinary practices for engaging the reader

Step 1

Select two or three journal articles in your discipline, articles you are reading for your research.

Step 2

Read quickly through them with a view to identifying and highlighting any practices of the type in Table 9.2. Think about the impact such practices have on you as reader. Can you see the insider *ethos* at work in these practices?

Approaching a book publisher

Perhaps you are writing your thesis with a view to having it published, or the examiners of your thesis have suggested publication. First bear this point in mind:

- Discuss early on with your supervisor and other colleagues ways in which you might reasonably modify the writing of your thesis to cut down on the amount of rewriting you will have to do for book publication.

While finding an interested publisher is certainly not easy, the degree of difficulty could depend on the *marketability* of your proposed book. I have known a few students who had publishers interested well before completing their theses because their research was very topical and of high interest to a wider audience. But this is not usual.

TABLE 9.2 **Strategies for engaging the reader**

Strategy	Examples
Using inclusive first person, indefinite and second person pronouns	'**One might argue** that in order to understand the codes, the learner needs to become …' '**We know,** however, it is only in the last few years that …' **We can readily see** that there are two kinds of …' 'If you concede that mental properties have causal powers … then you **must consider** the causal role of mental properties to be somehow dependent on the causal role of physical properties.'
Making references to shared knowledge – perhaps to concede a point only to turn the reader towards your own argument	(The adverbial phrase *of course* seems important here.) '**Of course,** we know that the indigenous communities of today have been reorganized by the Catholic church in colonial times and after.' 'The **obviously** correct relation between these two lengths is …' 'Chesterton **was of course wrong** to suppose that …' 'It is **of course important** to encourage practitioners to become more reflective about their day-to-day activities as X has done but there are other ways of changing professional practices.'
Using directives	(Includes imperatives, and obligation modals referring to actions of the reader – for example, must, ought, should, have to, need to, etc.). '**A distinction must be made** between …' '**What we now need to examine** is whether there is more to constancy than this.' '**Hence it is necessary to understand** the …'
Using questions both real and rhetorical	'Real' questions are not all that common, but are sometimes set up to generate interest and provoke reader thought in concluding comments: 'Do these findings mean that the current approach needs to be modified or that an entirely new approach needs to be developed?' (The 'rhetorical' question is more commonly found. It may be used in an introduction to 'establish a niche') 'How can these findings be reconciled? Our goal in this paper is to offer an explanation of these …' (Or as a transition device, say between paragraphs) 'What is it then that the Zapatistas want?' (Note comments in 'Interparagraph linking' in Chapter 4 on using the rhetorical question as a transition device)
Using asides addressed to the reader (sometimes marked off from the ongoing flow of the text)	'And – **as I believe many TESOL [Teaching English as a Second Language] professionals will readily acknowledge** – critical thinking has now begun to make its mark …' '**It is worth noting in passing,** that the conscience of those engaged in the moral condemnation that accompanied such reporting does not seem to have been greatly troubled by …'

Source: Collated from Hyland, 2001

STRATEGIC CONSIDERATIONS

If you are planning to approach a publishing house, then consider these points:

- Publishing houses have different requirements. They are not likely to welcome whole theses being forwarded, although some (but not all) will accept electronically a full manuscript of a re-worked thesis at the point of approach. Well-known publishers have websites; so do clarify the precise steps you need to take in approaching any particular publisher.
- You will need to produce a 'Proposal'. Again proposal formats are different for different publishing houses; you should be able to download these from the Web. Do write to specific requirements under the given sub-headings. You should also be able to identify on the site the appropriate editor to whom your proposal should be sent, and whether or not it is acceptable to do this by email.

> **Your proposal will be important in sparking initial interest, so do give it careful thought.**

- Proposals usually contain information of this type:

  (a) A synopsis of your intention in producing the book – its justification, its importance or its topicality.

  (b) A comparison of competitive publications in your area: how your manuscript differs, what it has to offer that others don't, its unique qualities.

  (c) A table of contents outline; perhaps an introduction and/or a sample chapter.

You will certainly need to address the issue of the **intended market** and some questions you will need to grapple with in this regard are:

- Who do I see as my potential audience of readers?
- How broad might the base of this audience be? Is interest likely to be generated beyond my subject speciality (a good idea in the current marketing climate)? If yes, among what types of readers and why?
- Why might people want to read my book instead of another on the same or a cognate subject?

- Why might they want to read my book alongside already published books on the subject? What am I adding in terms of subject value?
- Is my book likely to be included as a compulsory or recommended text for any course/s?

Talk over these questions with colleagues before writing your proposal. If your proposal is accepted (perhaps after being sent for peer review – see the next section), you will then confront the challenge of turning your thesis into a book:

- At this point, stop thinking in terms of your thesis; start thinking in terms of a manuscript you want to publish.
- Talk to as many academic colleagues as you can (particularly those who have published books) for advice on what they think you will need to take into account during the rewrite for publication.
- As you have an entirely new audience (no longer your thesis examiners), the introduction will need to be reshaped to address their interests. Also, a book typically has less detail and a less rigorously formal style than a thesis. Of course the nature of your audience will impact on the extent of rewriting required. A more specialist academic audience would involve less reworking than would be the case for a broader, more general readership.

Coping with peer review

It is highly likely your paper will be sent to reviewers if you are approaching a scholarly journal, and almost certain your book proposal will be sent for review.

Journal editors are concerned to select papers they consider most representative of the journal's interests (scope and aims), and the best available to maintain their reputation. Publishing houses too have reputations to maintain, and they are very interested in the market place, so your intended market *will* matter. The higher the status of the journal or the more prestigious the publishing house, the more advantage the editors have in selection, and the more care they are likely to exercise in ensuring they make the best possible choices. This is where referees come in.

Many quality journals are called refereed journals, meaning that articles published in them have been reviewed by outside referees or readers before acceptance for publication. Editors of these journals select papers from those they receive and send them on to reviewers, who are scholarly experts in the field of research being addressed in your paper. Publishing houses have a similar procedure with book proposals.

WHAT REVIEWERS LOOK AT

Referees of your journal manuscript or book proposal will be asked to address questions of this type (I have not separated articles from books here because for more academic publications similar types of questions will be asked, although questions specific to your particular book proposal or article may be included):

- Is there a relevant and informative title – 'eye-catching' may also be appropriate in some cases? Is there a clear and concise abstract? (An abstract is not always required, even for certain peer-reviewed journals, as some students in both the arts and sciences point out.)
- Is the article likely to have the right appeal for journal readers? Or is the book likely to appeal to the intended market as laid out in the proposal? Do you think they would actually buy it and why?
- Does the research reported on contribute new, innovative and/or significant insights? As suggested above, this needs to be foregrounded in your abstract and/or introduction.
- Does the introduction provide appropriate and sufficient context, in terms of breadth and depth, to put the audience in the picture? Are the foci, objectives and (perhaps) methodology or procedure all clearly laid out?
- How sound is the methodology or how well integrated is the theory? (if relevant)
- Does the paper/book evidence logical rigour? (for example, in terms of the validity of arguments, or interpretations of results or data, including speculations that arise from these, etc.).
- Are the coverage and use of references in the paper/book adequate, and are the referencing details correct?

- Is the paper/book well written? (for example, clearly focused, well organized and coherently developed, concisely written, correct grammar/spelling, etc.).
- Does the style of the book have the right appeal for the intended audience? (for example, use of sophisticated disciplinary terminology will not suit a broader, more general audience).
- What do you see as the strengths/weaknesses of this paper/book?
- Are there any ways in which the paper/book can be improved?
- Should the paper/book be published? revised? not published? why or why not?

DEALING WITH THE OUTCOME OF PEER REVIEW

Acceptance Your paper has been accepted as it is, or with only minor revisions, after review by referees. Or you have been offered a contract on the basis of peer review of your book proposal. Congratulations.

Revision They are interested – great – but you are asked to make substantial revisions. As you read the reviewers' reports, you could experience a confusion of feelings (outrage, embarrassment, anger, disappointment, etc.), as is common. Do not be surprised if the criticisms of both content and style are extensive; this is not unusual. Put the reviewers' reports aside for a few days until you have calmed down; until you have recovered from having your work picked over in such a humbling way; until you have regained your equilibrium and a bit more objectivity.

When you return to your manuscript:

- Attend to minor criticisms.
- Consider carefully all substantive criticisms. After detailed consideration of these, implement worthwhile suggestions. Do be prepared to justify your position, probably to the editor, with respect to suggestions you do not wish to take up. Some criticisms might seem to you to miss the point, to be off the point, or to be unbalanced or biased.
- With a book, you may be asked to write a response to reviewers' reports detailing how you will address criticisms and suggestions for improvement. It could be that

not until you have done this will your proposal be taken to a 'Proposal meeting' where it will be decided whether or not to offer you a contract.

- Be prepared for the possibility of having your manuscript go back and forth between yourself, editors and reviewers several times as you try to meet suggested improvements and negotiate with them.

Peer review can be harrowing. But it can also be a useful learning process if you approach it that way. Of course, if your thesis is to be a set of published articles, peer review prior to publication is bound to secure positive examination.

Rejection Your paper/book proposal has been reviewed and rejected, and you are discouraged. This is understandable. But do not let the rejection bruise your confidence too badly; even experienced authors confront rejection at times. This need not be the end of the story for you, and will not be if you think of the process of getting published as a tough training course, with you just starting out.

If, along with the rejection notification, the editors have not included the reports from the peer reviewers, write and ask for them. With this feedback you can now consider reworking your manuscript to send elsewhere, or the editors might already have suggested more appropriate journals or publishers to contact, which I strongly advise you to do. You now have the advantage of peer review input in your second attempt at publication. Keep trying. Do not give up too easily.

CASE STUDY
Example

Box 9.1 Not all publishers get it right: be persistent

A classic case is my former colleagues' book *Essay Writing for Students, by* Clanchy and Ballard. This was rejected by six publishers – 'well written, but students won't buy it', 'there's no market' – before being accepted by a seventh. Over twenty years later, the book is still in print, has sold nearly 100,000 copies, is in its third edition (1997), in both Australia and the UK, and has now been translated into Spanish!

Electronic publishing (eJournals)

Electronic publication may be an attractive option for you given that many research areas now have well-established and respected online journals, some of which are refereed. Electronic journals of this type usually provide clear instructions for author publication, usually along similar lines to those required for publication in print journals. The discussions above will apply equally to the context of ePublications where journals are of a high standard.

If, however, you are thinking to publish electronically, do take some care. There is an element of instability in this avenue of publishing. An eJournal I had thought looked promising disappeared after publishing just two issues, consigning the papers published in it to oblivion. In assessing the likely continuity and quality of an eJournal, consider questions of this type:

- How long has the journal been established?
- Is the journal a peer review journal? If not, what quality controls (if any) seem to be in place?
- Does the journal have official backing from a *recognized* educational institution (there *are* bogus institutions out there), a recognizable and prestigious society, or perhaps a government organization?
- Does it have an editorial board, and do you recognize any of these people as being distinguished scholars in your research area, or important government/ organization officials?
- What signifiers of quality can you identify from the site itself, and in papers already published on the site?

Do seek a second opinion from your supervisor when considering a site about which you are uncertain.

Forming a publication syndicate

A variation on organizing a thesis writing group (see Chapter 7) is to form a 'publication syndicate', as laid out by D. Royce Sadler (1999). Doing this would be particularly useful if you and other students in your research group are producing a set of published articles as a thesis.

The general idea is to discuss members' draft manuscripts in structured meetings organized by the convenor of the group. As Sadler points out:

> The syndicate itself simply consists of a group of like-minded [students] who agree to act cooperatively to further their mutual scholarship and publication. The members should be committed to the task of accelerating the production of either manuscripts for publication in academic journals, or chapters for publication in edited books. (1999: 144)

In such a group, it would be possible to take up many of the issues discussed in this chapter at relevant points in the publication process, to give each other feedback on drafts, to encourage each other, and to share difficulties and triumphs along the way.

Summary Comments

- If you are hoping for an academic career, it is strongly advised that you do publish during the course of your thesis, even where publication is not viewed as mandatory.
- Reduce the possibility of having your manuscript rejected by determining the appropriateness of the journal targeted and by studying the composition processes of articles already published in your journal of choice.
- As your book proposal will be vitally important in arousing the interest of the publishing house editor, follow the publisher's requirements precisely and give careful thought to its construction.
- The peer review process can be hard on students. But even if criticisms of your manuscript are many, appear unduly harsh or even unfair at times, try not to let your confidence plunge. Push through all disappointments and deal constructively with all criticisms. Think of the whole process as a tough training course that will leave you better positioned for future publication.

Appendix 1 Words and phrases for developing discussions

To list, or show 'time' relationships

First/second/third, etc.	Previously	Now
After that	Last/finally	Afterwards
When	Next/My next point	Meanwhile
Before	Earlier	Presently *or* currently

To add information

Furthermore	Also	Besides
Moreover	As well	Another reason/ factor/point is
In addition	Similarly	

To show a causal (cause and effect) relationship

So	Since this is so	Therefore
Consequently	Hence	Due to
Thus	Because of this	It follows
For	As a result…	The 'if/then' construction

To draw a 'conclusion'

This implies/suggests/indicates/shows/establishes/demonstrates/confirms, etc.

It can be inferred that	To sum up	In summary
In conclusion	It can be concluded that	To summarize

To clarify a previously stated idea

In other words
To put this another way
Put succinctly
That is
In effect
By this I mean
(Or simply restate the idea in a different way)

To introduce a 'contrasting' or 'qualifying' idea

In contrast
However
Even so
Unlike
Conversely
Nevertheless
On the other hand
Yet
But
Although
Alternatively
Whereas (then bring in contrast)

To provide an 'example'

For example
..., including ...
For instance
..., such as ...
To illustrate
..., as is illustrated by ...

Appendix 2 Example of a detailed thesis outline

This detailed thesis outline originally included a full table of contents with sub-headings, as well as an end bibliography, which I have omitted. But I suggest you do include sub-division headings if you are writing an outline of this type.

This outline was followed by the student in the writing of the thesis, though slight modifications of objectives and procedures were made in some chapters, as might be expected. I have inserted explanatory comments in square brackets into the original text at some points. Adapt the introduction to suit your specific research needs (not all students need to write a 'problem statement').

Chapter 1: Introduction

This study **focuses on** sustainable forestry management in X* particularly its special forest management approach in Y as embodied in the Strategic Environmental Plan (SEP) Law **[tells *what* the thesis is about]**. It examines whether the forest management approach under the SEP Law has made a difference to the management of the forest of Y in areas such as decentralization, local government involvement and local people's participation in achieving sustainable forestry **[tells *why* the research was undertaken]**. It is **my thesis** that sustainable forest management provided for in the implementation of the Strategic Environmental Plan (SEP) Law for Y does not adequately address the importance of institutional integration (between national and provincial), the need for improved human and technical capacity at the local government level and people's participation **[states the overall thesis – as in argument]**. Following on this thesis, there is an attempt to develop an alternative forest management approach, which applies the lessons of Y under SEP Law, and those of earlier forest management initiatives in X.

---

*Author's note: X refers to a particular country, and Y refers to a particular province in that country.

THE PROBLEM

[Lays out the problem addressed in the thesis]

The realization of the need to protect forest resources and to involve local people in its management has caused a major shift in the approach of the forestry sector in X to a more people-oriented approach. In the past, strong arguments have been put forward that government policies can encourage exploitation (particularly excessive logging) and development programmes that are inconsistent with sound forest resource management. The government has managed forest resources without a clearly defined framework aimed at harmonizing the many policies affecting forest resource use and confined forest benefits to the privileged few, and thus exacerbated forest depletion [reference].

In 1992, in Y a new approach to resource management was trialled. This was a 'landmark' piece of legislation that brought together multisectoral efforts in effecting a serious and sustained agenda to provide for continuous existence of ecological resources in Y. Specifically, this approach was embodied in the Strategic Environmental Plan (SEP) for Y. The SEP has a comprehensive framework for sustainable development compatible with protecting and enhancing the natural resources and sustaining local communities [reference]. This approach was complemented by the passage of the Local Government Code (LGC), which states that all national agencies and offices are to conduct periodic consultations with appropriate local government units, non-government and people's organizations and other concerned sectors of the community before any project or program is implemented in their respective jurisdictions. The LGC has given local officials authority to carry out and enforce environmental and forest protection laws. This seems to be a very progressive resource management policy where, if it were to be successfully harmonized with other initiatives that strive to strengthen local communities, forest degradation in Y might be arrested.

Despite such positive developments, however, recent experiences indicate that these kinds of approaches are far from being realized in practice. This is attested to by the data gathered and events witnessed during my 10-month fieldwork in Y in X. It is also reinforced by comments made by international researchers, Z and Q [reference], that the SEP is principally a strategy for environmental protection with a strong development element, and not a development strategy with a strong environmental element.

What is to be done? According to P [reference], X's forestry policy formulation is characterized as 'a vicious cycle.' He noted that 'when a provision of a regulation is violated, another regulation is handed down to curb further violation of the said provision instead of strengthening the implementation system'. Nevertheless, many researchers have claimed that 'X has drafted some of the most progressive resource management policies in Asia' [reference]. Hence, these policies are something to be acknowledged and learned from [reference]. This study undertakes a rigorous analysis of the social and institutional processes necessary for successful forest management under the SEP. It also considers practical action needed to improve the effectiveness of forest management under the SEP. Hence, I would like to canvass the possibility that this approach could be a 'virtuous one' and not the 'vicious cycle' once again. The study aims to achieve the objectives as set out below.

RESEARCH OBJECTIVES

[Relating to why the reasearch was undertaken]

1 To document, examine and analyse the post-war development concepts and their internal relationships. To examine how these development concepts have contributed to shaping the forestry sector and the perceived role of this sector in development as defined in the forest and development theories and relevant literature.

2 To analyse the institutional arrangements which support decentralized structure in achieving sustainable forestry management in Y.

3 To examine local government involvement in terms of technical and administrative capacity in an attempt to decentralize forest management in Y.

4 To critically evaluate the participation of the local community and the rights system provided to maintain the local community in terms of secured access to forest resources while at the same time sustaining the forest.

THESIS STRUCTURE

[Tells *how* the discussion is organized in the thesis]

Chapter 1 introduces the study by presenting the background of the study. It also presents the research thesis, problem and objectives. Chapter 2 outlines the evolving role of forestry in development. The chapter also examines how the practice of forestry in many developing countries has been influenced by the evolution of concepts and thoughts concerning development. These include the shift of development thought from development as economic growth to social objectives and, more recently, as sustainable development. Chapter 3 presents an historical account of forest management practice in X from industrial to social forestry approaches to community forest management. It examines how these forest management approaches have produced effects that worked against the goal of sustainable forestry management. This chapter also introduces SEP Law and analyses the potential of this Law to achieve sustainable forestry management.

Chapter 4 provides an overview of the three case study sites as a general background for the data-analysis chapters to follow. It discusses how and why the case study sites were selected, and the research procedures used during the fieldwork. Methodological issues of reliability and validity are also discussed. As well, it provides details of data collection. The chapter concludes by identifying key issues for data analysis.

Chapters 5, 6 and 7 constitute the three, core analytical chapters. Using the three case study sites, these chapters explore the nature of the institutional arrangements that underpin decentralized structures; local government involvement in terms of administrative and technical capacity and the practices behind local people's participation. The overall purpose is to determine the most effective strategies for managing forest resources under the SEP Law of Y. Chapter 8, the concluding chapter, summarizes the findings of this study and their implications. It reviews the objectives raised in Chapter 1 and points out issues needing further research.

[As you read through the following chapter introductions note the effort the writer puts into clarifying for the reader *precisely* what he will be doing in each chapter and why. He makes multiple use of such words as *introduces*, *outlines*, *examines*, *presents*, *analyses*, *provides an overview*, *discusses*, *concludes*, *purposes*, *objectives*, *summarizes*, *reviews*, *illustrate*, *etc.* (highlight these yourself as you read). He also indicates, at appropriate points parts of his argument: *This shows*; *It is shown*; *It is argued*, though you may not be sure about your argument/s if you are at an earlier stage of thesis writing than he was.]

Chapter 2: The evolving role of forestry in development

This chapter outlines the conceptual framework of the thesis, laying out the concepts of development and the evolving role of forestry in development from development as economic growth to social objectives and more recently, as sustainable development. Specifically, the chapter examines the development concepts and their internal relationships, and analyses how these development concepts have contributed to shaping the forestry sector, as well as the perceived role of this sector in development. The evolving theory and practice of economic development have influenced the use of natural resources including the forests, in many developing countries; hence, this chapter reviews how thinking about economic development has evolved over the past fifty years. These development theories are drawn upon to better understand how development has evolved from development as economic growth to social objectives and to sustainable development. The discussion shows how such theories have influenced thinking about forestry, and consequently, become instrumental in the development of forestry models from industrial forestry to forestry for local needs (or social forestry) to community forestry models.

This chapter concludes by discussing forest management based on the principles of sustained yield and multiple use. This section is presented in order to show that these principles are relevant in attempts to implement social and community forestry. The history of forest policy and management in X, as discussed in Chapter 3, illustrates this point.

Chapter 3: Forestry and development – the case of X

Chapter 3 explores the historical context of forestry development in X from industrial forestry to social forestry, to community forestry in the context of the ideals of sustainable forest management. Specifically, this chapter analyses forest-based development in X within five major periods in order to understand various reasons for forest degradation as experienced in the country. This chapter shows how forestry development in X is administered in a technocratic fashion that has failed to take into account the social dimensions of forest management. Finally, this chapter introduces the development of the SEP for Y as a new forest management approach for sustainable forestry.

Chapter 4: The research methods and the research case study area

The major objectives of this chapter are: discussion of the methodology, the philosophy behind the use of the case study approach, the advantage of qualitative research, and the research procedures; and the methodological issues of reliability and validity. The chapter also presents the biophysical and social environment of Y in order to examine the implications for sustainable forest management. The chapter concludes by laying out the key issues for data analysis as derived from the literature and initial content data analysis of the present study.

Chapter 5: National–provincial institutional arrangements affecting the SEP Law

Chapter 5 explores institutional arrangements that underpin a decentralized forest management structure in the implementation of SEP Law set up to achieve sustainable forestry. Specifically, this chapter examines the extent of power of the PCSD [a council for sustainable development] invested in the SEP Law. This shows that the SEP Law confers upon the PCSD the same power and authority as that of the national DENR [Department of Environment and Natural Resources], which has led to conflict between the two agencies. Hence, it is essential to critically evaluate the nature of the conflict existing between the DENR and PCSD. Following this analysis, the Chapter examines the existing institutional arrangements between the PCSD and the national DENR. The objective is to show that control over Y's forest resources has remained in the hands of the national DENR, which reinforces the centralized decision making that has worked against the national policy on decentralization and sustainable forestry.

At the outset, the Chapter covers the SEP Law in the context of the national decentralization policy with a view to showing how the SEP Law has the potential to achieve decentralized and sustainable forestry management. The roles of the national DENR and PCSD are examined. This is to show that the PCSD has the same power and authority as the national DENR. However, through presenting the case of communal forest of [municipality 1], this chapter clearly shows that a conflict prevails wherein the DENR undermines the authority of the PCSD as defined in the SEP Law. As well, this chapter examines the opinions of the DOJ [a legal ruling] about the conflict of power between the DENR and the PCSD to show that control over Y's forest management is still centralized despite an attempt to implement the SEP Law. The chapter concludes that the national DENR has not only become more active and powerful but has also reinforced its dominance through the arrangement made between PCSD and DENR, where PCSD is only recommendatory and DENR has the power to approve. In effect, in terms of forest protection and management, there is really no change is so far as the decentralization policy of the government is concerned.

Chapter 6: The local government involvement

This Chapter covers, at the outset, the roles of the local government in forest management based on the national policy of decentralization in order to clarify the responsibility of the local governments as provided for in the new LGC as against the national responsibility of the DENR, the lead agency for forest management. This is presented with the end view of determining the extent of the decision-making power of local governments to carry out newly assigned roles. The analysis shows that the powers devolved to the LGUs [Local Government Units] are more apparent than real. In other words, while the LGC devolves responsibility to the LGUs, the LGC has failed to provide for corresponding powers to accomplish the new roles, which, in fact, reinforces the power of the national DENR because the LGC states that the acts of the LGUs are subject to control, supervision and review of the DENR. It is shown that LGUs are subject to weak political will and leadership, have entrenched traditional attitudes and perceptions, lack technical and human capacities, have limited finances and local corruption prevails. Historically, this situation has resulted in massive forest destruction, particularly during the peak of the industrial forestry era that happened in the country.

Given these problems at the local government level, there is now a question of whether sustainable forestry management can occur under these circumstances. Community forestry as an offshoot to further the goals of sustainable forestry is being piloted in Y. However, evidence from the present study indicates that the goals to achieve sustainable forestry are far from being realized in practice. Thus, the next chapter explores local community participation and the provision of resource use rights access to forest resources in the community forestry program in [municipality 2].

Chapter 7: People's participation and resource use rights

This chapter examines the nature of participation of the community in the implementation of the community forestry program of the national DENR in Y. It does this by assessing the resource use rights systems provided to sustain the local communities while protecting the forest resources in Y and by analysing a case study of a local community in [municipality 2], where an NGO was contracted by the national government (DENR) to organize the community in the area.

In detail, this chapter evaluates the resource use rights system as provided for in the implementation of a community forestry program, that is, the *Community Forest Management Agreement (CFMA)*, a 25-year resource access agreement. This allows assessment of how this instrument has encouraged the local community to participate in the community forestry program. As well, there is a critical evaluation of how the use of CFMA has worked against the realization of the goals of community forestry, SEP Law and sustainable forestry management. Instead of enhancing the local community control over the forest resources, the use of CFMA has reinforced control over these resources by the national DENR. Consequently, in practice, CFMA has not arrested forest degradation despite the emphasis on sustaining Y's forest resources.

The chapter also explores the nature of local people's participation and the role of *non-government organizations (NGOs)* to determine their levels of success in the implementation of community forestry in Y. It examines the extent of NGO involvement in community forestry implementation. The purpose is to establish the positive and negative perceptions of NGOs as experienced in the implementation of a pilot community forestry program of the DENR under the SEP Law for Y. It is shown that NGOs can only contribute and become effective partners of the government if they have enough knowledge, skills and resources to undertake the roles expected of them. The chapter also engages issues raised by the local community and local government officials in the implementation of the community forestry program. These include: the need to define who the real beneficiaries in the implementation of community forestry are, and address unfulfilled promises of the government to the local community in terms of providing them access to forest resources. It is argued that in the implementation of community forestry in Y, the provision of CFMA as the resource access instrument has reinforced the control and authority of the national DENR over the management of Y's forest. Also, the involvement of NGOs has allowed the national DENR to fulfil its agenda, but the local community has not been able to meet its agenda. This has worked against community forestry, decentralization and sustainable development principles.

Chapter 8: Conclusions and recommendations

This chapter will provide the conclusion of the study. It will summarize the major findings of the thesis, address in more detail the exigent need to improve the SEP Law and point out other issues needing further research.

References and further reading

Bakhtin, M. (1986) *Speech genres and other late essays (*eds C. Emerson and M. Holquist, tans. V.W. McGee). Austin, TX: University of Texas Press.

Ballard, B.A. (1995) *The quality of the ANU PhD thesis: an analysis of a sample of examiners' reports.* Occasional paper, The Graduate School: The Australian National University.

Bazerman, C. (1988) *Shaping written knowledge: the genre and activity of the experimental article in science.* London: University of Wisconsin Press.

Berkenkotter, C. and Huckin, T. (1995) *Genre knowledge in disciplinary communication: cognition/culture/power.* Hillsdale, NJ: Lawrence Erlbaum.

Brown, R. (1997) *How to prepare a literature review*. Graduate Research College, Southern Cross University. http://www.scu.edu.au/research/grc/PostGrad/lit-review.htm [accessed 2 August 2001]

Christian, R., Davies, K., de Chazal, J., Krebs, E. and Melbourne, B. (1997) *PhD supervision: a guide for students and supervisors.* Canberra, Australia: The Australian National University.

Clanchy, J. and Ballard, B. (1997) *Essay writing for students: a practical guide*, 3rd edn. Melbourne: Longman.

Covey, S. (1994) *The seven habits of highly effective people.* New York: Simon and Schuster.

Cryer, P. (1996) *The research student's guide to success.* Buckingham: Open University Press.

Davis, L. and McKay, S. (1996) *Structures and strategies: an introduction to academic writing.* Melbourne: Macmillan Education Australia.

Denscombe, M. (1998) *The good research guide: for small-scale social research projects.* Buckingham: Open University Press.

Downes, S. (2003) *Stephen's guide to the logical fallacies* http://www.intrepidsoftware.com/fallacy/welcome.php [accessed 25 February 2004]

Fairclough, N. (1992) 'The appropriacy of "appropriateness"', in N. Fairclough (ed.), *Critical language awareness.* London: Longman.

Hyland, K. (1999) 'Disciplinary discourses: writer stance in research articles', in C. Candlin and K. Hyland (eds), *Writing texts: processes, and practices.* London: Longman. pp. 99–121.

Hyland, K. (2000) *Disciplinary discourses: social interactions in academic writing.* London: Longman.

Hyland, K. (2001) 'Bringing in the reader: addressee features in academic articles', *Written Communication*, 18 (4): 549–74.

Jordan, R.R. (1980) *Academic writing course*. London: Collins.

Kaufer, D., Geisler, C. and Neuwirth, C. (1989) *Arguing from sources: exploring issues through reading and writing*. New York: Harcourt Brace Jovanovich.

McCloskey, D. (1985) 'Economical writing', *Economic Inquiry*, 23: 2. (Extracted from *PCI Fulltext*, published by ProQuest Information and Learning Company, 2002. pp. 187–221.)

Murray, R. (2003) *How to survive your viva*. Buckingham: Open University Press.

Perry, C.P. (1998) *A structured approach to presenting PhD theses*. Thesis resource paper. http://www.scu.edu.au/schools/gcm/ar/art/cperry.html [accessed 27 January 2004]

Phillips, E. and Pugh, D.S. (1994) *How to get a PhD: a handbook for students and their supervisors*, 2nd edn. Buckingham: Open University Press.

Preece, R. (1994) *Starting research: an introduction to academic research and dissertation writing*. London: Pinter.

Sadler, D.R. (1999) *Managing your academic career: strategies for success*. Australia: Allen and Unwin.

Strunk, W. Jr and White, E.B. (2000) *The elements of style*, 4th edn. Boston, MA: Allyn and Bacon.

Swales, J.M. (1990) *Genre analysis*. Cambridge: Cambridge University Press.

Tufte, E. (2003) 'PowerPoint is evil: power corrupts. PowerPoint corrupts absolutely', *Wired Magazine*, Issue 11.09. September. http://www.wired.com/wired/archive/11.09/ppt2.html [accessed 2 November 2002]

Watts, M. (2003) *The holy grail: in pursuit of the dissertation proposal*. Dissertation proposal workshop: Process and parameters. Institute of International Studies, UC Berkeley. http://globetrotter.berkeley.edu/DissPropWorkshop/process/ [accessed 8 December 2003]

Further reading

Alley, M. (1996) *The craft of scientific writing*, 3rd edn. New York: Springer. (Despite the scientific emphasis, this publication contains much information useful for academic writing in general.)

Alley, M. (2000) *The craft of editing: a guide for managers, scientists, and engineers*. New York: Springer. (Again, this volume reaches beyond 'science' in providing much useful information and strategies for taking control of the editing process.)

Boddington, P. and Clanchy, J. (1999) *Reading for study and research*. Melbourne: Longman. (A small but compact volume that covers well the intricacies of reading effectively and efficiently in an academic context.)

Buzan, T. and Buzan, B. (2000) *The mind map book*, rev. edn. London: BBC Worldwide. (Buzan, the founder of mind mapping, provides a detailed understanding of what it means to mind map, and the multiple uses to which this 'tool' can be put.)

Fowler, H.R. and Aaron, J.E. (2001) *The little, brown handbook*, 8th edn. New York: Longman. (This volume is anything but little. It is rather a detailed and comprehensive coverage of academic writing that works hard at living up to its claim: 'answers all your questions about writing'.)

Marsen, Sky (2003) *Professional writing: the complete guide for business, industry and IT.* London: Palgrave Macmillan. (A very useful guide if you want to extend your writing skills to meet the challenges of writing in the professional contexts mentioned.)

Moxley, J.M. and Taylor, T. (eds) (1997) *Writing and publishing for academic authors*, 2nd edn. London: Rowman and Littlefield. (This volume provides additional information to that which I have covered, including strategies for enhancing scholarly productivity, the value of freewriting, publishing research reports and essays and writing grant proposals.)

Smedley, C.S., Allen, M., Briggs, H., Hale, N.S., Hoffman, C. and Laughton, D. (1993) *Getting your book published.* London: Sage. (This book provides valuable insights into the processes of academic publishing from the perspectives of the staff of a large publishing house with international reach. A must if you are considering book publication.)

Speague, J. and Stuart, D. (2000) *The speaker's handbook*, 5th edn. Forth Worth, TX: Harcourt College Publishers. (This is a remarkably tight and comprehensive volume that covers almost everything you might ever need to know about presenting and public speaking. Might well be seen as a companion volume to *The little, brown handbook*).

Swales, J.M. and Feak, C.B. (1994) *Academic writing for graduate students: essential tasks and skills.* Ann Arbor, MI: University of Michigan Press. (While this volume was developed as a course for non-native speakers of English, it has a wealth of useful strategies and practical exercises that could benefit other graduates too.)

Index

Indexed by Caroline Eley